HEBREWS:

From Flaw~e~d to Flawless
FULFILLED!

A Commentary
by *T. Everett Denton*
on the New Testament Epistle
Commonly Called "Hebrews"

Copyright © 2012
T. Everett Denton

Printed and Bound in
The United States of America
ISBN: 9781468006506

*Dedicated to all
Berean-minded,
Lovers of the Lord!
~ Acts 17:11*

Abbreviation Explanation

/ = "&" or "or" or "and/or"
AD = After the Birth of Christ (AD always precedes the date.)
BC = Before Christ (BC always succeeds the date.)
aka = "also known as" or "otherwise known as"
ca. = short for circa. = "around" or "approximately"
cf. = see, confer, consult, compare
e.g. = "such as" or "for example" or "for instance"
esp. = especially
et al. = "and others" (people)
etc. = "and others" (things) or "and so on" or "and so forth"
fr. = from
i.e. = "in other words" or "that is"
lit. = "literal" or "literally"
LXX = "The Septuagint" or "the Greek Old Testament"
NC = New Covenant
NT = New Testament
OC = Old Covenant
OT = Old Testament
p. = page number
v. = verse
vv. = verses
v. 2f = verse 2 and the next verse
vv. 2ff = verses 2 and the following verses
viz. = namely
no. = number
nos. = numbers
w/ = with

Table of Contents

Preface i
Introduction...iii
Outline vi

Chapter One
- Verses 1-3 1
- Verses 4-9 9
- Verses 10-14 17

Chapter Two
- Verses 1-4 25
- Verses 5-11 33
- Verses 12-18 41

Chapter Three
- Verses 1-6 49
- Verses 7-19 57

Chapter Four
- Verses 1-13 65
- Verses 14-16 73

Chapter Five
- Verses 1-3 77
- Verses 4-10 81
- Verses 11-14 89

Chapter Six
- Verses 1-3 94
- Verses 4-12 97
- Verses 13-20 105

Chapter Seven
- Verses 1-10 113
- Verses 11-19 121
- Verses 20-28 129

Chapter Eight
- Verses 1-5 139
- Verses 6-13 143

Chapter Nine
- Verses 1-10 151
- Verses 11-15 161
- Verses 16-28 169

Chapter Ten
- Verses 1-18 179
- Verses 19-31 189
- Verses 32-39 199

Chapter Eleven
- Verses 1-7 207
- Verses 8-19 215
- Verses 20-31 225
- Verses 32-40 235

Chapter Twelve
- Verses 1-3 245
- Verses 4-13 253
- Verses 14-21 261
- Verses 22-29 269

Chapter Thirteen
- Verses 1-8 277
- Verses 9-17 285
- Verses 18-25 293

Summary 300

Preface

Why another commentary on Hebrews? Well, a casual perusal of the remarks on just the initial verses will instantly demonstrate why this work has been deemed necessary by many who have heard/read this material over the past six years.

With the objective of performing a detailed study of this magnificent New Testament epistle, I have read/studied many writings and collected numerous bound volumes on Hebrews over the last few decades; from that experience, I believe I can accurately state that this exposition is different —in its approach—from any other *bound* work on Hebrews ("bound" because there are at least two good major web-works similar in approach at bereanbiblechurch.org/hebrews.htm and christinyou.net/pages/hebrewsindex.html). Since this work is different, and since it's so important to do this, I beg the reader to consult <u>every</u> reference provided within this commentary.

Furthermore, it has become my conviction that *The Epistle to the Hebrews* is the single most important piece of New Testament literature relative to an accurate understanding of biblical eschatology (end-times) and soteriology (salvation). As long as the foundational theological information in this treatise is misunderstood, misapplied, and mistaught (long before interpreting *The Book of Revelation* is ever attempted), God's people—we—will not enjoy the contentment that our Lord intended for us to experience. Hence my prayer is that all who open this book will also open their minds to the approach employed that they, like the Acts 17:11 Bereans, may also be commended by their God for displaying such a life-changing attitude.

The original studies from which this book is compiled were presented in PowerPoint format. Presently, these studies may be downloaded (and even used without authorization) from ASiteForTheLord.com/id2.html, a website through which I may also be contacted.

(Unless otherwise noted, the *New King James Version* [NKJV] has been employed throughout this work.)

If any of my readers should discover anything in these pages believed to be a doctrinal falsehood or even a typo or grammatical error, please don't hesitate to share it with me for corrections in the next edition. It will be appreciated. Email me via my website: ASiteForTheLord.com or at tedenton64@hotmail.com.

An Introduction to Hebrews

The author of this magnificent piece of literature has been debated for centuries. Due to my own immense desire for at least some degree of certainty concerning the identity of this writer, I dove into my own significant investigation of this matter and have concluded that the Apostle Paul was the author of *The Letter to the Hebrews*. Instead of relating the details of my research, I will merely convey a few of the primary reasons for my decision, leaving the reader to more of his/her own in-depth study if he/she feels the need for such.

From the writing of this epistle itself, what follows are a few characteristics that may be determined about the author: {1} Like Paul he was a Jew (note first person plural in 2:1-9; 4:14-16; etc.). {2} Like Paul he was in Italy (13:24). {3} Like Paul he was close to Timothy (13:23). {4} Like Paul he was highly educated (he was a better writer than any other New Testament writer). {5} Like Paul he was not an immediate disciple of Christ (2:3, cf. 1 Cor. 15:8). And {6} like Paul he was very well acquainted with the Law of Moses, quoting from it some 30 times and echoing it some 50 times. (It's doubtful that any Christian writer was better acquainted with the Old Testament than Paul; cf. Acts 22:3, 5:34, & Php. 3:4-5.)

There are at least twelve similarities of expression and thought in Hebrews to the undisputed writings of Paul; for examples, referencing the prophetic statement "THE JUST SHALL LIVE BY FAITH" is unique to Paul (cf. Rom. 1:17, Gal. 3:11, & Heb. 10:38), and the ending benediction "GRACE BE WITH YOU ALL" was used by Paul in every letter, but not by any other writer. Hebrews 10:30 in particular seems to clinch Paul's authorship because this exact same paraphrase of Deuteronomy 32:35-36 is also found in Romans 12:19. (For further information on this, consult James Burton Coffman's commentary on Hebrews 10:30.)

Here's what we know about the author from sources outside this letter. A study of such will demonstrate that all of early Christianity attributed it to Paul from the beginning; in AD 95 Clement of Rome even quoted from Hebrews in the context of another of Paul's letters. Peter, who wrote his epistles to Jews (1 Pet. 1:1 & 2 Pet. 3:1), said in his second letter that Paul had also written to these Jews (2 Pet. 3:15); and no other known letter better qualifies for this statement than Hebrews.

This epistle was sent out from Italy (13:24), probably from Rome where Paul was imprisoned for a while (perhaps along with Timothy, 13:23a) and where it seems the only church in Italy was located at the time.

This epistle was penned sometime in the early to mid AD 60s, just before Paul left Rome (13:23) after his imprisonment there around AD 62 (when he wrote his prison letters), but before the acute persecution that began in AD 64 under Nero reached them, for, according to 12:4, they had yet to experience bloodshed for Christ, which _very_ likely would've happened once Nero came into the picture.

This epistle's content (and its title) unquestionably establishes that the recipients of this writing were Jewish Christians.

This epistle was written to prevent its recipients from returning to Judaism (2:1-4, 3:12-13, 4:1-3, 11, 14, 6:1-2, 10:23-31, 12:1-3, 12-16, & 13:13-15). This may explain why Paul didn't identify himself: such a letter would likely provoke more persecution than he was already enduring; besides, the recipients knew who the author was (cf. 6:9 & 13:18-23).

This epistle contains unanswerable proof for the superiority of Christ and His law (of liberty) over that of Moses and his law (of bondage), thus fulfilling the author's purpose.

This epistle's purpose will be more readily grasped by means of an examination of its background, beginning of course with Jesus—its central theme.

Jesus came on the scene fulfilling every Messianic prophecy. The Jews, in general, rejected Him as their Messiah, so He warned them of the impending doom of their idolized city and temple. In order to shut Him up, they crucified Him, but that failed because the church He promised to build was inaugurated within two months after His death. The Jews, again in general, likewise rejected His church which only induced her members to preach the same message of doom to their rejectors as did their Leader. So in order to shut them up, the Jews went about trying to rid their world of Christianity.

This persecution was initially led by the zealous Saul of Tarsus, who later became known as Paul the Apostle. Although some of the worst Jewish persecution lasted from the establishment of the church (AD 30) until Saul was converted (AD 34, cf. Acts 9:1-31), there was always persecution of Christians (especially Jewish ones) in one form or another wherever anti-Jesus Jews were found in their world—the Roman Empire.

Growing weary of the acute pressure to turn their backs on Christianity and return to Judaism, these Hebrew Christians (likely in Jerusalem itself) were privileged to receive a letter from Paul in this regard. Besides, there would soon be an even greater 3.5-year wave of persecution once Nero (who was married to a Jewess) allied himself with anti-Christian Jews to eradicate all Christians. (Since Paul, during the time of this epistle [ca. AD 63], was probably in Rome while rumors of this alliance were spreading, it's likely that he "got wind" of this ominous information, providing him with even more motivation to write. And of course logic dictates that if one is attempting to encourage persecuted souls, he doesn't reveal that their maltreatment is only about to become worse.)

No wonder there are six paragraphs of warning within this work, warnings which become stronger as the letter progresses—from neglect to desertion: {1} A Warning Against Neglect (2:1-4); {2} A Warning Against Unbelief (3:7-19); {3} A Warning Against Carelessness (4:1-13); {4} A Warning Against Immaturity (5:11–6:20); {5} A Warning Against Willful Sin (10: 26-31); and {6} A Warning Against Desertion (12:12-29).

Hebrews isn't altogether negative in nature, however; in fact, it's actually more positive than negative. So in order to appreciate the positive context, consider the following overview/outline of this impressive epistle:

THE SUPERIORITY OF CHRIST'S PERSON & PRIESTHOOD (1:1–7:28)
    THE SUPERIORITY OF CHRIST'S PERSON (1:1–4:13)
        Christ Is Superior to the Prophets (1:1-3).
        Christ Is Superior to the Angels (1:4–2:18).
        Christ Is Superior to Moses (3:1-19).
        Christ Is Superior to Joshua (4:1-13).
    THE SUPERIORITY OF CHRIST'S PRIESTHOOD (4:14–7:28)
        Christ Is Superior to Aaron (4:14–6:12).
        Christ Is Superior to Melchizedek (6:13–7:10).
        Christ Is Superior to Levi's Priesthood (7:11-28).

THE SUPERIORITY OF CHRIST'S PACT AND PRINCIPLE (8:1–13:25)
    THE SUPERIORITY OF CHRIST'S PACT (AGREEMENT/COVENANT) TO MOSES' (8:1–10:18)
        Christ's Covenant Has Superior Promises (8:1-13).
        Christ's Covenant Has a Superior Sanctuary (9:1-15).
        Christ's Covenant Has a Superior Sacrifice (9:16-28).
        Christ's Covenant Has Superior Results (10:1-18).
    THE SUPERIORITY OF CHRIST'S PRINCIPLE (FAITH) TO MOSES' (10:19–13:25)
        Christ's Faith-Principle Is a Response to Superior Things (10:19-39).
        Christ's Faith-Principle Prompts Superior Actions (11:1-40).
        Christ's Faith-Principle Establishes a Superior Relationship (12:1-29).
        Christ's Faith-Principle Is the Basis for a Superior Way of Life (13:1-25).

The key-word of Hebrews is obvious: "better," used 13 times; but there are 2 other significant words throughout: "perfect" and "eternal." The original word for "perfect" is used 14 times, and the original word for "eternal" is used 19 times. Thus Jesus and Christianity are <u>better</u>, for they grant a <u>perfect</u> standing before God, the blessings of which are <u>eternal</u> in nature.

Hebrews 1:1-3

As noted in the introduction, the student should keep in mind that this letter was sent to Jewish Christians who were being fiercely pressured into returning to Judaism. So Paul composed this letter of encouragement to remain faithful to Christ and Christianity by initially appealing to Jesus' preeminence over their beloved prophets (cf. outline on previous page).

> **VERSES 1-2A: GOD, WHO AT VARIOUS TIMES AND IN VARIOUS WAYS SPOKE IN TIME PAST TO THE FATHERS BY THE PROPHETS, HAS IN THESE LAST DAYS SPOKEN TO US BY HIS SON...**

The phrase **AT VARIOUS TIMES** literally means "in many parts," simply meaning that God's revelations concerning salvation were given to mankind a piece at a time, not all at once; in fact, Isaiah 28:13 records that 'THE WORD OF THE LORD WAS '... HERE A LITTLE [AND] THERE A LITTLE.'" The phrase "in many parts" indicates that God's revelations were progressive, provided to man as He deemed fitting, beginning of course with the Adam of the OT ("THE FIRST ADAM," 1 Cor. 15:45) and ending with the Adam of the NT—Jesus ("THE LAST ADAM," 1 Cor. 15:45).

The phrase **IN VARIOUS WAYS** means that God's revelations were imparted via several techniques. For examples, "Amos gave God's message by oracles and direct statements from God, Hosea by typical experiences in his own life, Habakkuk by argument and discussion, Malachi by questions and answers, Ezekiel by strange and symbolic acts, Haggai by sermons, and Zechariah by signs" (Edward Fudge on Hebrews 1:1 in *Our Man In Heaven*). Now, however, the types/shadows of the Old Testament that Peter said the prophets and angels desired to understand (1 Pet. 1:10-12) have been fulfilled and made clear in/through Jesus.

The phrase **IN TIME PAST** is interesting. There were two words in Greek for "old": αρχαιος meaning "old in point of time," and the one Paul chose here, παλαιος, meaning "old in the point of use, worn out, ready to be displaced by something new" (Kenneth Wuest's *Word Studies in the Greek New Testament*). So a major (if not the main) point for these Hebrews to get was that God gave His revelation of redemption in two primary stages. The purpose of the first stage (the Old Testament) was merely to prepare mankind (by means of His people, the Israelites) for salvation, and it was in its very last phases of fulfillment at the time of this writing (cf. 1:11, 8:13, & 12:25-28). The purpose of the second stage (the New Testament) reveals how the first stage was being fulfilled through/by the Messiah. Today, while the Old Covenant had been provisional, the New Covenant is eternal (cf. 13:20).

The phrase **TO THE FATHERS** may have reference only to the fathers of the Mosaical age, yet (because God even called Abraham a prophet, Gen. 20:7) I believe it may easily include the patriarchs, leaders, elders, and others of both the ages (i.e. before and after Moses) covered by the Old Testament.

The phrase **BY THE PROPHETS** literally means "in the prophets"; in other words, a prophet was God's medium of revelation, as Peter wrote, "PROPHECY ... CAME BY ... HOLY MEN OF GOD ... AS THEY WERE MOVED BY THE HOLY SPIRIT" (2 Pet. 1:20-21).

The phrase **IN THESE LAST DAYS** literally means "in the last of these days"; in fact, the original word for "LAST" here refers to "the outermost point." Bar saying, "IT IS THE LAST HOUR" (1 John 2:18), it's very difficult to get any closer to the end than that.

Just as the Jews divided their history into two periods—the time before Messiah and the time after, so Paul divided it into two periods: {1} "THESE DAYS" of 1:1 and "THE PRESENT TIME" of 9:9 referred to the time in which he lived, while {2} "THE TIME OF REFORMATION" of 9:10, "THE WORLD TO COME" of 2:5, "THE AGE TO COME" of 6:5, and "THE CITY TO COME" of 13:14 referred to the perfected kingdom which was on the horizon (cf. 10:37 & 12:28).

God spoke to man through His Son at "THE TIME OF THE END" of the first period (cf. Daniel); later in 9:26 Paul even said Jesus sacrificed Himself at "THE END OF THE AGES" (cf. Marvin Vincent's *Word Studies of the New Testament*). Earlier, to the Corinthians, Paul (while addressing them about people of the Old Covenant age) informed them that they—the Corinthians—were actually those "UPON WHOM THE ENDS OF THE AGES" had come (1 Cor. 10:11).

The phrase **BY HIS SON** is literally "in His Son." What's the significance? The contrast that Paul meant for his readers to catch is that, at the close of that age, God had fully and finally spoken in a son—His own Son—instead of in mere prophets. The previous revelations were in prophecies, types, and shadows, but an impersonal revelation of a person is always an imperfect one; so God sent "A SON," because only a personal revelation of a person can be a perfect revelation. After all, logic dictates that the authority of one's son should be the most respected (cf. Mark 12:1-12).

> **VERSE 2B: ...HIS SON, WHOM HE** (GOD THE FATHER) **HAS APPOINTED HEIR OF ALL THINGS...**

In order for Jesus to be the **HEIR**, there were two conditions: {1} He must be God's Son; Psalm 2:7-8 have Jesus quoting His Father as saying to Him, "'YOU ARE MY SON, TODAY I HAVE BEGOTTEN YOU.... I WILL GIVE YOU THE NATIONS FOR YOUR INHERITANCE, AND THE ENDS OF THE EARTH FOR YOUR POSSESSION.'" And {2} there must be something to inherit; similar to Psalm 2, the parable in Luke 19:12-27 speaks of Jesus as receiving a kingdom (fulfilling numerous prophecies, of course). Another thing Jesus inherited is mentioned right here in Hebrews 1:4: "HE HAS BY INHERITANCE OBTAINED A MORE EXCELLENT NAME."

Being the chief heir, Jesus is Lord of all, or as here "ALL THINGS." (Cf. Gal. 4:1 & Acts 10:36 where Peter used this phrase to refer to Jesus as now being Lord of the Gentiles as well as the Jews, thus "ALL NATIONS" per Psalm 2; cf. Rev. 15:4, 21:24-26, & 22:2.)

What did Paul mean by the phrase **ALL THINGS**? Probably he not only meant all peoples, but also all things related to the promised kingdom, such as Jesus' being crowned Prophet, Priest, and King.

Thus, *the idea of Jesus inheriting the material universe was never the point.*

> **VERSE 2C:** ... **THROUGH WHOM** (JESUS) **ALSO HE** (GOD THE FATHER) **MADE THE WORLDS**...

Since the Greek term for **MADE** can mean either "created" or "arranged" (as in 11:3), it must be interpreted by its context; so consider the following concerning the original terms for "world" and "worlds."

The word for "world" in 10:5 is the Greek term for "planet" (κοσμος [cosmos], cf. 11:7); the word for "world" in 1:6 is the Greek term for "inhabitants" (οικουμενε); and the word for "worlds" here in 1:2 is the Greek term for "ages" (αιον [eon]); so, depending on the contextual usage of each word, these then range from the planet, to an age or the ages of the planet, to the people of an age or the ages of the planet.

(Side-note: While κοσμος is the term for planet Earth, in the Bible it's quite often used metaphorically of [a certain group of] inhabitants [e.g. 1 Cor. 1:20ff]; conversely, οικουμενε nearly always refers to inhabitants. Although αιον indirectly includes people, *it always refers to an age and never to the material planet Earth or the universe* [cf. Mat. 24:3 for one of numerous examples].)

The important/indisputable point is that the Greek word for **WORLDS** here is not the term used to include our planet—it's the term for "ages"; besides the fact that "ages" is the correct translation, there are other reasons for it to be rendered as such. Firstly, "ages" is plural, meaning that not only does "**WORLDS**" make this an unnatural statement, but (unless Hebrews is the only place) the Bible never speaks of God as creating "the worlds" plural; but, as will be seen soon, this book does concern two covenant ages or two covenant worlds.

Secondly, since Paul chose the Greek word for the physical creation in 10:5 wherein he wrote of Jesus coming into the world, then he obviously knew the difference; in fact, there seems to be a definite distinction between these terms in 9:26: Jesus "THEN WOULD HAVE HAD TO SUFFER OFTEN SINCE THE FOUNDATION OF THE WORLD [κοσμος]; BUT NOW, ONCE AT THE END OF THE AGES [αιον], HE HAS APPEARED TO PUT AWAY SIN BY THE SACRIFICE OF HIMSELF." Even here, when Paul wanted to refer to the natural creation and its beginning, he used the word κοσμος instead of αιον. A synonym for "AGES" here would be the word "TIMES" in Ephesians 1:10 in which Paul wrote of God's work of gathering together "ALL THINGS" in Christ in the fullness of the "TIMES."

So, in this context, the word **MADE** means "arranged" or "ordered," not "created," signifying that God arranged and/or ordered the ages as they commenced and progressed.

> **VERSE 3A: ...WHO** (GOD'S SON), **BEING THE BRIGHTNESS OF HIS** (GOD THE FATHER'S) **GLORY AND THE EXPRESS IMAGE OF HIS PERSON...**

This is a prime example of the utter impossibility to fully or accurately describe God in human terms; this is why God chose to inspire men to utilize such an enormous amount of symbolic language in the Bible to describe Him as well as numerous gifts (such as the kingdom) emanating from Him.

The phrase **THE BRIGHTNESS OF HIS GLORY** essentially means that the Son is the light itself which radiates from its source—God; the following phrase, **THE EXPRESS IMAGE OF HIS PERSON**, simply expands upon this by signifying that the Son was/is the exact replica or facsimile of God's reality or nature. An intriguing detail about this phrase is that the Greek for "EXPRESS IMAGE" is the term χηαρακτερ (character) which, in early times, referred to the image that an engraving or stamping tool left behind; in other words, as we use the word "character" today, it's that by which a person may be recognized (cf. John 1:14 & 14:7-9).

VERSE 3B: ...AND UPHOLDING ALL THINGS BY THE WORD OF HIS POWER...

Because the English word **UPHOLDING** is actually too passive to accurately communicate the meaning of Paul's word-choice, a better English translation would be "maintaining," indicating that Paul was conveying the idea that Jesus was <u>actively</u> upholding "ALL THINGS." How? By fulfilling them!

To what does the phrase **ALL THINGS** have reference? Well, if we keep our interpretation in strict context, it has reference to everything concerning man's redemption down through the ages. See, verse two speaks of the Son's inheritance of "ALL THINGS." What "THINGS"? The things of the material universe? Of course not! Rather "ALL THINGS" relative to His becoming Prophet/Priest/King over His own kingdom or house (cf. 3:6).

In direct relation to that, in verse 2 above it speaks of Jesus as arranging/ordering the ages to bring about redemption in the kingdom that He was to establish and rule over as the rightful heir. Then, in the previous phrase, Paul wrote of how Jesus, obviously primarily in His human form, was the exact representation of God. And why did He come? To redeem man. Lastly, in the following phrase, Paul spoke of our sins being cleansed by Jesus who sat down at God's right hand.

So how could the "ALL THINGS" here have reference to the material universe? It couldn't. And here's the point: Not only did God the Son arrange/order the ages (v. 2), but (especially at the time of this epistle) He was also maintaining everything by keeping all His promises and fulfilling all the prophecies made throughout those ages, consequently qualifying Him to inherit "ALL THINGS."

What about the phrase **THE WORD OF HIS POWER**? Well, it must be observed that the original term for "WORD" here isn't the usual term λογος (logos) but ρηεμα (rhema as in 11:3), meaning "command." This denotes that everything in redemptive history was being sustained, upheld, and/or fulfilled by the authority of God's Son and according to His plan.

Just as through His inspired word He made promises and provided prophecies, He, by virtue of the power of that word, would/did make good on—and <u>fulfill</u> <u>them</u> <u>all</u>—by vindicating His church/people in the fall of Judaism. (Luke 21:22 records Jesus' promise that "'THESE ARE THE DAYS OF VENGEANCE WHEN <u>ALL</u> <u>THINGS</u> WHICH ARE WRITTEN WILL BE FULFILLED'").

> **VERSE 3C: ...WHEN HE HAD BY HIMSELF PURGED OUR SINS** [CF. 10:12], **SAT DOWN AT THE RIGHT HAND OF THE MAJESTY ON HIGH...**

The supplied phrase **BY HIMSELF** is better as "<u>through</u> Himself."

The Greek for the phrase **PURGED OUR SINS** more literally reads, "having made a cleansing of sins," He then sat down.

To sit at **THE RIGHT HAND** of a ruler denoted a place of highest honor and authority (cf. 1 Kgs. 2:19 & Mat. 20:20-23).

The phrase **THE MAJESTY** means The Majestic One, obviously a reference to God the Father.

The phrase **ON HIGH** can be understood by looking at two other passages in this letter: Hebrews 8:1 speaks of Jesus as He "WHO IS SEATED AT THE RIGHT HAND OF THE THRONE OF THE MAJESTY IN THE HEAVENS," and Hebrews 9:24 speaks of Jesus as appearing "IN THE PRESENCE OF GOD" in "HEAVEN ITSELF." (By the way, "ON HIGH" is equivalent to Heaven, while "HEAVENS" is a generic term that must be determined by context.)

Jesus' sitting down at God's right hand is significant for two reasons: {1} it's a reference to Jesus taking over the office of high priest, and {2} instead of <u>never</u> being able to sit down as the Levitical high priests in their tabernacle duties, Jesus <u>was</u> able to sit down (cf. Acts 7:56): Paul wrote that "CHRIST HAS NOT ENTERED THE HOLY PLACES MADE WITH HANDS ... BUT INTO HEAVEN ITSELF, NOW TO APPEAR IN THE PRESENCE OF GOD FOR US; NOT THAT HE SHOULD OFFER HIMSELF OFTEN, AS THE HIGH PRIEST ENTERS THE MOST HOLY PLACE EVERY YEAR WITH BLOOD OF ANOTHER—HE THEN WOULD HAVE HAD TO SUFFER OFTEN...; BUT NOW, ONCE AT THE END OF THE AGES, HE HAS APPEARED TO PUT AWAY SIN BY THE SACRIFICE OF HIMSELF" (9:24-26).

His sitting at this point in time signified that such is where He'd remain while He, as Revelation 17:17 indicates, directed His campaign against His enemies (Heb. 10:13) and purified His bride for her wedding (Heb. 10:14): in 2:8 Paul wrote about all things being subjected under Jesus' feet, and how that, at the time of this epistle, such had yet to be accomplished (though by Paul's choice of the imminent term μελλω [mello], 2:5 [at which this term is discussed in more detail] indicates that its accomplishment was on the horizon).

IN SUMMARY, Paul began his encouragement of these persecuted Christians by demonstrating Jesus' superiority to the prophets for seven reasons:

1. *He's God's final spokesman—Prophet.*
2. *He's heir of all things related to the kingdom.*
3. *He's the One through whom the ages were arranged.*
4. *He's the One through whom everything was fulfilled.*
5. *He's God's light and His exact representation.*
6. *He's the One who cleansed our sins—Priest.*
7. *He's the One who is at God's right hand—King.*

Hebrews 1:4-9

Beginning at this point, the more detailed development of Paul's argument is introduced. The goal was to illustrate the superiority of the New Testament Agent between God and man—Jesus Christ—over that of the Old Testament agents between God and man—Moses and angels. Although Paul mentioned prophets in verse 1, he began with angels in verse 4, moving on to Moses later in chapter 3.

As indicated in the introductory outline, Paul's discussion of Jesus over angels is in 1:4–2:18. Although chapters would be too long to use the following, this lengthy section may be divided into three parts: *An Affirmation of Jesus' Superiority* (1:4-14), *An Admonition Based on Jesus' Superiority* (2:1-4), and *An Explanation of Jesus' Superiority* (2:5-18).

Having established in verses 1-3 that Jesus is the new/eternal Prophet, Priest, and King, Paul continued to build.

> **VERSE 4:** ...HAVING BECOME BETTER THAN THE ANGELS, AS HE HAS BY INHERITANCE OBTAINED A MORE EXCELLENT NAME THAN THEY.

The phrase **HAVING BECOME BETTER** implies that Jesus was, at one time, human, which of course corresponds to the comments at verse 3 earlier, namely that when Paul spoke of Jesus being the exact replica of God, He was referring to Him in His human state. Later in 2:9 Paul wrote of Jesus as being "MADE A LITTLE LOWER THAN THE ANGELS FOR THE SUFFERING OF DEATH ... THAT HE ... MIGHT TASTE DEATH FOR EVERYONE." In other words, He had to become human in order to die for us, thereby fulfilling God's will and being made worthy of His inheritance.

The word **BETTER** here refers to Jesus' superiority in position of authority over angels. Paul obviously brought this up here because the Jews boasted greatly in the Law of Moses which was supplied via the ministry of angels (cf. Deu. 33:2, Psa. 68:17, Gal. 3:19, & Acts 7:52-53); in fact, in this very context Paul recognized this, saying that the old law was "SPOKEN THROUGH ANGELS" (2:2).

Paul continued on by saying that Jesus **HAS BY INHERITANCE OBTAINED A MORE EXCELLENT NAME THAN** the angels, which means that, as John 1:14 notes about Jesus, He's "THE ONLY BEGOTTEN OF THE FATHER," or, as the NIV says, "THE ONE AND ONLY"; in other words, regardless of the honor involved in being an angel of God by creation or being a son of God by adoption, only Jesus possesses the unique relationship of being an actual Son of God. So what's the "NAME"? It's "SON."

> **VERSE 5:** FOR TO WHICH OF THE ANGELS DID HE EVER SAY, "YOU ARE MY SON, TODAY I HAVE BEGOTTEN YOU"? AND AGAIN, "I WILL BE TO HIM A FATHER, AND HE SHALL BE TO ME A SON"?

Paul first referred to Psalm 2, a Psalm which (according to ancient Jewish doctors of the Law) applies solely to the Messiah; besides, Peter applied the first three verses to Jesus in Acts 4:25-26. (Specifically here, Paul quoted from Psalm 2:7.)

When it says **TODAY I HAVE BEGOTTEN YOU**, the word "TODAY" refers to the contents of Psalm 2:6 where God said of Jesus, "'I HAVE SET MY KING ON MY HOLY HILL OF ZION,'" while the word "BEGOTTEN" refers to Jesus' resurrection—that which qualified Him to be that King of Zion.

How may we know that "BEGOTTEN" refers to Jesus' resurrection? Easy: this same quote was used by Paul in Acts 13:33-34 where he applied it this way: "'GOD ... RAISED UP JESUS.... AS IT IS WRITTEN IN THE SECOND PSALM, "YOU ARE MY SON, TODAY I HAVE BEGOTTEN YOU."'" Further, in Romans 1:4 Paul again wrote that Jesus was "DECLARED TO BE THE SON OF GOD ... BY THE RESURRECTION FROM THE DEAD."

The point here is that Jesus was confirmed as the prophesied Son of God who would be King by the fact that God raised Him from spiritual death and seated Him as King over His own spiritual house (1:3 & 3:6); in other words, Jesus, after having borne the sin of others, was the first**born** into spiritual or fellowship life toward God, uniquely qualifying Him for the office of perpetual King as well as perpetual High Priest. In fact, in Colossians 1:18 this same apostle plainly stated that Jesus is "THE FIRSTBORN FROM THE DEAD THAT IN ALL THINGS HE MAY HAVE THE PREEMINENCE." (There's that "ALL THINGS" idea again.)

The second Old Testament passage Paul brought to the fore is a prophecy in 2 Samuel 7:4-17 or 1 Chronicles 17:4-15 (two accounts of the same incident). This prophecy from God to David concerned the coming of One who would build and preside over the house/temple of God "FOREVER."

Although David's son, Solomon, built God's temple in Jerusalem, neither he nor anyone else in David's lineage, except Jesus, fulfilled the prophecy of this passage in its entirety. We can know this because Solomon's temple, as well as the city of Jerusalem, has long been destroyed.

> **VERSE 6: BUT WHEN HE AGAIN BRINGS THE FIRSTBORN INTO THE WORLD, HE SAYS, "LET ALL THE ANGELS OF GOD WORSHIP HIM."**

THE FIRSTBORN here is an obvious reference to Jesus. But what does "FIRSTBORN" mean? It usually signifies "the first child born into a family." So, in this resurrection-birth connection, Jesus is called the firstborn of all God's spiritual children. (We'll get more in-depth into this subject beginning with 2:10.)

Other passages (e.g. Rev. 1:5 & Col. 1:18 where Jesus is spoken of as "THE FIRSTBORN") make it clear that Jesus is the firstborn of those resurrected from among the dead ones. Does that mean He was the first to ever be resurrected physically? Of course not; we know there were others. Rather, by raising Jesus who suffered sin-death for all mankind (2 Cor. 5:21), God made Him who committed no sin (1 Pet. 2:21) to be the first one raised to reconciliation-life toward God from among those who were unreconciled (death = separation) due to the sin of which they couldn't rid themselves while on Earth.

So, being the firstborn of those to be reconciled to God (cf. Mat. 27:46), Jesus became the preeminent One—the King, the Captain, the Heir of "ALL THINGS," the "ALL THINGS" Jesus gladly shares with those who've been adopted as His brethren and God's children into His House (cf. Rom. 8:29 which speaks of the elect—the remnant—as the firstborn ones).

Some feel that when Paul wrote, **WHEN GOD AGAIN BRINGS THE FIRSTBORN INTO THE WORLD**, he was referring to Jesus' physical birth—His first coming; however, it's much more likely that he was referring to what's generally called His "second coming." Following are a few reasons for this: {1} The placement of the word **AGAIN** in the text leans towards this interpretation; {2} the word **BRINGS** is in the future tense, future to this AD 63 epistle; {3} at the time of this particular coming, Jesus would already be the **FIRSTBORN** of resurrection-life; and {4}, in the context of Deuteronomy 32:43, which is the background for this, Moses was speaking about God's vengeance against His enemies. In other words, the type/anti-type principle here wouldn't work for Jesus' first coming to die for sin, but it would work for His second coming to take vengeance on His rejectors and enemies.

Even if Paul had Psalm 97:7 in mind, the context there still lends toward the same conclusion that the reference is to the Messiah and His reign as King in His kingdom, something that wouldn't occur until His enemies were vanquished and His kingdom thereby established in its fullness at His second coming in the near future of this epistle's recipients (cf. Heb. 10:37 & 12:28). (Other passages indicating a future coming of the kingdom in this sense are 2 Tim. 4:1 & 18, Acts 14:22, 2 The. 1:5, Heb. 12:28, & 2 Pet. 1:10f.) Besides, the only place in the Bible where one can find angels worshipping Jesus is at His return in vengeance (Rev. 5:11-14, cf. Php. 2:9-11), not at His birth.

Regardless to when this has reference, the point is that God would cause the angels to worship Jesus at that time; and they would worship Him because He's greater than they are.

Let's briefly consider the words "world" and "worlds" again at this point: "WORLD" in 10:5 is the Greek term for "planet" (κοσμος, where we get "cosmos"); "WORLDS" in 1:2 is the Greek term for "ages" (αιον, where we get "eon"); and "WORLD" here in 1:6 is the Greek term for a "people" (οικουμενε, where we get "economy," the etymology of which refers to "a managed household"). Hence the idea here is that Jesus would (soon, v. 5) come into (receive) His own people to govern, a kingdom of which He would of course be King (cf. Luke 23:42 as well as Luke 19:12ff).

> **VERSE 7: AND OF THE ANGELS HE SAYS, "WHO MAKES HIS ANGELS SPIRITS AND HIS MINISTERS A FLAME OF FIRE."**

The terms **ANGELS** and **MINISTERS** are simply two words which refer to the same personages; the term for "ANGELS" means "messengers," while the term for "MINISTERS" means "servants" and is the term from which we get "liturgy," the word which is used for the religious ministry of the Old Testament priests.

Since the Greek word for **SPIRITS** can be translated as "winds," "breaths," or "spirits," then it must be translated according to context. Based on a study of this context, I share with the reader my thoughts as follows: πνευματα ("pneumata") in this verse should be translated as "winds" because {1} every other major translation translates it as "winds"; {2} the verb "MAKES" is in the present tense, meaning either that God was still at the time of this epistle in the business of creating these beings (something for which there's no Scriptural authority) or that He uses them to create or to become winds or flames of fire (e.g., Judges 13:20) or whatever else He so desires; and {3} the context of Psalm 104:4 (the verse Paul echoed here) speaks of natural phenomena such as waters, clouds, and fire.

Whether its translated as "spirits" or "winds," the main point is still unmistakable: Jesus, the One who is the only begotten and the express image of God, the One who was crowned as King and is worshipped by angels (who themselves are not allowed to be worshipped) is, therefore, superior to them.

> **VERSES 8-9:** BUT TO THE SON HE SAYS, "YOUR THRONE, O GOD, IS FOREVER AND EVER; A SCEPTER OF RIGHTEOUSNESS IS THE SCEPTER OF YOUR KINGDOM. YOU HAVE LOVED RIGHTEOUSNESS AND HATED LAWLESSNESS; THEREFORE GOD, YOUR GOD, HAS ANOINTED YOU WITH THE OIL OF GLADNESS MORE THAN YOUR COMPANIONS."

Note the status of Jesus here: He is **GOD**. He's called "GOD" by God the Father in both verses 8 & 9. Consider the syllogisms that follow:

Major Premise: Only God is to be worshipped (Deu. 10:20 & Mat. 4:10).

Minor Premise: Angels are commanded by God to worship Jesus (Heb. 1:6).

Therefore: Jesus is God, meaning that He is deity in His very nature (cf. John 1:1).

                                                               ☙ ❧

Major Premise: Only God is to be worshipped (cf. above).

Minor Premise: Like men (Acts 10:25f), angels are not to accept worship (Rev. 19:10 & 22:9).

Therefore: Unlike Jesus, angels are not deity.

The **THRONE** spoken of here is the one Jesus inherited from His forefather, King David. God had promised David that his throne would last forever (Psa. 89:35-37); later, Gabriel told Mary that her Son would reign over His father David's throne forever, and to His kingdom there would be no end (Luke 1:32-33, cf. 2 Pet. 1:11). Besides, David's throne/kingship over physical Israel was merely a type of God's or Jesus' throne/kingship, the anti-type (cf. Acts 2:30 & 33).

As is perfectly illustrated in Esther 4:11, the **SCEPTER** was a sign of kingly authority; since Jesus doesn't bear a literal scepter as earthly kings did/do, the point here is that His kingdom is governed with/by/in perfect righteousness (Isa. 9:7).

The Greek word for **ANOINT** is the base term for "Christ" (which translates as "Messiah") and means "anointed One."

An anointing was usually an official, public ceremony when a prophet (1 Kings 19:16), a priest (Num. 3:3), or a king (1 Kings 1:34 & 39) was appointed to his respective office with a perfumed oil. (Ironically, a prophet and a priest anointed Solomon as David's successor in 1 Kings 1.) Instead of being anointed with an earthly oil, Jesus was anointed with the Holy Spirit (Mat. 3:16), and not just to be King (Rev. 17:14), but also Prophet (Deu. 18:15-18) and High Priest (Heb. 4:14).

The phrase **OIL OF GLADNESS** brings to mind the festivities of joy that accompanied the coronation of a king. In Hebrews we can see this joy in both the Son (who was crowned King) and in His Father (who crowned Him): in 12:2 we can see the pleasure of King Jesus when Paul wrote that Christ, "FOR THE JOY THAT WAS SET BEFORE HIM, ENDURED THE CROSS ... AND ... SAT DOWN AT THE RIGHT HAND OF THE THRONE OF GOD," and here in 1:9 one reads about the joy of the Father—how He crowned His Son as King with more joy than He had ever crowned the previous kings of Israel (Christ's **COMPANIONS**). And certainly it would be careless to fail to recall the words of Father-God when the Spirit descended upon Jesus as a dove: "'THIS IS MY BELOVED SON IN WHOM I AM WELL PLEASED'" (Mat. 3:17). Surely one reason for this is that Jesus was anointed, not only as King, but also as Prophet and Priest. (For more information on this topic, see *Why Was Jesus Baptized* at http://ASiteForTheLord.com/id7.html.)

Speaking of joy, this quote of Paul here in Hebrews is from the 45th Psalm which depicts another occasion of joy, for it's a wedding sonnet addressed to an Israelite king.

IN SUMMARY, Jesus is superior to the angels because...

1. *He is God's Son, an angel is not.*
2. *He is to be worshipped, an angel is not.*
3. *He is served by angels, being neither below nor even equal to them.*
4. *He is God, an angel is not.*
5. *He was given an eternal kingdom to rule as its King, an angel was not.*

16

Hebrews 1:5

Hebrews 1:10-14

Back in verses 4-9 Paul began teaching *Jesus' Superiority to Angels* (cf. 1 Pet. 3:22). At verse 10 his argumentation for this continues, beginning with a quotation of Psalm 102:25-27.

> **VERSES 10-12:** "YOU, LORD, IN THE BEGINNING LAID THE FOUNDATION OF THE EARTH, AND THE HEAVENS ARE THE WORK OF YOUR HANDS. THEY WILL PERISH, BUT YOU REMAIN; AND THEY WILL ALL GROW OLD LIKE A GARMENT; LIKE A CLOAK YOU WILL FOLD THEM UP, AND THEY WILL BE CHANGED. BUT YOU ARE THE SAME, AND YOUR YEARS WILL NOT FAIL."

As people are prone to do when they fail to embrace the interpretive principle of "audience relevance," this passage is generally interpreted literally. But I want to share with you why this passage is actually <u>not</u> alluding to the extinction of the material world, but to the removal of the Jewish world; it's about the removal of Old Covenant life and its supersession by New Covenant life. Let's consider all three contexts: **THE REMOTE CONTEXT** (the Bible), **THE ADJACENT CONTEXT** (the epistle and paragraph adjoining the text), and **THE IMMEDIATE CONTEXT** (the passage itself).

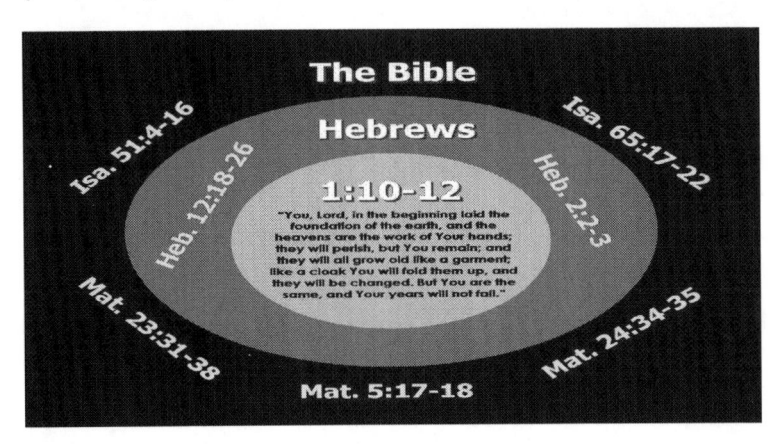

THE REMOTE CONTEXT reveals that "THE HEAVENS" and "THE EARTH" are used in combination frequently to refer to the life, the government, the economy, or the "WORLD" of the Old Covenant people; after all, like various other Bible covenants, it was a covenant between God in Heaven and men on Earth.

God once reminded the Israelites of His covenant with them by saying, "'I AM THE LORD YOUR GOD, WHO DIVIDED THE [RED] SEA [when they were baptized into Moses, 1 Cor. 10].... I HAVE PUT MY WORDS IN YOUR MOUTH; I HAVE COVERED YOU WITH THE SHADOW OF MY HAND THAT I MAY PLANT THE HEAVENS, LAY THE FOUNDATIONS OF THE EARTH, AND SAY TO ZION, "YOU ARE MY PEOPLE"'" (Isa. 51:15-16).

In the same context when prophesying about His new law to come, God said that "'LAW WILL PROCEED FROM ME, AND I WILL MAKE MY JUSTICE REST AS A LIGHT OF THE PEOPLES. MY RIGHTEOUSNESS IS NEAR, MY SALVATION HAS GONE FORTH, AND MY ARMS WILL JUDGE THE PEOPLES; THE COASTLANDS WILL WAIT UPON ME, AND ON MY ARM THEY WILL TRUST. LIFT UP YOUR EYES TO THE HEAVENS, AND LOOK ON THE EARTH BENEATH. FOR THE HEAVENS WILL VANISH AWAY LIKE SMOKE, THE EARTH WILL GROW OLD LIKE A GARMENT, AND THOSE WHO DWELL IN IT WILL DIE IN LIKE MANNER; BUT MY SALVATION WILL BE FOREVER, AND MY RIGHTEOUSNESS WILL NOT [like the Law] BE ABOLISHED'" (Isa. 51:4-6).

When promising the establishment of a new covenant with a new people, God said, "'I [WILL] CREATE NEW HEAVENS AND A NEW EARTH,'" and "'THE NEW HEAVENS AND THE NEW EARTH WHICH I WILL MAKE SHALL [unlike the old heavens and earth] REMAIN BEFORE ME'" (65:17 & 66:22). Incidentally, in Isaiah 65 God had predicted that the new creation (the New Covenant and New Jerusalem) would come when Israel had filled the measure of her sin and was destroyed (v. 7). And when did that transpire? It transpired in September of AD 70.

Jesus said to the Jews, "'YOU ARE SONS OF THOSE WHO MURDERED THE PROPHETS. FILL UP THEN THE MEASURE OF YOUR FATHERS' GUILT'" (Mat. 23:31b-32); then, after referring to their impending demise, He said, "'ASSUREDLY I SAY TO YOU, ALL THESE THINGS WILL COME UPON THIS GENERATION.... SEE! YOUR HOUSE IS LEFT TO YOU DESOLATE'" (vv. 36 & 38). A few verses later, Jesus spoke more at length of this approaching doom by predicting the fall of Israel's world—their heaven and earth—when He said that "'THE POWERS OF THE HEAVENS WILL BE SHAKEN'" (24:29) and "'THIS GENERATION WILL BY NO MEANS PASS AWAY TILL ALL THESE THINGS ARE FULFILLED. [YOUR] HEAVEN AND EARTH WILL PASS AWAY, BUT MY WORDS WILL BY NO MEANS PASS AWAY'" (24:34-35).

(Side-note: It's intriguing that in Genesis 2:4, immediately after God created Adam, the author said, "THESE ARE THE GENERATIONS OF THE HEAVENS AND EARTH WHEN THEY WERE CREATED, IN THE DAY THAT THE LORD GOD MADE THE EARTH AND THE HEAVENS" (KJV). Is this just coincidental? Or is there perhaps some generally overlooked connection that should be investigated further?)

In Luke's account of this warning, he logged Jesus as saying, "'THESE ARE THE DAYS OF VENGEANCE (i.e. retribution) THAT ALL THINGS WHICH ARE WRITTEN MAY BE FULFILLED'" (21:22); and what's even more interesting is that, when this is all put together, Matthew 5: 17-18 make perfect sense: "'DO NOT THINK THAT I CAME TO DESTROY THE LAW OR THE PROPHETS. I DID NOT COME TO DESTROY BUT TO FULFILL. FOR ASSUREDLY I SAY TO YOU, TILL HEAVEN AND EARTH PASS AWAY, ONE JOT OR ONE TITTLE WILL BY NO MEANS PASS FROM THE LAW TILL ALL IS FULFILLED.'" In other words, Jesus wasn't talking about the physical world, but about the covenant world of the Jews; since Jesus said that heaven and earth couldn't pass away until the Law was fulfilled, then—since the material world is still extant—He was talking about the Jewish world system, not the physical universe.

It's also important to note that Psalm 102 itself (the passage Paul quoted) implies that he was referring to something that would occur on Earth not to Earth, meaning that he wasn't referring to the extinction of creation: the verse following Paul's quote says, 'THE CHILDREN OF YOUR SERVANTS WILL CONTINUE; THEIR DESCENDANTS WILL BE ESTABLISHED" (v. 28, cf. v. 18).

Moving on to **THE ADJACENT CONTEXT**, note how all this information from the remote context tallies to Hebrews in general. Hebrews was written to—yes, Hebrews, Jews—God's Old Covenant people who became His New Covenant people, a people who were being relentlessly pressured to turn back to Judaism by Judaizers. To these Hebrews, Paul wrote of the fulfillment of numerous prophecies about the change of covenants. In 12:18, 22, & 26-28 he wrote, "YOU HAVE NOT COME TO THE MOUNTAIN THAT MAY BE TOUCHED AND THAT BURNED WITH FIRE [Mt. Sinai].... BUT YOU HAVE COME TO MOUNT ZION AND TO THE CITY OF THE LIVING GOD, THE HEAVENLY JERUSALEM.... NOW HE HAS PROMISED, SAYING, 'YET ONCE MORE I SHAKE NOT ONLY EARTH, BUT ALSO HEAVEN.' NOW THIS, 'YET ONCE MORE,' INDICATES THE REMOVAL OF THOSE THINGS ... BEING SHAKEN ... THAT THE THINGS WHICH CANNOT BE SHAKEN MAY REMAIN. ...WE ARE RECEIVING A KINGDOM THAT CANNOT BE SHAKEN" (effectively fulfilling Joel 3:16-17).

The book of Hebrews itself verifies that Paul not only knew about "THE HEAVENS AND EARTH" phrase being a Hebraism (a Jewish idiom), denoting a government or covenant world, but he also used it in this manner. Sticking for a moment with Hebrews 12, notice something interesting concerning 1:10-12 by comparing...

HEBREWS 2:2-3A	HEBREWS 12:25
IF THE WORD SPOKEN THROUGH ANGELS PROVED STEADFAST AND EVERY TRANSGRESSION & DISOBEDIENCE RECEIVED A JUST REWARD, HOW SHALL WE ESCAPE IF WE NEGLECT SO GREAT A SALVATION?	DO NOT REFUSE HIM WHO SPEAKS. FOR IF THEY DID NOT ESCAPE WHO REFUSED HIM WHO SPOKE ON EARTH, MUCH MORE SHALL WE NOT ESCAPE IF WE TURN AWAY FROM HIM WHO SPEAKS FROM HEAVEN.

Not only is there an unmistakable correlation, but the contexts of both passages are similar in subject-matter as well: both of these statements are made in the contexts of "THE HEAVENS AND EARTH" ideology. Consider the statement of 1:14 about how the angels worked for those who would inherit salvation; certainly it can be agreed that such was meant to apply to people on Earth.

One other detail here is that this interpretation also perfectly corresponds to previous comments on 1:2 & 1:6 concerning the different ways the word "world" is used in Hebrews as well as elsewhere → 1:2 speaks of how God orchestrated the ages for His redemptive purpose, while 1:6 speaks of the citizens of King Jesus' kingdom age; then in 2:5 Paul stated that "THE WORLD [kingdom, 1:6] TO COME" of which he spoke—in his time, seven years before the AD 70 consummation of all things—would, unlike the Old Covenant kingdom, not be managed by angels (cf. 2:5, etc.).

Lastly, consider **THE IMMEDIATE CONTEXT** of 1:10-12, which was borrowed from Psalm 102:25-27. In this passage itself there are also hints that Paul had the covenant world—not the material world—in mind.

The phrase **IN THE BEGINNING** (v. 10) is not as definite as the same phrase found in Genesis 1:1 (in Hebrew or Greek); it actually merely means "of old" (which, incidentally, is the way it's rendered in Psalm 102:25); in other words, the phrase could take one's mind back to literal/physical creation, or—more likely in this context—it could merely take him back to the formation of the covenant between God and His people Israel, at least as far back as Abraham and Moses, if not all the way back to Adam himself who, as the head of God's people, was the first in a covenant relationship with Him (cf. Hosea 6:7 where "MEN" should be translated as "Adam").

Besides that, the portion of Psalm 102 that Paul quoted is a verse of hope sang just before Israel's restoration to Zion after being held captive in Babylon, a type which perfectly corresponds to the anti-type of how mankind was enslaved in sin before Jesus brought complete redemption, not only by ratifying a new covenant, but also by removing the old one in AD 70.

The ideas in 1:11-12 of the heavens and earth perishing, growing old, being rolled up, and changed are found later in 8:13 where seemingly everyone agrees Paul had the passing of the old law and the establishing of the new law in mind: "IN THAT HE SAYS, 'A NEW COVENANT,' HE HAS MADE THE FIRST OBSOLETE. NOW WHAT IS BECOMING OBSOLETE AND GROWING OLD IS READY TO VANISH AWAY." (Incidentally, the only other place the term for "ROLLED UP" is used in the NT is in Rev. 6:12-17 which perfectly parallels Mat. 24 & Luke 21.)

In Second Corinthians 3:7-13, Paul, again in the context of the new law superseding the old law, spoke of how the old law was—at the time he wrote—"PASSING AWAY," while the new law (which was in existence simultaneously with the old law for that generation [cf. Gal. 4:21-31]) would remain. Likewise, Jesus said that the heavens and earth (the old law) would pass away, but His words (the new law) would remain (Mat. 24:35); that is, it would endure the shaking (Heb. 12:25-28) which that generation (Mat. 24:34) would experience.

> **VERSE 13: BUT TO WHICH OF THE ANGELS HAS HE EVER SAID, "SIT AT MY RIGHT HAND TILL I MAKE YOUR ENEMIES YOUR FOOTSTOOL?"**

In the Greek, the word for **SIT** here is in the present tense, implying that it would be better understood as to "be sitting" or "remain seated," expressing permanency. Jesus sat down (past tense) in verse 3, and He was meant to continue sitting; in fact, in the same Psalm there's another quote to which Paul alluded in 5:6, one which speaks of Jesus as being the High Priest "FOREVER."

(Important side-note: The word **TILL** isn't used here as "a point of termination," meaning that Jesus would no longer sit on the throne after His enemies were made His footstool, for then He'd have no need of the footstool created for Him out of His enemies; rather, "TILL" [as in various other passages such as 1 Tim. 4:13] is used here as "a point of reference," meaning that no end to the object or task under consideration is to be inferred.)

Verse 13 is the crowning argument of Paul as to why Jesus is superior to angels: the fact that on Jesus was conferred the highest of all honors possible—to sit and remain seated at the right hand of God—proves beyond dispute that Jesus is superior to every being in existence, except God Himself, and then the only difference appears to be in position of authority (cf. 1 Cor. 15:28).

Listen to Daniel 7:13-14, noting how it corresponds to the context of this study; Daniel described his prophetic vision this way: "BEHOLD, ONE LIKE THE SON OF MAN COMING WITH THE

CLOUDS OF HEAVEN! HE CAME TO [actually 'as'] THE ANCIENT OF DAYS, AND THEY BROUGHT HIM NEAR BEFORE HIM. THEN TO HIM WAS GIVEN DOMINION AND GLORY AND A KINGDOM THAT ALL PEOPLES, NATIONS, AND LANGUAGES SHOULD SERVE HIM. HIS DOMINION WAS AN EVERLASTING DOMINION WHICH SHALL NOT PASS AWAY, AND HIS KINGDOM THE ONE WHICH SHALL NOT BE DESTROYED." Peter wrote that "JESUS CHRIST ... HAS GONE INTO HEAVEN AND IS AT THE RIGHT HAND OF GOD, ANGELS, AUTHORITIES, AND POWERS HAVING BEEN MADE SUBJECT TO HIM" (cf. 1 Pet. 3:22). (For reasons why "to the Ancent of Days" should perhaps be translated "as the Ancient of Days," cf. B. E. Reynolds' article at http://www.biblicalstudies.ru/OT/05.pdf; see also Issac Leeser's 1853 translation of the Hebrew Bible.)

Question about Hebrews 1:13: "Who exactly are/were His enemies?" According to Jesus, His enemies included Jews who rejected Him: in a prophetic parable about them in Luke 19:27, He said, "'BRING HERE THOSE ENEMIES OF MINE WHO DID NOT WANT ME TO REIGN OVER THEM, AND SLAY THEM BEFORE ME.'" Then in 20:17-19, when speaking to the chief priests and scribes, He told of how He, as the chief cornerstone, would grind His rejectors to powder. Paul spoke of the unbelieving Jews as "ENEMIES OF ... CHRIST" (Php. 3:18, cf. Rom. 11:28). (Judaism was Satan's Synagogue, according to Jesus in Rev. 2:9 & 3:9.)

Another item that might be included in the "ENEMIES" would be found in First Corinthians 15:26 which literally reads, "The last enemy being [at the time of the letter] rendered powerless is death." (This death is spiritual or sin-death, for verse 56 says that "THE STING OF DEATH IS SIN, AND THE STRENGTH OF SIN IS THE LAW"; since the Law has long since been fulfilled/abolished, and since we still experience physical death, then spiritual/fellowship death is the topic under consideration.)

The **FOOTSTOOL** motif here is an allusion to the ancient custom of placing one's foot on the neck of a defeated enemy (cf. Jsh. 10:22-25); some of the more haughty victors used their defeated enemies as stools from which to mount their horses.

In 10:12-13 Paul wrote of Jesus, saying that "THIS MAN, AFTER HE HAD OFFERED ONE SACRIFICE FOR SINS FOREVER, SAT DOWN AT THE RIGHT HAND OF GOD, FROM THAT TIME WAITING TILL HIS ENEMIES ARE MADE HIS FOOTSTOOL."

> **VERSE 14: ARE THEY** (THE ANGELS) **NOT ALL MINISTERING SPIRITS SENT FORTH TO MINISTER FOR THOSE WHO WILL INHERIT SALVATION?**

The word **ALL** was likely used in order to emphasize that even the highest ranking angel is still subject to Christ (1 Pet. 3:22) and, in a sense, even to His kingdom subjects (cf. 2:5); after all, it says here that angels were serving Christians. In fact, as mentioned in the remarks at verse 7, the original term for **MINISTER** is from a word that referred to the work of the Old Testament priests for God's people.

The phrase **SENT FORTH** means "sent repeatedly" and implies that Jesus was the One with the authority to send, while the angels merely fulfilled the role of servants-sent.

The word **FOR** means "for the sake of," meaning that angels weren't sent to minister to Christians, but for Christians; this verse, then, doesn't support the idea that each Christian has his own personal angel.

The word **WILL** literally means "about to," perhaps referring to all that the angels did for the first generation Christians in the book of Revelation, meaning that angels were being sent repeatedly during this period of transformation for those who were on the verge of inheriting (AD 70) the salvation of God's redemptive plan (cf. Eph. 1:10-14).

Thus by returning to the old law, these Hebrews would in essence be going back to a law that came through the agency of mere angels, being under the authority of Christ, the One they were being pressured to leave. Interestingly, in his discussion to the Colossians about Judaizers, Paul advised them to not be carried away into the worship of angels (Col. 2:18), meaning that they needed to cling to the substance —Christ Himself, not a mere shadow of Him (Col. 2:17).

IN SUMMARY: Jesus is superior to angels because He's unchanging from everlasting to everlasting; He corresponds to Yahweh in Psalm 102:25; and on only Him was conferred the highest honor of sitting and remain seated at God's right hand!

Hebrews 2:1-4

Although Paul hadn't finished his work of contrasting Jesus with angels (he continued this through chapter 2), he paused at the beginning of this chapter long enough to provide the first of the six warnings in this letter (cf. intro. p. v.)

The word **THEREFORE** in 2:1 tells us that this warning to these Jewish Christians was based on what he had already said in chapter 1, namely that—since God had appointed Jesus as their Prophet, Priest, and King—it was necessary that they reverse their backsliding course!

> **VERSE 1:** WE MUST GIVE THE MORE EARNEST HEED TO THE THINGS WE HAVE HEARD LEST WE DRIFT AWAY.

The word for **MUST** refers to a "need," not necessarily in the sense of being required by a command, but a need that's required by eternal self-preservation.

The word for **HEED** is means "to mind" or "hold the mind to" something, indicating that they needed to give more attention to spiritual matters than they were (cf. Heb. 5:11-12). This word was commonly used for bringing a boat to land, as if one had a rope attached to a boat and was pulling it in to safety. It's translated as "beware" in Matthew 7:15, indicating that there's danger in the path of the one who isn't minding his course.

The phrase **THE THINGS WE HAVE HEARD** refers to the good news of salvation through Jesus: Paul was exclaiming, "That for which we Jews have hoped/prayed for generations has finally arrived, so let's don't take it for granted now!"

Though suitably rendered, due to context the English phrase **LEST WE DRIFT AWAY** doesn't seem to divulge the true intensity of meaning found in its Greek counterpart; in other words, Paul didn't seem to be referring to mere absent-mindedness such as drifting along like tumbleweed that has no mind of its own. Rather, this was a purposeful releasing of themselves from their ties to Jesus, resulting in the danger of being swept away into the same calamity toward which the Jews who had never accepted Christ in the first place were headed. As a matter of fact, the original term for **DRIFT** here was used to describe a river that flowed away from and escaped its natural channel, usually due to flooding; and that fits the picture in Revelation 12:15f where persecution is depicted as coming against the church like a flood. The point is, the phrase **LEST WE DRIFT AWAY** conveys that these Jewish brethren had recognized/accepted that God's redemptive plan was being fulfilled in their lifetime by means of Jesus of Nazareth, but (due to pressure from the Judaizers) they had begun to let it slip from their grasp.

The original term for **DRIFT** was also used at times in reference to someone who let something slip his mind, which indicates a relation of this word to the term for **HEED**; it seems that, because of the flood of persecution in their time, they were like the man of James 1:23-24 who saw himself in the mirror of God's Word, but then deliberately turned away in order to forget what he saw.

These brethren were admonished to not be like dead wood that's swept away to its destruction, but to be like powerful ships, fighting the current of their generation. In fact, Jesus Himself warned them to "'STRIVE [as if swimming upstream] TO ENTER THROUGH THE NARROW GATE'" (Luke 13:24), and Peter warned them to be saved from that generation (Acts 2:40).

VERSE 2-3A: FOR IF THE WORD SPOKEN THROUGH ANGELS PROVED STEADFAST, AND EVERY TRANSGRESSION AND DISOBEDIENCE RECEIVED A JUST REWARD, HOW SHALL WE ESCAPE IF WE NEGLECT SO GREAT A SALVATION...

The word **IF** here (from ει, instead of εαν) means "since."

THE WORD SPOKEN THROUGH ANGELS, as mentioned in the study of verse 4, refers primarily to the Law being given from God to Moses via angels (cf. Acts 7:30, 38, & 52-53).

Paul said that **THE WORD** had been **PROVEN**. How? Through all the miracles which attended it (cf. Acts 7:30, 35-36, and Heb. 12:18-21 & 25-26).

The word for **STEADFAST** means "valid"—from God, therefore "reliable."

The word for **TRANSGRESSION** refers to a stepping over the line, which is done when one (as Romans 2:23 translates it) breaks a/the law; this is the sin of commission, where one, in a spirit of rebellion, refuses to be bound by one or more laws.

The word for **DISOBEDIENCE** refers to a refusal to listen or to discover what's expected of him (as if "ignorance is bliss"); this is the sin of omission, where one, also in a spirit of rebellion, merely allows information to "DRIFT" by him. Related to this, "hearing" and "obeying" are often used interchangeably in the Bible.

> Exodus 15:26 has God saying to the Jews to "'DILIGENTLY HEED THE VOICE OF THE LORD YOUR GOD AND DO WHAT IS RIGHT IN HIS SIGHT, GIVE EAR TO HIS COMMANDMENTS AND KEEP ALL HIS STATUTES.'"

> Jeremiah 32:23 is an example of both sins listed here in Hebrews 2:2: the weeping prophet, when praying to God for his people, said, "'THEY HAVE NOT HEARKENED TO YOUR VOICE OR WALKED IN YOUR LAW.'" (It's interesting that most versions replace "HEARKENED" with "obey"; cf. Jer. 35:16-17.)

> In Acts 7:57-58 there's a perfect example of people who refuse to hear: concerning those who murdered Stephen
> it reads: "THEY CRIED OUT WITH A LOUD VOICE, STOPPED THEIR EARS, AND RAN AT HIM WITH ONE ACCORD; AND THEY CAST HIM OUT OF THE CITY AND STONED HIM."

The phrase for **JUST REWARD** refers to the payment of proper wages, giving one what he has earned or what's coming to him, whether good or bad (cf. Rom. 6:23). Obviously in this context it signifies punishment that fits the crime (cf. Rom. 3:8), something of which only the Creator of man and law would have proper knowledge.

The question **HOW SHALL WE ESCAPE?** was a rhetorical one to these Jewish Christians, a question that demanded a negative answer: "We cannot escape." It seems that Paul was implying to them that this was something they should have learned over the centuries.

The word for **NEGLECT** takes us back to the idea of allowing something to just drift by or away; in other words, by losing their faith and gradually releasing themselves from their ties to Jesus, they'd end up with no recourse, no way to secure their salvation before it was too late, especially since the end-time was so very close.

See, the **SALVATION** Paul wrote of here didn't just refer to the purging of their sin as alluded to in 1:3 (that which would be fulfilled in its entirety at Jerusalem's imminent destruction, Luke 21:28), but it also referred to their salvation from the approaching slaughter of the Jews. Here's why: Firstly, Paul had just referred to the physical punishments of the Jews under the Old Testament, the most of which of course resulted in an eternal sentence since physical death was involved. But, secondly, in Hebrews 10, where he essentially expanded upon 2:2-3, Paul warned of the coming Jewish destruction which was prophesied in the Old Testament and which, again, would include their eternal destruction.

After talking about how God would forget the sins of those who had accepted and stuck it out with Christ in Hebrews 10:17, Paul went on in verses 26b-30 to apply a prophecy of Moses about the Jews' destruction to the time of his writing, which, incidentally, corresponds well to Peter's words in Acts 2:40 to: "'SAVE YOURSELVES FROM THIS GENERATION'" (cf. Luke 17:25 w/ Luke 21:32).

Another way we can know that this was specifically/primarily referring to Judaism's end is that Paul also applied to his generation a prophecy about that end from Habakkuk 2:3-4, saying, "'YET A [very, very] LITTLE WHILE, AND HE WHO IS COMING WILL COME AND WILL NOT TARRY.'" (The phrase for "A LITTLE WHILE" literally means, "in a very, very short time"; some versions, such as the *New English Bible*, acknowledge this by reading, "'FOR SOON, VERY SOON, HE WHO IS TO COME WILL COME, AND HE WILL NOT DELAY.'") It's just very important we remember, as we study this and other New Testament letters, that these brethren lived during the very crossroads of God's redemptive plan.

Exactly how was this salvation **GREAT**? This could be answered in a variety of ways from other Scriptures, but since Paul went on to describe what he was thinking about in this particular context, we'll just follow his lead.

VERSE 3B: ...WHICH AT FIRST BEGAN TO BE SPOKEN BY THE LORD AND WAS CONFIRMED TO US BY THOSE WHO HEARD HIM...

The word **WHICH** points back to the salvation of the prior clause, the great salvation that "FIRST BEGAN TO BE SPOKEN BY THE LORD" Jesus when He lived on Earth. This doesn't mean that salvation had never even been alluded to before, for it had been spoken of in numerous prophecies retroactive all the way to Adam/Eve (Gen. 3:15, cf. Gal. 3:8); it's just that it was a mystery—something not very clear—until, as Paul put it, Jesus "BROUGHT LIFE AND IMMORTALITY TO LIGHT THROUGH THE GOSPEL" (2 Tim. 1:10). But, since their salvation at this time included their deliverance from Jerusalem's destruction, it could also be considered "GREAT" from that standpoint.

So another positive contrast of Jesus to the angels is that the message of angels was given in a shroud of mystery, while the message of Christ was given in the clarity of crystal. Besides that, it was **CONFIRMED**, a word which means the same thing as the phrase "PROVEN STEADFAST" in verse 2.

The phrase **THOSE WHO HEARD HIM** is of course a reference to the apostles who followed Jesus from His baptism to His crucifixion (cf. 1 John 1:1-3 & 2 Pet. 1:16-18).

Since Paul brought up how the Old and <u>unclear</u> Law provided by angels was confirmed as truly from God to their satisfaction by various miracles, he went on to write of how the New and <u>clear</u> Law provided by Christ and His apostles was likewise confirmed through various miracles.

> **VERSE 4: ...GOD ALSO BEARING WITNESS BOTH WITH SIGNS AND WONDERS, WITH VARIOUS MIRACLES, AND GIFTS OF THE HOLY SPIRIT, ACCORDING TO HIS OWN WILL?**

The phrase **GOD ALSO BEARING WITNESS** doesn't mean that God was bearing witness separate/apart from Jesus and His apostles, but along with/through/by means of them. So when Jesus or a lone apostle needed a second witness as the Law required (Deu. 19:15, etc.), God was there to be that substantiating Witness.

Referring to the witness of miracles by God for the apostles, Jesus told them that He (who is also God) would be their Witness to the end of the age (Mat. 28:20). How can we know this statement of Jesus was in reference to miracles? Because Mark's parallel account in 16:17-18 indicates this. Notice the following two charts of comparison.

MATTHEW 28:18-20	**MARK 16:15-20**
Go make disciples (v. 19).	Go preach the Gospel to every creature (v. 15).
Baptize them (v. 19).	He who is baptized will be saved (v. 16).
I'm with you daily—even to the end of the age (v. 20). How? →	Signs will follow (v. 17). Jesus confirmed the Word by signs (v. 20).

Mark 16:16-20	Hebrews 2:1-4
Preaching went out to the world (v. 20).	Paul said to give heed to what's been heard (v. 1).
Jesus spoke of being saved (v. 16).	Paul wrote about salvation (v. 3).
Jesus spoke of unbelievers being condemned (v. 16).	Paul spoke of the penalty for neglecting salvation (v. 3).
The Lord had spoken to them (v. 19).	Paul said it was spoken by the Lord (v. 3).
Jesus said that signs would follow (v. 17).	Paul said it was confirmed (v. 3).
The Lord confirmed it by signs (v. 20).	Paul said God witnessed to it with signs (v. 4).

The word **BOTH** here in Hebrews 2:3b may be confusing until one takes a careful look at the original language. In other words, since the term "BOTH" concerns two things, how does it fit in this verse which concerns at least three things: signs, wonders, and miracles? After scrutinizing the Greek, one will discover that the word, as usual, actually only modifies {1} Jesus and {2} His apostles in the previous clause.

Furthermore, though **SIGNS, WONDERS, AND MIRACLES** were differing feats that were executed, they also pictured different things accomplished by supernatural feats in sight of an audience: for example, to one person the healing of a lame man would be a "sign"—a miraculous confirmation of the authority of the miracle-worker; to another person the healing of a lame man would be a "wonder"—something that got his attention in order to hear what the miracle-worker had to say; and to still another person the healing of a lame man would be a "miracle"—a work from God, the only One who possesses the power to perform such supernatural feats. Another way to put this is that supernatural occurrences may be described as "SIGNS" in their purpose (affecting the intellect), "WONDERS" in their nature (affecting the emotions), and "MIRACLES" in their origin (producing faith).

Speaking of "origin," the term for **MIRACLES** (the word from which the English term "dynamite" is derived) actually refers to "powers" of God; Jesus and the apostles always gave glory to God for the power that worked in/through them.

The word **GIFTS** suggests the idea of distribution, meaning that the Holy Spirit had and utilized the authority to distribute the various miraculous gifts, something Paul wrote about at length in First Corinthians 12:4-11.

So due to all the wondrous ways in which Jesus transcends the prophets and the angels (including, as discussed in the first chapter, His being the perfect Savior), these brethren were expected to not only be more grateful to God than ever before, but also to demonstrate their gratefulness more than ever before by not neglecting that which God had given them at such great cost! As Jesus Himself said in Luke 12:48, "'TO WHOM MUCH IS GIVEN, FROM HIM MUCH WILL BE REQUIRED'" or expected.

Because they, under the persecutorial pressure of Jewish-rejectors, had begun losing their determination, Paul was telling them that if there had ever been a time in their history when they needed to pay attention to their relationship with their God, that time was now—in the mid AD 60s when the end of their old age/world was on the verge of meeting its purposed conclusion!

Hebrews 2:5-11

So far in Hebrews, Paul has referred to Jesus as being God (1:1-6), as being the King of a new kingdom (1:7-9), and as the One through whom the old world was exchanged for a new one, bringing a great salvation not to be neglected (1:10–2:4). Now, with that new world (that "NEW HEAVENS AND EARTH") in mind, he continued to write:

> **VERSE 5: FOR HE HAS NOT PUT THE WORLD TO COME, OF WHICH WE SPEAK, IN SUBJECTION TO ANGELS.**

The word **FOR** here makes the warning of 2:1-4 a connector between chapter 1:1-14 and 2:5-18; in other words, 2:5-18 present even more reasons why the recipients of this letter should avoid forsaking Christ—the main reason being that only through Christ can man enjoy a relationship with His Creator (cf. John 14:6). Remember 1:14 which indicates that this salvation/reconciliation was still on its way at the time of this letter (cf. notes on that verse). This salvation would be "THE TIME OF REFORMATION" (9:10; cf. "THE TIMES OF RESTORATION" in Acts 3:19ff).

As mentioned back in the notes for 1:6, the Greek term for **WORLD** here isn't the word for "planet" or the word for "age," but οικουμενε, a term that refers to "a certain people" of a certain age of planet Earth—a kingdom of citizens.

According to Greek Lexicons, the original root term for the phrase **TO COME** (μελλω) means "about to come" or "at the point of coming"; yes, it's a relative term, but if it ever does refer to a time outside of one's own generation, then it's the exception to the rule.

Notice how this word is translated in a few passages in the *New King James Version*:

> Speaking of seconds, John wrote, "I WAS ABOUT TO WRITE" (Rev. 10:4).
>
> Speaking of minutes, Luke wrote, "AS THE DAY WAS ABOUT TO DAWN" (Acts 27:33).
>
> Speaking of hours, Luke wrote that "THE SEVEN DAYS WERE ALMOST ENDED" (Acts 21:27).
>
> Speaking from a few days to several months, Jesus cautioned the church at Ephesus to "'STRENGTHEN THE THINGS THAT ... ARE READY TO DIE'" (Rev. 3:2).

In Hebrews alone this word is found at least 10 times such as...

> "THOSE WHO WILL [are about to] INHERIT SALVATION" (1:14).
>
> "THE POWERS OF THE AGE [about] TO COME" (6:5).
>
> "CHRIST CAME AS HIGH PRIEST OF THE GOOD THINGS [about] TO COME" (9:11).
>
> "THE LAW, HAVING A SHADOW OF THE GOOD THINGS [about] TO COME" (10:1).
>
> "FIERY INDIGNATION WHICH WILL [is about to] DEVOUR THE ADVERSARIES" (10:27).
>
> "HERE WE HAVE NO CONTINUING CITY, BUT WE SEEK THE ONE [about] TO COME" (13:14).

It's interesting that every time the phrase "about to" is found in the NKJV in reference to time (23 times) it's translated from the Greek word μελλω. (Romans 15:19 is the only other instance where "about to" is found, and in that verse it has reference to a preaching circuit.) This implies that the phrase **THE WORLD TO COME** referred to the new heavens and earth, the new world or kingdom of Christ in which could be found the great salvation. (A more in-depth study of the Greek term μελλω can be found on my website: www.ASiteForTheLord.com/id15.html.)

There were two "worlds" during this period of transition: the Jewish and the Christian—the one that was going to win out (cf. Heb. 12:25-28 & Gal. 4:21-31). Here are some of the differing phrases by which this kingdom is called in the New Testament Scriptures:

- The Kingdom of Christ (Eph. 5:5)
- The Jerusalem from Above (Gal. 4:26)
- The Heavenly Jerusalem (Heb. 12:22)
- Mount Zion (Heb. 12:22)
- The World to Come (Heb. 2:5)
- The New Heavens and Earth (Rev. 21:1)
- The New Jerusalem from Heaven (Rev. 21:2)
- A Heavenly Country (Heb. 11:16)
- The City of the Living God (Heb. 12:22)

And Many Others

The word for the phrase IN SUBJECTION refers to an economy, a system of administration, which corresponds perfectly to the original term (οικουμενε) for "WORLD" here—a kingdom of subjects (those "IN SUBJECTION").

So the kingdom Jesus died to establish for man's salvation wouldn't be under the dominion of angels like the kingdom of the Old Testament; it, as originally intended, would be under man's dominion (cf. Rev. 22:5), meaning it wouldn't be administered (or proclaimed) by angels, but by man.

> **VERSES 6-8B:** BUT ONE TESTIFIED IN A CERTAIN PLACE [PSA. 8:4-6], SAYING, "WHAT IS MAN THAT YOU ARE MINDFUL OF HIM OR THE SON OF MAN THAT YOU TAKE CARE OF HIM? YOU MADE HIM A LITTLE LOWER THAN THE ANGELS; YOU CROWNED HIM WITH GLORY AND HONOR AND SET HIM OVER THE WORKS OF YOUR HANDS. YOU HAVE PUT ALL THINGS IN SUBJECTION UNDER HIS FEET." FOR IN THAT HE PUT ALL IN SUBJECTION UNDER HIM, HE LEFT NOTHING THAT IS NOT PUT UNDER HIM.

Though I've thought otherwise at times, this passage refers to humanity, not to Jesus, for at least four reasons: {1} The original word for **MAN** here isn't the Greek word (ανερ) for an individual man (like Jesus), but the Greek word (ανθροπος) for mankind; {2} Psalm 8:4-6 are about mankind in general, because it goes on to refer to creation; {3} The question "What is man that You [God] are mindful of and care about him?" clearly implies that a class of being less than God is under consideration; and {4} the contrasting word **BUT** between verses 8 & 9 here in Hebrews 2 indicates that Jesus became part of mankind in order for man to be reconciled to his Creator.

The phrase **THE SON OF MAN** here isn't a reference to Jesus this time, but rather a reference to the earthly nature of the children of Adam—those of the dust of the earth; notice a parallel in Psalm 144:3: "LORD, WHAT IS MAN THAT YOU TAKE KNOWLEDGE OF HIM? OR THE SON OF MAN THAT YOU ARE MINDFUL OF HIM? MAN IS LIKE A BREATH ... LIKE A PASSING SHADOW."

The phrase **TAKE CARE** is from the Greek word επισχοπος, the word from which the Episcopal church gets its name and which is translated as "BISHOP" (1 Pet. 2:25) and "OVERSEER" (Acts 20:28). This care-taking of man is the result of God's mindfulness of man.

The clause **YOU MADE HIM A LITTLE LOWER THAN THE ANGELS** is defined by verse 9 to mean (at least in part) that man is capable of dying, while angels aren't: "JESUS ... WAS MADE A LITTLE LOWER THAN THE ANGELS FOR THE SUFFERING OF DEATH."

The statement that **YOU HAVE PUT ALL THINGS IN SUBJECTION UNDER HIS FEET** would more literally read, "You place (not 'have placed') all things in subjection under his feet." This is important because, unlike the way it reads in English, taking it this way doesn't necessitate that those things were still under man's feet. Besides, verse 8 goes on to say that things are not under man, at least not at the time of Paul's writing.

To say that **HE LEFT NOTHING THAT IS NOT PUT UNDER HIM** means that, in the beginning, mankind was meant to be the very highest of all earthly beings, the only one with a special relationship to his Creator; but, since he was careless with this relationship, it would need to be restored through Christ, thus the rest of verse 8 and verse 9 read as follows:

> **VERSES 8C-9: BUT NOW WE DO NOT YET SEE ALL THINGS PUT UNDER HIM. BUT WE SEE JESUS, WHO WAS MADE A LITTLE LOWER THAN THE ANGELS, FOR THE SUFFERING OF DEATH CROWNED WITH GLORY AND HONOR, THAT HE, BY THE GRACE OF GOD, MIGHT TASTE DEATH FOR EVERYONE.**

The original Greek of verse 8c reads more like this: "BUT NOT AS YET ARE WE SEEING ALL THINGS HAVING BEEN SUBJECTED TO HIM." So Paul was implying that this Psalm was actually an indirect prediction of what would be accomplished in Christ—the very event these brethren were "about to" experience (1:14 & 2:5)—the time when mankind could finally have and hold onto a (sinless) relationship with His Creator.

As one compares Psalm 8 with this text, he discovers wherein at least part of man's dominion in Eden had lain: Adam had the choice to be and remain in a (holy/sinless) relationship with God, an idea Paul brought up again in 8:10-11. So being helplessly lost, Paul wrote, **WE SEE JESUS** who is the answer to man's sin-problem. Incidentally, since this is the first time the name of the person Paul had been describing for 20+ verses is mentioned in this letter, it seems that he was building up to this very statement—**WE SEE JESUS!**

Paul then wrote that **JESUS ... WAS MADE A LITTLE LOWER THAN THE ANGELS FOR THE SUFFERING OF DEATH.** Verse 14 puts it like this: "AS THE CHILDREN HAVE PARTAKEN OF FLESH AND BLOOD, HE [Jesus] HIMSELF LIKEWISE SHARED IN THE SAME, THAT THROUGH DEATH HE MIGHT DESTROY HIM WHO HAD THE POWER OF DEATH, THAT IS, THE DEVIL." And verse 17 puts it like this: "HE HAD TO BE MADE LIKE HIS BRETHREN ... TO MAKE PROPITIATION FOR THE SINS OF THE PEOPLE." So not only was/is Jesus the Son of God/Deity/King/Savior, but He was also—at one time and in order to beget or bring about the great salvation—<u>a man</u>.

In this context, being **CROWNED WITH GLORY AND HONOR** likely corresponds to the idea just discussed, namely the idea of being holy; in other words, by His own will and as a man, Jesus died sinless. (Besides, in the original it's *"having been crowned"*; and in Psalm 8 man's crown of honor and his dominion are interlaced.)

The phrase **TASTE DEATH** simply means to experience death, but its apparent origin is from one of the various forms of execution; Socrates, for example, was forced to taste, or drink from, a cup of poison.

In the context of some of the very same ideas (1 Cor. 15:24-28), First Corinthians 15:21-22, 45, & 47-49 read, "SO YOU SEE, JUST AS DEATH CAME INTO THE WORLD THROUGH A MAN, ADAM, NOW THE RESURRECTION OF THE DEAD [ones] HAS BEGUN THROUGH ANOTHER MAN, CHRIST. EVERYONE DIES BECAUSE ALL OF US ARE RELATED TO ADAM, THE FIRST MAN. BUT ALL WHO ARE RELATED TO CHRIST, THE OTHER MAN, WILL BE GIVEN NEW LIFE (NLT). ... SO IT IS WRITTEN, 'THE FIRST MAN ADAM BECAME A LIVING BEING'; THE LAST ADAM A LIFE-GIVING SPIRIT.... THE FIRST MAN WAS OF THE DUST OF THE EARTH, THE SECOND MAN FROM HEAVEN. AS WAS THE EARTHLY MAN, SO ARE THOSE WHO ARE OF THE EARTH; AND AS IS THE MAN FROM HEAVEN, SO ALSO ARE THOSE WHO ARE OF HEAVEN. AND JUST AS WE HAVE BORNE THE LIKENESS OF THE EARTHLY MAN, SO SHALL WE BEAR THE LIKENESS OF THE MAN FROM HEAVEN (NIV).

The Last Adam, Jesus, gained the victory (1 Cor. 15:57) through the blood of His cross over the enemy under whose attack the first Adam had gone down in defeat. Being sinless and raising Himself out from under sin's consequence—"death," the Last Adam made it possible for the saints of all ages to share in His glory (cf. Rom. 5:12-19).

> **VERSE 10:** FOR IT WAS FITTING FOR HIM, FOR WHOM ARE ALL THINGS AND BY WHOM ARE ALL THINGS, IN BRINGING MANY SONS TO GLORY, TO MAKE THE AUTHOR OF THEIR SALVATION PERFECT THROUGH SUFFERINGS.

As a defense against Judaizers who said such things as, "'WE HAVE HEARD FROM THE LAW THAT THE CHRIST REMAINS FOREVER. SO HOW CAN YOU SAY, "THE SON OF MAN MUST BE LIFTED UP?"'" (John 12:34), Paul simply said it was because **IT WAS FITTING**, a phrase which likely means that, because of the justice and mercy within God's nature, this is the way He chose to save us, regardless if we understand it. Besides, Paul argued that their own Law prophesied of it as occurring in this fashion: in Hebrews 10:5-7 he wrote, "CHRIST, WHEN HE CAME INTO THE WORLD, SAID [to His Father], 'YOU DIDN'T WANT ANIMAL SACRIFICES AND GRAIN OFFERINGS, SO YOU HAVE GIVEN ME A BODY SO THAT I MAY OBEY YOU. NO, YOU WERE NOT PLEASED WITH ANIMALS BURNED ON THE ALTAR OR WITH OTHER OFFERINGS FOR SIN. ... LOOK, I HAVE COME TO DO YOUR WILL, O GOD—JUST AS IT'S WRITTEN ABOUT ME IN THE SCRIPTURES'" (NLT).

So, since it's true that their own Scriptures attested to this, why did the Jews say that they were taught from the Law that their Messiah would live forever? Well, all we have to do is remember that they thought of the Messiah's kingdom as a physical kingdom, and since His kingdom was to never be destroyed, they also believed this Messiah from God would live forever, certainly not die on a cross!

The pronoun **HIM** is undoubtedly a reference to God the Father—also the subject of the first part of verse 11.

The phrase **ALL THINGS** here should likely be associated with the next phrase—the **BRINGING** [OF] **MANY SONS TO GLORY**, reminiscent of Romans 8:29 where Paul said that Jesus would be "THE FIRSTBORN OF MANY BRETHREN." (Cf. the comments at 1:5 concerning "begotten.")

The word **GLORY** is equal to the word **SALVATION** in the next clause, which means that, through Christ, man can possess his intended glory, namely a relationship with his immortal Creator apart from sin which only separates them; being separated from Him who is immortal (1 Tim. 6:16) means not having immortality ourselves.

The word **BRINGING** may be better understood as "leading" in this context; after all, sort of like the pied piper, one "brings" those he "leads." By the way, the word for **AUTHOR** literally means "leader" and was used to refer to the commander of an army who went ahead of his men, blazing the trail for them; this is why the KJV translated it as "CAPTAIN" (cf. Heb. 5:8-9, 6:20, & 12:2).

By means of His suffering/death, Jesus was made **PERFECT** or completely qualified. Thus God's Son preceded the saved on the road to Heaven; in fact, Jesus Himself said that He is the road or the way (John 14:6), and in Hebrews (10:20) Paul spoke of Jesus as the new and living road or way into the presence of God, the road sprinkled with the blood of Jesus; in other words, Jesus is both the leader on the road and the road itself (cf. Isa. 35:8).

> **VERSE 11: FOR BOTH HE WHO SANCTIFIES AND THOSE WHO ARE SANCTIFIED ARE ALL OF ONE, FOR WHICH REASON HE IS NOT ASHAMED TO CALL THEM BRETHREN.**

The phrase **OF ONE** literally means from or out of one source or origin—God the Father; in other words, since both Jesus and the saints (the "SONS" in v. 10 & the "SANCTIFIED" of v. 11) can call God "Father" (Gal. 4:6), Jesus isn't ashamed to call them His "BRETHREN." Incidentally, the word **BRETHREN** here is from a term meaning "from the same womb," which, in this context, is reminiscent of Peter's words about saints taking part in "THE DIVINE NATURE" (2 Pet. 1:4)—the nature of God (Heb. 12:10) and big brother Jesus (cf. notes on 1:8).

The point is that Jesus wasn't so divine that (as the Judaizers implied) He wouldn't allow Himself to become a human and suffer the humiliation of dying on a cross—for that's exactly what He did, and He isn't ashamed to call sanctified humans His brethren. So God, the greatest being imaginable, is also the most humble imaginable—one of the many ironies about Yahweh around which most Jews just couldn't seem to wrap their minds. (Cf. Php. 2:6-9.)

Hebrews 2:12-18

Genesis informs us that God created man in His own image and with a dominion which included a relationship with his Creator that none else on Earth possessed; however, God, apparently wanting to be loved by man without an innate compulsion (like robots) to do so, provided him with a free will that he used to choose self over God.

Since man broke his relationship with his Creator by opting to commit sin, and since through thousands of years following that decision it was demonstrated that no mere human could restore that relationship, Jesus, God's Son, then came on the scene to repair it for him.

In studying 2:5-11 one learns that Jesus is superior to angels for two reasons: {1} He—as God and not an angel—became human in order to mend man's relationship to his Creator, thereby reestablishing his initial dominion; and {2} He was crowned as eternal King over the kingdom which consists of those who desire that mended relationship with God through His Son (which of course is the only way to possess it, John 14:6).

Upon approaching the remainder of Hebrews chapter 2, one must also remember that most Jews had trouble not only with God becoming a man, but also with Jesus being the fulfillment of the Messianic prophecies, especially since He died a criminal's death by crucifixion—*for surely that was confirmation that He couldn't have been the promised King!*

Although Hebrews 2:12-18 continue the same subject-matter of verses 5-11, they close out Paul's argumentation for the superiority of Jesus over angels.

> **VERSE 12: "I WILL DECLARE YOUR NAME TO MY BRETHREN, IN THE MIDST OF THE CONGREGATION I WILL SING PRAISE TO YOU."**

Since Paul just stated in verse 11 that Jesus isn't ashamed to call sanctified ones His brethren, he went on to support his assertion by the use of three Old Testament quotations, the first from a well-known Messianic verse: Psalm 22:22. The Messiah was prophesied as saying to God, "I WILL DECLARE YOUR NAME"; to **DECLARE ONE'S NAME** simply means to speak of the character of the person behind the name.

The phrase **TO MY BRETHREN** is obviously the phrase that Paul meant to emphasize here; just as David wrote hundreds of years prior, the coming Messiah, right alongside His New Covenant age siblings (v. 11), would unashamedly worship their mutual Father.

The original term for the phrase **SING PRAISE** is actually the term from which we get our word "hymn" (ηψμνεσω); even so, it doesn't <u>necessarily</u> mean to sing, for it can also merely mean "to praise," as the term is actually translated in Psalm 22:22 and even here in some versions such as the RSV.

> **VERSE 13: AND AGAIN: "I WILL PUT MY TRUST IN HIM." AND AGAIN: "HERE AM I AND THE CHILDREN WHOM GOD HAS GIVEN ME."**

(Side-note: Lest one loses sight of it, the main point here is that Jesus, because He became one of us, had to depend upon God just as other human beings, not for redemption from sin that He committed of course, but in order to be made completely qualified to lead us—sinners—to salvation, v. 10).

These two separate quotes are from Isaiah 8:17-18: the first indicates that Jesus, as God's Son, placed His trust in God His Father, while the second indicates His close link to God's other children who are placed under Jesus' guardianship as the elder brother.

> **VERSE 14: INASMUCH THEN AS THE CHILDREN HAVE PARTAKEN OF FLESH AND BLOOD, HE HIMSELF LIKEWISE SHARED IN THE SAME, THAT THROUGH DEATH HE MIGHT DESTROY HIM WHO HAD THE POWER OF DEATH, THAT IS, THE DEVIL.** (CF. 1 JOHN 3:8.)

The phrase **FLESH AND BLOOD** was used by ancients to describe humanity in contrast to deity.

The original word for **SHARED** refers to the voluntary acceptance of becoming human. (There's a different Greek term for being born human without the choice of being so.)

The original word for **DESTROY** literally means "to render inoperative or ineffective as if no longer existing"; this word is rendered as "WITHOUT EFFECT" in Romans 3:3.

The word for **POWER** here isn't the term meaning "authority"; it's actually an antonym for **DESTROY**, for while "to destroy" means "to render powerless," **POWER** here is the word for "strength." Look at it this way: In Genesis 3:15 God said that the head of the foe (here **THE DEVIL**, meaning opposer/slanderer) would be crushed by the Messiah; but, in the process of that crushing, the Christ's heel would be wounded, meaning that crushing the enemy would come at a price—a brief separation from the Father (Mat. 27:46). Why? Because on the cross Jesus bore the sin which brought about the death/separation of the two parties in the first place (cf. Gen. 2:15-17 & 3:1-24). So Christ, by taking sin upon Himself in His sacrifice, began the process of, as Paul wrote in First Corinthians 15:26, *rendering* sin-death *powerless* (note present tense of the Greek), a process that was accomplished when the Law had been fulfilled at the demise of the Old Covenant Temple and its Holy City ca. AD 70 (1 Cor. 15:56). Incidentally, by "sin-death" is meant the severing of fellowship between God and man; thus, by fulfilling/eliminating the Law which gave sin its power, thereby in turn stripping sin of its power—death/separation, all who so choose may be reconciled to (made friends again with) the Father. (For in-depth studies on 1 Cor. 15 & 2 Cor. 5, see http://ASiteForTheLord.com/id15.html.)

Jesus' death/resurrection/ascension, the destruction of the temple/Jerusalem, the fulfillment/consummation of the Old Covenant world/life, all conspired to bring about the total crushing of the enemies of God and man and their relationship to one another: not only was that which was physical and temporal—the Jesus-hating Jews—taken care of, but also that which was spiritual and eternal—sin and its ensuing death—was taken care of (at least for those who accept this graciously offered gift of God). Just reflect on how great an encouragement it was to the Christians in Rome (who were also suffering persecution) when, ca. AD 57, Paul told them that "THE GOD OF PEACE WILL CRUSH SATAN UNDER YOUR FEET SHORTLY" (Rom. 16:20).

> **VERSE 15:** [JESUS BECAME A MAN, THAT THROUGH DEATH HE MIGHT] **RELEASE THOSE WHO, THROUGH FEAR OF DEATH, WERE ALL THEIR LIFETIME SUBJECT TO BONDAGE.**

The word **RELEASE** means "to set free from something."

The word **FEAR** is a translation of the Greek word from which we get "phobia," and, as John wrote, "FEAR INVOLVES TORMENT" (1 John 4:18).

The phrase **SUBJECT TO BONDAGE** means "held in slavery."

Humans without Christ are slaves to fear—the fear of separation from the Creator for all eternity (what many call "spiritual death"), something that's sealed by physical death if reconciliation isn't realized beforehand. No wonder Job looked upon death as "THE KING OF TERRORS" (Job 18:14).

Death as the result of sin (Rom. 6:23) was made even more clear and potent by means of the Law (Rom. 7), because it didn't offer salvation, only condemnation (Gal. 3:19); this was the main flaw of the Law (Heb. 8:6-7), not that the Law itself was faulty, but (because man couldn't fulfill righteousness or become righteous through the Law, Rom. 7:4), it was inadequate to reconcile him to God.

In fact, notice how Christ's overcoming death was joined with the destruction of the Law in First Corinthians 15:55-56: "THE STING OF DEATH IS SIN, AND THE STRENGTH OF SIN IS THE LAW. BUT THANKS BE TO GOD WHO GIVES US THE VICTORY THROUGH OUR LORD JESUS CHRIST." So Jesus came on the scene as a human who lived the Law perfectly, thereby fulfilling all righteousness (cf. Mat. 3:15) as well as the prophecies concerning the One who would bring in a new law of grace and life; by means of this accomplishment, He abolished the Law of sin and death (Rom. 8:2) which provided the enemy with his great advantage over man. Now through Christ there's a blessing found in the idea of death (Rev. 14:13).

> **VERSE 16:** FOR INDEED HE DOES NOT GIVE AID TO ANGELS, BUT HE DOES GIVE AID TO THE SEED OF ABRAHAM.

The word **INDEED** here isn't the usual one which means "truly"; this one carries with it a sense of praise, as if Paul were saying, "Isn't it amazing?!"

Since Paul was writing to Jewish Christians, and since he had just stated in verse 9 that Jesus died for all races, we know he used the phrase **SEED OF ABRAHAM** rhetorically; the truth is, as Paul said in Romans and Galatians, anyone—Jew or not—who chose/chooses to place his faith in Christ is a child of Abraham (Gal. 3:9 & 29).

According to Kenneth Wuest (who authored *Word Studies in the Greek New Testament*), the idea in this extended context seems to be that "Jesus, in His work on the cross, didn't provide for the salvation of fallen angels, but for the salvation of fallen human beings. In perfect righteousness, He passed by fallen angels, and in infinite mercy and condescension, He stooped to provide salvation for man. He passed by the superior being to save the inferior being."

> **VERSE 17:** THEREFORE IN ALL THINGS HE HAD TO BE MADE LIKE HIS BRETHREN THAT HE MIGHT BE A MERCIFUL AND FAITHFUL HIGH PRIEST IN THINGS PERTAINING TO GOD TO MAKE PROPITIATION FOR THE SINS OF THE PEOPLE.

The phrase **HE HAD TO BE MADE** must not be interpreted to mean that Jesus was obligated to save man who willingly broke bonds with Him, for justice would have prevailed if He had not done so. So what does it mean? This verse itself explains it to mean that (due to Jesus' mercy—His desire to save us regardless) He had to be made human in order to fulfill the requirements of that salvation, meaning He had to keep His own laws perfectly.

The phrase **LIKE HIS BRETHREN** refers not to simulation, but to assimilation, meaning that Jesus, who's 100% God, was also, at one time, 100% man—**IN ALL THINGS** or in every way.

The phrase **THAT HE MIGHT BE A MERCIFUL AND FAITHFUL HIGH PRIEST** means that He's compassionate, constituting Him a faithful High Priest; this means that, by becoming or being human Himself, He could truly sympathize with us (4:15).

The high-priesthood of Christ is the keynote of the book of Hebrews; it was alluded to in 1:3, but this is the first time it's mentioned directly, setting the tone for the rest of the book.

Having shown that Christ came to deliver mankind from the fear of death, Paul here showed that this was achieved in His role as High Priest, something that's very fitting since in the Old Testament the fear of death was especially connected with the approach to God of an impure worshipper (Num. 18:3).

This fear was relieved or removed by the intervention of the Levitical priest, because it was his duty to discharge the service of the tabernacle that there might be no outbreak of divine wrath on the children of Israel (Num. 18:5); in other words, the work of the priesthood was not without its stress!

Perhaps in part because of the stress involved in this job, compassion as an attribute of priests isn't found in the Old Testament; on the contrary, the fault of the priests was their frequent lack of sympathy for the people (cf. Hos. 4:4-9). In the latter part of Jewish history (i.e. in the New Testament times), priests—especially the Sadducees—were notoriously unfeeling and cruel, so the idea of a compassionate (as well as a faithful) high priest was very appealing to Jewish readers.

The phrase **THINGS PERTAINING TO GOD** (as defined by the next phrase) simply refers to Jesus as fulfilling ... once and for all time ... the conditions of God concerning the reconciliation of man; Jesus—who's merciful to man and faithful to God—is our sacrifice on Earth and our High Priest in Heaven.

The word **PROPITIATION** is more recognizable to us today by the term atonement (at-<u>one</u>-ment), a term actually invented specifically as a translation for "that which or for one who restores," in this case the relationship between God and man (Heaven and Earth) that was marred by sin; as John wrote of Jesus, "HE ... IS THE PROPITIATION FOR OUR SINS, AND NOT FOR OURS ONLY, BUT ALSO FOR THE WHOLE WORLD" (1 John 2:2). So Jesus became like us (Heb. 2:17) that we might become like Him (1 John 3:2).

(Much more along these lines may be found in the remarks on chapter five.)

> **VERSE 18: FOR IN THAT HE HIMSELF HAS SUFFERED, BEING TEMPTED, HE IS ABLE TO AID THOSE WHO ARE TEMPTED.**

Recalling that Paul was writing to suffering Christians, it only makes sense that he'd essentially ask them, "Why would Jesus become human, suffer, and die for you, only to forsake you?" which, by the way, is exactly the idea with which he ended the book in 13:5-6.

The point was that just because Jesus was gone from them in the flesh didn't mean that He was unconcerned and uninvolved in their lives; rather, as demonstrated in the story of Stephen's stoning when he saw Jesus "STANDING" (instead of sitting) at God's right hand, Paul wrote later in Hebrews 4:15 that Jesus is a truly sympathetic High Priest.

The phrase **HE HAS SUFFERED** brings to mind Luke 22:28 where Jesus seemed to imply to His apostles that His entire life, especially the 3.5 years of His ministry, was continually plagued with the suffering of trials: He said, "'YOU ARE THOSE WHO HAVE CONTINUED WITH ME IN MY TRIALS.'"

The phrase **HE IS ABLE** strikes at the heart of the matter: Jesus doesn't sympathize with us just because, as Deity, He's aware of everything, but also because, having been human, He experienced what they were experiencing (i.e. suffering). In fact, He warned His disciples, saying, "'SINCE THEY PERSECUTED ME, THEY WILL ALSO PERSECUTE YOU'" (John 15:20), and "'IN THE WORLD YOU WILL HAVE TRIBULATION; BUT BE OF GOOD CHEER, I HAVE OVERCOME THE WORLD'" (John 16:33).

The word **AID** here comes from a word which means to call for help or run toward a cry for help; these brethren needed to realize that, as Peter wrote, "THE LORD KNOWS HOW TO DELIVER THE GODLY OUT OF TEMPTATIONS" (2 Pet. 2:9) and that, as Paul wrote, "GOD IS FAITHFUL, WHO WILL NOT ALLOW YOU TO BE TEMPTED BEYOND WHAT YOU ARE ABLE, BUT WITH THE TEMPTATION WILL ALSO MAKE A WAY OF ESCAPE THAT YOU MAY BE ABLE TO BEAR IT" (1 Cor. 10:13).

The word for **TEMPTED** carries more the idea of being tried than tempted; these two concepts can't be entirely separated, but the idea of being tried by persecution fits the whole point of this letter much better than being tempted.

Hebrews 3:1-6

The last six sections in Hebrews have been concerned with *The Superiority of Christ's Person* in relation to the prophets and especially the angels. Beginning in 3:1, Hebrews now concerns itself with *The Superiority of Christ's Priesthood*. Paul initiated this argumentation with Christ's Superiority to Moses (who, according to Psalm 99:6, was a priest).

This chapter could be outlined as follows: *Christ is greater than Moses in His office* (3:1-2); *Christ is greater than Moses in His ministry* (3:3-6); and *Christ is greater than Moses in His reward* (3:7-19).

See, if Paul could prove that Jesus was/is superior to Moses, then how could they go back to Judaism when what Christ offered was so much greater than what Moses offered?

> **VERSE 1: THEREFORE, HOLY BRETHREN, PARTAKERS OF THE HEAVENLY CALLING, CONSIDER THE APOSTLE AND HIGH PRIEST OF OUR CONFESSION, CHRIST JESUS...**

The word **HOLY** describes something/someone who has been set apart by/for/and to God—a saint, someone who has been sanctified as mentioned in 2:11; an interesting point here is that New Testament people become brethren voluntarily through their decision to be holy, while Old Testament people were brethren because they were born as such (cf. 8:10-11), which leads to the next word.

The word **PARTAKERS** was discussed in 2:14 (where the verb form is translated as "SHARED"): this is the particular Greek word which refers to someone voluntarily taking something upon himself; in other words, these brethren weren't saved against their will—they chose to accept the calling of God. (This is the same word used in Luke 5:7 to refer to partners in the fishing business, as well as the same word used in Hebrews 3:14 to refer to partners of Christ [cf. 2:10-11 & Eph. 5:30].)

The phrase **HEAVENLY CALLING** conveys the concept found in Second Thessalonians 2:13-14 where Paul wrote, "WE ... GIVE THANKS ALWAYS FOR YOU, BRETHREN ... BECAUSE GOD ... FOR SALVATION THROUGH SANCTIFICATION ... CALLED YOU BY THE GOSPEL." And God, through this Gospel, called them to what? His "HEAVENLY COUNTRY" (as opposed to the earthly one of Canaan, 11:16) or "HEAVENLY JERUSALEM" (as opposed to the earthly one, 12:22), thereby making them citizens of Heaven (Php. 3:20).

The word **CONSIDER** means "to fix one's eyes upon" (cf. NIV). They were gradually moving their eyes away from Jesus and back to Moses (cf. 2:1). Later in 12:2 Paul told them to look to Jesus, the author and finisher of their faith (cf. 2:10).

The word **APOSTLE** refers to someone who was sent on a commission, especially by God. Just as Moses was sent by God to lead the people to the promised land of Canaan (Exo. 3:10 where, in the LXX, the word for "apostle" is used), Jesus was sent by God (1 John 4:14) to lead the people to the promised land of salvation (Heb. 2:10). So, just as Paul indirectly contrasted the first Adam and the Last Adam in chapter 2, here he contrasted the first apostle, Moses, with the second apostle, Christ.

Jesus is said here to be **THE APOSTLE AND HIGH PRIEST OF OUR CONFESSION**, which simply means that Jesus was the One they named in their confession when they were saved: in Romans 10:9-10 Paul wrote that "IF YOU CONFESS WITH YOUR MOUTH THE LORD JESUS ... YOU WILL BE SAVED. FOR ... WITH THE MOUTH CONFESSION IS MADE TO SALVATION." The word "CONFESS" means "to agree with another"; an example of this is when someone confesses Jesus as God's Son, for he's agreeing with God's own statement to that effect (Mat. 3:17 & 17:5).

A passage that corresponds very well with this verse is First Timothy 6:12 where Paul told Timothy to "LAY HOLD ON ETERNAL LIFE TO WHICH YOU WERE CALLED AND HAVE CONFESSED THE GOOD CONFESSION IN THE PRESENCE OF MANY WITNESSES."

Paul made it a point to refer to their previous confession of Jesus as the Christ—the Messiah, so now they were being urged to remain faithful to that confession; to these suffering Christians, he reiterated this toward the end of the book: "LET US HOLD FAST THE CONFESSION OF OUR HOPE [in Christ] WITHOUT WAVERING, FOR HE WHO PROMISED IS FAITHFUL" (10:23).

> **VERSE 2:** ...WHO WAS FAITHFUL TO HIM WHO APPOINTED HIM, AS MOSES ALSO WAS FAITHFUL IN ALL HIS HOUSE.

The first **WAS** in this verse should be translated as "is"—Jesus is faithful. (To mistranslate it as "was" is to teach that Christ's work was finished at the time of this writing when it wasn't.)

The word for **APPOINTED** literally means "to make"; in other words, just as God made Moses the apostle to the Jews and Aaron the high priest for the Jews (cf. 1 Sam. 12:6, esp. in the LXX), so He made Jesus both our Apostle and High Priest.

Moses was referred to here not only because he was the most revered character of the Old Testament, but also because he was the very representation of the Old Covenant, just as Christ is the very representation of the New Covenant.

The word **HIS** in the phrase **HIS HOUSE** refers to God, meaning that Moses was faithful in fulfilling his apostolic duties in God's Old Testament house (or church, Acts 7:38), which was the house or family of Israel; we can be certain of this because the first part of verse 2 is based on Numbers 12:7, where God said of Moses that "'HE IS FAITHFUL IN ALL MY HOUSE.'"

Since verses 2 & 5 allude to God's Old Covenant house of which Moses was a part, and since verse 6 alludes to the New Covenant house over which Jesus resides, then it seems obvious that the first part of verse 2 alludes to the faithfulness of Jesus who was set in position—not in but—over God's house.

To encourage faithfulness in them, Paul was thus indicating that his persecuted audience needed to fix their eyes upon the faithfulness of Jesus, who, because He never failed, was even more faithful than their beloved Moses.

> **VERSE 3:** FOR THIS ONE HAS BEEN COUNTED WORTHY OF MORE GLORY THAN MOSES, INASMUCH AS HE WHO BUILT THE HOUSE HAS MORE HONOR THAN THE HOUSE.

The **ONE** here is of course Jesus. So by bringing this all closer together, Paul was saying, "consider Jesus ... because He has been counted worthy of even more glory/honor/praise than the great Moses."

The word **INASMUCH** could simply be replaced by the word "just." More literally, the last part of verse 3 could read, "just as the builder has more honor than the house itself"; the *New Living Translation* reads, "JUST AS A PERSON WHO BUILDS A FINE HOUSE DESERVES MORE PRAISE THAN THE HOUSE ITSELF."

> **VERSE 4:** FOR EVERY HOUSE IS BUILT BY SOMEONE, BUT HE WHO BUILT ALL THINGS IS GOD.

After wrestling quite a while with verses 3-4, I've come to the conclusion that verses 3b-4 are merely a parenthetical analogy brought to Paul's mind by his reference to a house in verse 2. This would mean that Paul wasn't teaching anything doctrinal, such as the notion that Jesus built the Old Testament house of Israel; rather, he was merely illustrating how Jesus was worthy of more honor than Moses. Besides, in the flow of thought, verses 5 & 6 are what actually follow 3a which teaches that Christ is a son over God's house, while Moses was a mere servant in God's house.

Furthermore, even though he always returned, Paul often digressed from his main point, which is what it seems he did in verse 4: it's a short and slight (though illustrative) digression of his flow of thought, which brought glory for everything (old and new) ultimately to God.

So this verse may be reworded thusly: "Consider Jesus who is worthy of more respect than Moses (just as a builder is more worthy of honor than his building; after all, every house is built by someone, although ultimately all things are of God)."

> **VERSE 5:** AND MOSES INDEED WAS FAITHFUL IN ALL HIS HOUSE AS A SERVANT, FOR A TESTIMONY OF THOSE THINGS WHICH WOULD BE SPOKEN OF AFTERWARD...

In verse 2 Paul pointed his readers to Numbers 12:7 where one learns that Moses was faithful in God's house, but just not in what capacity; so here in verse 5 Paul pointed his readers to Numbers 12:8, because in it God described the position Moses faithfully fulfilled in the Old Covenant house—he was a mere "SERVANT."

The original word for **SERVANT** here in Hebrews isn't the usual one which means "slave"; rather, it carries with it the idea that Moses was what he was and did what he did voluntarily and conscientiously.

Since the word **TESTIMONY** will come up various times in Hebrews, one should be sure to understand what it means at this point; and to do that, he must go back 4,000 years to Abraham, the first man ever to be circumcised. ("To circumcise" means "to cut around"). So why did God devise the idea of circumcision? Because He made a promise to or a covenant with Abram that through his seed the Messiah would eventually arise; the cutting off of some superfluous skin on the genitalia (the base term for "generation," by the way) was thus a logical choice (cf. Gen. 15 & 17).

Since that organ bore the sign of a promise of God Himself, there was therefore nothing better at the time upon which one could make an oath, thus the incident in Genesis 24:2-3 which concerned Abram's lineage: Abraham "SAID TO THE OLDEST SERVANT OF HIS HOUSE, ... 'PLEASE PUT YOUR HAND UNDER MY THIGH, AND I WILL MAKE YOU SWEAR BY THE LORD, THE GOD OF HEAVEN AND THE EARTH, THAT YOU WILL NOT TAKE A WIFE FOR MY SON FROM THE DAUGHTERS OF THE CANAANITES.'"

An adult may now instantly perceive how the word "testimony" developed: terms like testify and testimony are rooted in the word "testicles"—the term for the reproductive glands that produce <u>seed</u>. In fact, all this was so important at the time that there was a law given concerning the chopping off of one's hand if that hand attempted to chop off a man's genitals (Deu. 25:11-12). The whole point here is that testimony, being associated with an oath made on a sign of God's covenant (much like the hand on the Bible in court today), was <u>not</u> to be taken lightly!

Although much of Hebrews deals with it, the typology found within the Law of Moses is directly alluded to for the first time in 3:5. Hebrews 8:5 speaks of the Old Testament priests who served "THE COPY AND SHADOW OF THE HEAVENLY THINGS, AS MOSES WAS DIVINELY INSTRUCTED WHEN HE WAS ABOUT TO MAKE THE TABERNACLE. FOR GOD SAID, 'SEE THAT YOU MAKE ALL THINGS ACCORDING TO THE PATTERN SHOWN TO YOU,'" and he did ... conscientiously. Speaking again of that tabernacle, 9:9 says it was "SYMBOLIC FOR THE PRESENT TIME." Later of the Law, 10:1 says it was "A SHADOW OF THE GOOD THINGS TO COME." Even Colossians 2:17 speaks of various things in the Law as "A SHADOW OF GOOD THINGS TO COME, BUT THE SUBSTANCE [that which casts the shadow] IS OF CHRIST," which is reminiscent of John 5:46 where Jesus said, "'IF YOU BELIEVED MOSES, YOU WOULD BELIEVE ME, FOR HE WROTE ABOUT ME.'" Moses once said to Israel, "'THE LORD ... WILL RAISE UP FOR YOU A PROPHET LIKE ME'" (Deu. 18:15); so Jesus shined the light (2 Tim. 1:10), while Moses worked in its shadows (Heb. 8:5); or one could say that Jesus was the light (John 9:5), while Moses was His shadow.

The question Paul seemed to be implying to his readers is this: "If Moses created things that typified Jesus and His church, and if Moses prophesied of Jesus and His new way, and if Moses himself was a type of the very Jesus whom you confessed as the Christ, why are you even considering the notion of returning to Judaism? Wouldn't that be a slap even in the face of Moses, much less Christ?"

The main point is this: Although he was commendably faithful, Moses was merely a servant of God, not the Son of God.

> **VERSE 6: ...BUT CHRIST AS A SON OVER HIS OWN HOUSE, WHOSE HOUSE WE ARE IF WE HOLD FAST THE CONFIDENCE AND THE REJOICING OF THE HOPE FIRM TO THE END.**

While Moses was a servant <u>in</u> God's house, Jesus is a Son **OVER** God's house.

The word **OWN** is not in the original, and the parallelism in this context indicates that this house belongs to God; this means that Christ is a Son whom God placed in authority over His house. This isn't to say that the kingdom or church doesn't belong to Christ, for it does (cf. 2:13); it's just that such isn't the analogy Paul was making in this particular context. In fact, it's interesting that the New Testament never calls the church "the house of Christ," but always "the house of God" (cf. Eph. 2:19, 1 Tim. 3:15, Heb. 10:21, & 1 Pet. 4:17).

The tense of the phrase **WHOSE HOUSE WE ARE** carries with it the idea of "whose house we are and will continue to be ... if we hold fast to the end." (Incidentally, by saying that Christians are now the house of God, Paul was implying that the Jews—minus the remnant—were no longer God's house!)

The phrase **HOLD FAST** is from a nautical term which meant to "hold one's course," being translated "MADE FOR SHORE" in Acts 27:40.

Perhaps most importantly in this verse, What was **THE END** Paul had in mind? Well, the Greek term meant more than just the termination of something—it actually referred to the consummation, the ultimate goal, or the fulfillment of something which had been in the works; in other words, it wasn't merely a reference to their deaths, but rather to how that everything in their history—including what they were going through at this very point in time—had a purpose which reached its goal or found its fulfillment, consummation, or "END" surrounding the events of AD 70 (cf. remarks at 2:14).

There are at least two other times in Hebrews when Paul alluded to this "END." In Hebrews 3:14 he wrote, "WE HAVE BECOME PARTAKERS OF CHRIST, IF WE HOLD THE BEGINNING OF OUR CONFIDENCE STEADFAST TO THE END." And in 6:11 he wrote, "WE DESIRE THAT EACH ONE OF YOU SHOW THE SAME DILIGENCE TO THE FULL ASSURANCE OF HOPE UNTIL THE END." Also in this vein, in 10:25 Paul implied that they could "SEE" this end-time coming.

It's worth reiteration that Paul wasn't referring to their individual deaths after which they would await some end-of-time consummation of the universe, but to the very ever-present probability of their living up to and hopefully even through this "END" that Paul in 10:37 said would "NOT TARRY," but (per the original language) would come in "A VERY, VERY LITTLE WHILE." This should bring to mind how that Jesus even indicated to His disciples in John 21:15-24 (esp. v. 22) that the beloved apostle John could very well live to witness this end which would be when the Lord returned, meaning that it was an <u>age</u>-ending, not a <u>time</u>-ending, event.

And John wasn't the only one in this generation about whom something was said leading readers to believe that others would live to see "THE END." Paul told Timothy to "KEEP THE COMMANDMENTS ... UNTIL THE APPEARING OF THE LORD" (1 Tim. 6:14). If Paul wasn't convinced that the Lord's coming was soon, at hand, etc., then why didn't he tell Timothy to keep the commandments till he died? According to the traditional position about the Lord's coming, wouldn't there have been much more of a chance of Timothy dying in the first century than of the Lord coming? So why was Paul convinced that Timothy would still be around when the Lord came, unless it was what the Lord had taught (e.g. Mat. 16:27-28, etc.)?

Paul told Titus to be "LOOKING FOR ... THE APPEARING OF THE ... SAVIOR JESUS CHRIST" (Titus 2:13). Doesn't this sound as if Paul was convinced that Titus would also be around when the Lord returned? Even further, why didn't Jesus exhort the Thyatirans to hold fast until their deaths (Rev. 2:25)?

Certainly such passages should make the Berean-minded (Acts 17:11) pause to reconsider what they've been taught.

Hebrews 3:7-19

In Hebrews 3:1-6 Paul began arguing for *Christ's Superiority to Old Testament Priests*, beginning with Moses (Psalm 99:6), arguing that Jesus is greater in His <u>office</u> (3:1-2) as well as in His <u>ministry</u> (3:3-6). In the remainder of this chapter, Paul argued that Jesus is greater in His <u>reward</u>.

Incidentally, this same passage is also the second of the six warnings found throughout this epistle. In 2:1-4 he warned against <u>neglect</u>, while in 3:7ff he warned against <u>unbelief</u>.

> **VERSES 7-9:** THEREFORE, AS THE HOLY SPIRIT SAYS, "TODAY, IF YOU WILL HEAR HIS VOICE, DO NOT HARDEN YOUR HEARTS AS IN THE REBELLION, IN THE DAY OF TRIAL IN THE WILDERNESS WHERE YOUR FATHERS TESTED ME, PROVED ME, AND SAW MY WORKS FOR FORTY YEARS...."

As mentioned in the comments on the previous verses, Paul often used parenthetical thoughts in his discussions, so one must be sure to interpret his writings with that fact in mind; for example, the word **THEREFORE** here connects directly to verse 12, making it read, "THEREFORE [that is, because Jesus is greater than the prophets, angels, and even Moses, if you want to remain God's house], BEWARE BRETHREN LEST YOU BECOME HARDENED THROUGH SIN AND DEPART FROM GOD."

Notice that, although verses 7-11 are taken from a Psalm of David (the 95th one and also verses 7-11), Paul attributed these words to the Holy Spirit then later to David (4:7).

Although the antecedent for **HIS** in Psalm 95 is God, here it's Jesus who of course is also God (1:8); this means that God, Jesus, and the Holy Spirit are all found in this passage.

For the phrase **IF YOU WILL HEAR HIS VOICE** the Hebrew has, "O THAT YOU WOULD HEAR HIS VOICE," emphasizing the eternal significance of listening to God; Paul put it as a conditional statement, meaning that they wouldn't be able to hear God if their hearts were hardened.

The idea of hardening one's heart is very well illustrated by the custom of branding animals: things such as needles will pierce a cow's hide, until it's branded; after that, it's nearly impossible to do so. Likewise, since God created man with a free will, God can't penetrate the heart of a person who has chosen to harden it against God's desire for him. To Timothy Paul wrote of people who had their consciences seared with a hot iron (1 Tim. 4:2).

The word for **REBELLION** means "to irritate, exasperate, or aggravate"; so, by their hardened hearts, those Jews of old stirred up God's wrath against them.

The word **TRIAL** actually has the definite article "the" before it in the Greek (literally, "the day of the trial"), meaning that Paul had a specific occasion in mind, that occasion being when the Jews complained to Moses concerning their lack of water in Exodus 17:1-7.

The Greek words for **TESTED** and **PROVED** are interesting in that, when combined, they mean that those Jews had put God to the test to see what evil or good there was in Him when they put Him to the test for the purpose of approving Him if He should meet their tests. Talk about a mouthful and adding insult to unbelief! They were like children who test their parents to see just how far they can be pushed!

According to *Vincent's Word Studies of the New Testament*, the original word for **AND** should probably have been translated "AND YET," meaning that, even though they continually put God to the test, He still worked with them for 40 years.

> **VERSES 10-11:** "THEREFORE I WAS ANGRY WITH THAT GENERATION AND SAID, 'THEY ALWAYS GO ASTRAY IN THEIR HEART, AND THEY HAVE NOT KNOWN MY WAYS.' SO I SWORE IN MY WRATH, 'THEY SHALL NOT ENTER MY REST.'"

The word **ANGRY** means "to reject due to being disgusted with" (which should make one think of Hebrews 10:31).

Notice that the Bible here defines a generation as 40 years! Even though this is true, countless people will do their best to find a way around this when it comes to passages such as Matthew 24:34 when Jesus spoke of His return as being within that—His—generation. (By the way, the Greek term for "generation" doesn't mean "race"; there's a different word for that.)

The words **GO ASTRAY** mean "to wander"; so just as they wandered in the wilderness, their hearts wandered away from God. Perhaps that's why God allowed them to experience what they did.

The word for **HEART** is where we get our word "cardiac"; this word, however, isn't speaking of the physical blood-pump, but of what it represented to the Jews—the mind, the seat of the affections, the will, and the understanding such as when we refer to someone's "understanding heart."

They hadn't known God's ways because they had forsaken Him while in captivity; then, to top it off, "THEY TURNED BACK TO EGYPT IN THEIR HEARTS," Stephen said to their descendents in Acts 7:39 before they stoned him to death.

The word **REST** here refers to a termination of nervous activity or struggle; for them it was the end of their physical struggle from oppression and wanderings in the wilderness, while for Paul's readers it was the end of their spiritual struggle against the enemies commented on in 2:14 (cf. Eph. 6:10-17, etc.).

The **REST** of physical Canaan was their inheritance (Deu. 12:9), while the **REST** of spiritual Canaan was their (as well as our) inheritance, corresponding to the subject discussed later in 6:12 & 9:15 (not to mention previously in 2:14 and context).

See, during the time in which Paul wrote, Christ (as a second Moses) was leading His people on a forty-year exodus out from under the law of sin and death and into the promised rest from sin and death; Abraham even looked beyond the physical land to a better, heavenly one (11:8-16). In other words, the church was on an exodus to the promised land; Christ was liberating and redeeming God's New Covenant people, transferring them into a new city—the new spiritual, heavenly Jerusalem—which would soon come (Heb. 13:14) and be the permanent home of God's newly redeemed. (For an in-depth study on The Kingdom, go to the following webpage: www.ASiteForTheLord.com/id15.html.)

Before moving on to verse 12, notice that Paul gave three exhortations based on verses 7-11: {A} in verses 12-19 he warned them to take heed; {B} in 4:1-10 he warned them to fear; and {C} in 4:11-13 he warned them to labor.

> **VERSE 12:** BEWARE, BRETHREN, LEST THERE BE IN ANY OF YOU AN EVIL HEART OF UNBELIEF IN DEPARTING FROM THE LIVING GOD.

The word **BEWARE** of course implies danger, and the idea behind its present tense is to "be constant in keeping a watchful eye open."

The word **LEST** refers to a fear that an event may occur, but it also carries with it here the suspicion that it will occur, especially since they were turning back one by one.

The phrase **IN ANY OF YOU** appealed to them as individuals: "Out of those of you who are left, take heed—beware!"

By connecting **AN EVIL HEART** with departing from God, Paul accused those who had already left as being evil to the core—the heart being one's core. There are two Greek words for "EVIL": one (κακος) is evil in the abstract, while the other, stronger one (πονερος) is evil in active opposition to good; the one Paul chose is the stronger one, meaning that he suspected some in his audience were about to act on their evil hearts and follow previous ones who had formerly left Christianity.

The phrase **OF UNBELIEF** means that disbelief is what causes an evil heart—it's a heart which has left God, taking the body with it; I say "disbelief" because the original word actually carries with it the idea of a purposeful refusal to continue to believe/trust.

The word for **DEPARTING**, transliterated, is "apostasy," meaning "to step away and stand aloof from." So the phrase **DEPARTING FROM ... GOD** is the result of a heart of distrust, reminiscent of the Jews who said, "'LET US SELECT A LEADER AND RETURN TO EGYPT'" (Num. 14:4).

Paul probably chose the adjective **LIVING** before "GOD" to indicate that life is only in God; so if they were to leave His house (v. 6), they would be rejecting the promised life—the inheritance of that house.

> **VERSE 13: BUT EXHORT ONE ANOTHER DAILY WHILE IT IS CALLED "TODAY," LEST ANY OF YOU BE HARDENED THROUGH THE DECEITFULNESS OF SIN.**

The word **EXHORT** means "to entreat, beseech, beg"; in other words, they were to beg one another to not go backward but forward. Notice how Christian fellowship is associated with keeping people from apostatizing.

Since they would very likely be killed by the Romans (or at the very least be taken captive into foreign lands if they went back to Judaism), they had the choice of being saved from all of that, along with all Christians—then and only then—before it was too late; that's the primary application of the word **TODAY** here.

Because the definite article "THE" is before the word **SIN** in the original, then the phrase **THROUGH THE DECEITFULNESS OF [THE] SIN** likely refers to the deceit found in the thinking of how the right thing would be to apostatize from Christ and return to Moses.

Isn't it interesting how unbelief and hardness of heart seem to go hand-in-hand in the Bible (cf. Mark 16:14, Acts 19:9, etc.)?

> **VERSES 14-15:** FOR WE HAVE BECOME PARTAKERS OF CHRIST IF WE HOLD THE BEGINNING OF OUR CONFIDENCE STEADFAST TO THE END, WHILE IT IS SAID, "TODAY, YOU WILL HEAR HIS VOICE, DO NOT HARDEN YOUR HEARTS."

Verse 14 is parallel to verse 6; the primary difference is that in verse 6 they were spoken of as belonging to Christ, while here Christ is spoken of as belonging to them, both of which of course were/are true (cf. the already-not-yet of John 14:19-23).

The word **PARTAKERS** is the same here as in 1:9, 2:14, and 3:1 where it was noted that it refers to a voluntary sharing in something with others; the idea is that they, of their own free will, chose to be fellow-owners of Christ.

As mentioned relative to verse 6, the word **END** here is translated from a word which means more than just a termination of something—it refers to a consummation, ultimate goal, or fulfillment of something that has been in the works; in other words, it isn't merely a reference to one's death, but how that everything in his history, including what he was experiencing at this time, had a purpose which found its fulfillment ca. AD 70. This was to what Paul was alluding in 6:11-12: "SHOW ... DILIGENCE TO THE FULL ASSURANCE OF HOPE UNTIL THE END, ... IMITATE THOSE WHO, THROUGH FAITH AND PATIENCE, INHERIT THE PROMISES." What promises? The promises made to Abraham (6:13-20, cf. 10:35-38).

Peter, also writing to suffering Jewish Christians, encouraged them in much the same way in First Peter 1:9, telling them to hold fast because soon they would receive "THE END" of their faith—"THE SALVATION OF THEIR SOULS"—the fulfillment of the promise to Abraham through the New Covenant (cf. Gal. 3: 15-29 & 4:21-31). So, again, what was "THE END" in mind here? It was the same "END" of which was spoken in Matthew 24:3, 13, & 34 when Jesus said that the old "HEAVENS AND EARTH"—the Old Covenant—would be destroyed. Why? Because that would bring an "END" to that which couldn't fulfill the promise to Abraham of a salvation/rest, that which Paul went on to discuss in chapter 4.

Therefore, they needed to hold steadfastly to **THE BEGINNING OF THEIR CONFIDENCE**, a phrase referring to that believing confidence with which they began their Christian lives; since the same word for **CONFIDENCE** is found in Hebrews 11:1, and since the idea of that verse fits here, let's read it: "FAITH IS THE SUBSTANCE [confidence] OF THINGS HOPED FOR, THE EVIDENCE OF THINGS NOT SEEN." Thus they were being urged by Paul to be resolute in holding fast while they had the opportunity to do so.

> **VERSE 16: FOR WHO, HAVING HEARD, REBELLED? INDEED WAS IT NOT ALL WHO CAME OUT OF EGYPT, LED BY MOSES?**

Here Paul was pointing out that those who rebelled back in Moses' day were, like these Hebrews, just beginning their journey; so if their forefathers could do it, they could do it.

Furthermore, there were so many of them in Moses' day who provoked God that it constituted nearly an entire generation of people; so, if an entire generation could apostatize, the few of them could as well.

> **VERSE 17: NOW WITH WHOM WAS HE ANGRY FORTY YEARS? WAS IT NOT WITH THOSE WHO SINNED, WHOSE CORPSES FELL IN THE WILDERNESS?**

This verse explains that the fate spoken of pertained only to those who sinned. And they sinned by rebelling against what they had heard from God.

Jude 5, written around the same time, says that "THE LORD, HAVING SAVED THE PEOPLE OUT OF THE LAND OF EGYPT, AFTERWARD DESTROYED THOSE WHO DID NOT BELIEVE"; and the word "believe" carries with it of course the idea of "TRUST"—even after all He had already done for them, they still didn't trust their God to take care of and fulfill His promises to them!

> **VERSES 18-19: AND TO WHOM DID HE SWEAR THAT THEY WOULD NOT ENTER HIS REST, BUT TO THOSE WHO DID NOT OBEY? SO WE SEE THAT THEY COULD NOT ENTER IN BECAUSE OF UNBELIEF.**

Disobedience leads to unbelief, and unbelief leads to disobedience; it's a vicious cycle in which Paul was warning these brethren to not allow themselves to get caught up.

In conclusion of this section, First Corinthians 10:1-12 seem appropriate: "Brethren, I do not want you to be unaware that all our fathers were under the cloud, all passed through the sea, all were baptized into Moses in the cloud and in the sea, all ate the same spiritual food, and all drank the same spiritual drink. For they drank of that spiritual Rock that followed them, and that Rock was Christ. But with most of them God was not well pleased, for their bodies were scattered in the wilderness. Now these things became our examples to the intent that we should not lust after evil things as they also lusted. And do not become idolaters as were some of them. As it is written, 'The people sat down to eat and drink and rose up to play.' Nor let us commit sexual immorality as some of them did, and in one day twenty-three thousand fell; nor let us tempt Christ as some of them also tempted and were destroyed by serpents; nor murmur as some of them also murmured and were destroyed by the destroyer. Now all these things happened to them as examples, and they were written for our admonition, on whom the ends of the ages have come. Therefore let him who thinks he stands take heed lest he fall."

Hebrews 4:1-13

In Hebrews chapter 3, Paul's point concerned *Jesus Being a Superior Priest to Moses*, not only in His <u>office</u> (3:1-2) and His <u>ministry</u> (3:3-6), but also in His <u>reward</u> or rest; now in chapter 4 (esp. vv. 1-11), Paul, in continuing the topic of Christ's superior reward or rest, dealt with *Jesus Being Superior to Joshua*, the one of course who brought Old Covenant Israel directly into the land of promised rest.

Paul's main purpose here was to warn his readers against forfeiting the soon coming spiritual—and eternal—reward, as their forefathers forfeited their physical—and ultimately their eternal—reward.

> **VERSE 1:** SINCE A PROMISE REMAINS OF ENTERING HIS (GOD'S) REST, LET US FEAR LEST ANY OF YOU SEEM TO HAVE COME SHORT OF IT.

The statement that **A PROMISE REMAINS OF ENTERING HIS REST** implies the idea of fulfillment; in other words (while the promise to Moses for a physical rest in Canaan is past, even fulfilled), Paul—in AD 63—was saying that "the promise of the entrance into God's rest is yet to be fulfilled."

If we simply replace the word **SEEM** with "appear," the next clause isn't too difficult to interpret: Paul would've been simply saying that they needed to get busy so that they wouldn't "appear" (or be found) outside the kingdom of rest or peace where the "DOGS" are (Rev. 22:15).

The word **FEAR** means the same thing as "BEWARE" in 3:12; speaking to Christians about Jews, Paul wrote, "BECAUSE OF UNBELIEF THEY WERE BROKEN OFF.... [SO] DO NOT BE HAUGHTY, BUT FEAR" (Rom. 11:20).

> **VERSE 2:** FOR INDEED THE GOSPEL WAS PREACHED TO US AS WELL AS TO THEM; BUT THE WORD WHICH THEY HEARD DID NOT PROFIT THEM, NOT BEING MIXED WITH FAITH IN THOSE WHO HEARD IT.

In order to get a good grasp on this, one should notice: {1} in the original text the definite article "THE" isn't found before the word "GOSPEL," and {2} the word **GOSPEL** simply means "good news," indicating that Paul was saying, "good news was preached to us as well as to them."

Since the context defines this good news, then we know Paul was writing about the physical rest for the generation which came out of Egyptian bondage and wilderness hardship <u>as well as</u> the spiritual rest for Paul's generation that was coming out of sin's bondage and persecution hardship.

The word for **MIXED** means "to unite one thing to another," simply meaning here that the good news of rest in Canaan promised to those of Moses' generation didn't benefit them because, due to unbelief and distrust in God, they rebelled against Him and thus failed to make it into that rest; this teaches us that the coin is two-sided: God's Word + Faith = Reward (cf. Mat. 7:26-27).

> **VERSE 3:** FOR WE WHO HAVE BELIEVED ENTER THAT REST, AS HE HAS SAID: "SO I SWORE IN MY WRATH, 'THEY SHALL NOT ENTER MY REST,'" ALTHOUGH THE WORKS WERE FINISHED FROM THE FOUNDATION OF THE WORLD.

When the last part of verse 2 is read along with the first part of verse 3, the contrast and meaning are clear: because of unbelief, those of Moses' day did <u>not</u> enter into rest, while, because of belief, those of Paul's day <u>were</u> entering into rest. (The Greek term for **ENTER** isn't only present tense, it's also passive, meaning that they were being carried into this rest; that is, at this point, Paul implied that they had not yet entered it, even though they were "about to" [cf. 1:14 & 2:5].)

By bringing up the promise, **I SWORE ... THEY SHALL NOT ENTER MY REST**, Paul was saying to them that "If God's promise against unbelievers was fulfilled, then surely His promise for believers will be fulfilled."

By the last clause, **ALTHOUGH THE WORKS WERE FINISHED FROM THE FOUNDATION OF THE WORLD,** it appears Paul was saying that, although God had worked out all things for the forefathers to enter their rest, He still forbade entrance to those who distrusted and disobeyed. If this is correct, then Paul was implying that God wouldn't hesitate in doing the same to them; in other words, no matter how much He put into providing them this rest, if they failed to be faithful, they would likewise not be allowed to enter.

> **VERSES 4-5: FOR HE HAS SPOKEN IN A CERTAIN PLACE OF THE SEVENTH DAY IN THIS WAY: "AND GOD RESTED ON THE SEVENTH DAY FROM ALL HIS WORKS"; AND AGAIN IN THIS PLACE: "THEY SHALL NOT ENTER MY REST."**

Since Paul here brought into his writing another "type" from Genesis 2:2, the picture becomes a little more complex, for not only does the Canaan-rest typify the Christian-rest, but the Sabbath-rest also typifies the Christian-rest.

The phrase **IN THIS PLACE** refers to David's statement that he quoted twice in this very context (3:11 & 4:3).

Hebrews in general (e.g. chap. 9) indicates that God's **REST** is the spiritual/eternal peace that's only found in His presence. The Jews who rebelled and didn't make it through the wilderness into Canaan also wouldn't make it into God's eternal presence; likewise, those who weren't faithful throughout the great tribulation of Paul's generation didn't make it into God's eternal kingdom of rest/peace (cf. Acts 14:22 & Rom. 14:17).

So here's the picture: Man and God enjoyed a peaceful and restful covenant relationship ... until man broke covenant (Hos. 6:7), thus destroying the peace and rest. God therefore was forced to go to work orchestrating man's reconciliation (cf. John 5:17). In the process of that work, He established seventh-day observance (Exo. 16) as a token of the previous state of rest. At this same time, Israel was on her way to a place of rest where she could freely worship God and keep His sabbaths (Exo. 21), all of which prefigured the time when that reconciliation would be finally/eternally accomplished in/through Jesus—the very One these first generation Jewish Christians were abandoning (cf. Heb. 10:25 & notes there).

> **VERSE 6:** SINCE THEREFORE IT REMAINS THAT SOME MUST ENTER IT, AND THOSE TO WHOM IT WAS FIRST PREACHED DID NOT ENTER BECAUSE OF UNBELIEF (LIT. DISOBEDIENCE)...

For clarity's sake, the design of this verse concludes in verse 9; in other words, "Since there are even now [AD 63] those who must enter God's rest, the promise of it still remains unfulfilled for the people of God."

Here's the thing: the **REST** pictured in Genesis 2:2 and Exodus 16 was never fulfilled during the Old Covenant age; but it was "about to be" fulfilled in the accomplished Kingdom of Heaven on Earth in the New Covenant age.

> **VERSES 7-8:** AGAIN HE DESIGNATES A CERTAIN DAY, SAYING IN DAVID, "TODAY," AFTER SUCH A LONG TIME, AS IT HAS BEEN SAID, "TODAY, IF YOU WILL HEAR HIS VOICE, DO NOT HARDEN YOUR HEARTS." FOR IF JOSHUA HAD GIVEN THEM REST, THEN HE WOULD NOT AFTERWARD HAVE SPOKEN OF ANOTHER DAY.

The word **AGAIN** just means that Paul was adding another parenthetical detail which, in this case, refutes the objection someone may make that the second generation during Joshua's time <u>did</u> enter the rest, fulfilling the promise.

The clause **HE DESIGNATES A CERTAIN DAY** means that God, through David, 500 years after Joshua—**A LONG TIME**, still had a specific rest in mind that obviously wasn't fulfilled by Joshua; this means that, although David conquered what Joshua didn't, David's land still wasn't the ultimate promised land. So the phrase **AS IT HAS BEEN SAID** refers to Paul's prior two quotes in 3:7-8 & 15 of Psalm 95:7-8.

The point here then is that if the promised rest was fulfilled by the second generation of those who left Egypt, then why did God promise it again 500 years later? In other words, the rest wasn't limited to the day of Moses and/or Joshua—that rest was merely a shadow of the true yet to come.

Thus Jesus isn't only greater than Moses who led the people to the Canaan-rest, but He's also greater than Joshua who took them into it, for the rest that Jesus (the NT Yeshua, by the way) provides is the real thing, a far greater rest than that of Joshua, a rest that isn't just found in Heaven itself, but also in the Kingdom of Heaven on Earth, for Jesus Himself said, "'COME TO ME ALL YOU WHO LABOR AND ARE HEAVY LADEN, AND I WILL GIVE YOU REST. TAKE MY YOKE UPON YOU, AND LEARN FROM ME ... AND YOU WILL FIND REST'" (Mat. 11:28-29).

(It would be helpful to also compare Luke 13:28-30 and Hebrews 11:9-10, 13, & 16 with this paragraph.)

VERSE 9: THERE REMAINS THEREFORE A REST FOR THE PEOPLE OF GOD.

It's interesting to note that Paul picked a different Greek word for **REST** here; in this verse (and in this verse only) Paul chose the word for "sabbath-rest," a term signifying the ideal rest once possessed in the beginning and which would be possessed again through Christ. Besides, this original word literally means "a keeping sabbath," indicating the true, spiritual, eternal, and heavenly rest made possible by the restoration of all things (cf. Acts 3:19-21 & Heb. 9:6-15).

(Side-notes: The word "sabbatical" that people sometimes use for "vacation" is also from this word. And, although Saturday was the weekly sabbath day, the word "sabbath" doesn't mean Saturday —it merely means "rest.")

VERSE 10: FOR HE WHO HAS ENTERED HIS REST HAS HIMSELF ALSO CEASED FROM HIS WORKS AS GOD DID FROM HIS.

This sentence would probably make more sense to us if it read, "For he who has entered God's rest has ceased from his works just as God did from His."

This verse is merely an illustration or a proverb, indicating that it doesn't mean to imply that anyone—as of AD 63—had yet entered into this rest (contradicting vv. 3 & 11); it only means that once someone did enter this rest he would—at that time—experience God's respite of salvation from works with regard to sin (9:39) and death (2:14-15).

The near fulfillment (Rev. 1:3 & 22:10) of the time of the Revelation 14:13 statement comes to mind: "'BLESSED ARE THE DEAD WHO DIE IN THE LORD FROM NOW ON.' 'YES,' SAYS THE SPIRIT, 'THAT THEY MAY REST FROM THEIR LABORS, AND THEIR WORKS FOLLOW THEM.'"

> **VERSE 11:** LET US THEREFORE BE DILIGENT TO ENTER THAT REST, LEST ANYONE FALL AFTER THE SAME EXAMPLE OF DISOBEDIENCE.

The word **DILIGENCE** means "to do your best, to give it your all" (the opposite of "DRIFTING" in 2:1); it means intensity of purpose followed by intensity of effort toward the attainment of that purpose.

Thus Paul was telling them that "Since there's a rest that's worth all your effort, since so many have failed in reaching God's rest through their unbelief, and since there's so much danger that you may fail also (especially in this time of great tribulation, Mat. 24:21), make every effort to reach this goal!"

> **VERSE 12:** FOR THE WORD OF GOD IS LIVING AND POWERFUL AND SHARPER THAN ANY TWO-EDGED SWORD, PIERCING EVEN TO THE DIVISION OF SOUL AND SPIRIT AND OF JOINTS AND MARROW, AND IS A DISCERNER OF THE THOUGHTS AND INTENTS OF THE HEART.

The term for **LIVING** might actually be better translated as "alive" (cf. Acts 7:38 & 1 Pet. 1:23), and the term for **POWERFUL** (the word for our "energetic") means "active" (cf. Isa. 55:10-11); thus, like God Himself, His Word is always alive and active.

Although this verse doesn't describe God's Word to be like a two-edged sword as in other places (e.g., Rev. 1:16 & 2:12), it seems implied by the words **PIERCE** and **DISCERN**. Since God's Word as a sword denotes the power of judgment (cf. Rom. 13:4), Paul was calling attention to the power of God's Word to judge (cf. next verse, Hos. 6:5, & John 12:48).

Why was God's Word called a double-edged sword? Perhaps the answer is found in that it was the judge of both the church and its enemies. Speaking of judgment on the first century church, ca. AD 65 Peter wrote, "THE TIME HAS COME

FOR THE JUDGMENT TO BEGIN AT THE HOUSE OF GOD" (1 Pet. 4:17a). Then, speaking of the enemies of the church, he went on to say, "AND IF IT BEGINS WITH US FIRST, WHAT WILL BE THE END OF THOSE WHO REFUSE TO OBEY THE GOSPEL OF GOD" (v. 17b)?

Paul said in 4:2 that the people of Moses' day, because they disobeyed God's Word, didn't gain any blessings from it, they merely suffered its curses. The people to whom Paul was writing here, however, still had time to be blessed from that which the Word offered in the promise of rest; but, if they refused to continue in the faith they had previously confessed (3:1, cf. 3:14), they too would suffer its curses (cf. Deu. 28 & cf. Rev. 1:3 w/ 22:18-19). So they could choose to either be blessed or cursed by God's words of exhortation.

The phrase **DIVISION OF SOUL AND SPIRIT AND OF JOINTS AND MARROW** would likely be better understood as follows: "God's Word is even able to divide the soul and spirit, right down to the joints and marrow." (The reader is left to perform his own in-depth study to verify this.) The phrase **JOINTS AND MARROW** appears to be a way of picturing for us the idea that God's Word is so powerful and sharp that it can get into the deepest nooks and crannies of our beings.

Since the word **PIERCING** is what Greek scholars call "a genitive of description," and since Paul didn't use the word "from" in this clause, then he wasn't saying that God's Word divides soul from spirit or joints from marrow. In fact, this clause isn't to be taken literally at all; it was merely a poetic way of saying that <u>no one can escape</u> (a thought that had begun in 2:1-3 and then carried through 4:13).

The word for **DISCERNER** carries with it the idea of "sifting," indicating that God's Word (that by which they were about to be judged) separates the good from the bad (cf. Mat. 13:47-50 & 25:31-33).

The third and last reason Paul gave here for being sure they were diligent to enter God's rest is in...

> **VERSE 13: AND THERE IS NO CREATURE HIDDEN FROM HIS SIGHT, BUT ALL THINGS ARE NAKED AND OPEN TO THE EYES OF HIM TO WHOM WE MUST GIVE ACCOUNT.** (CF. JER. 32:19.)

Since Jesus was the One to whom was given the power of judgment (John 5:22), and since He's the One into which the next verse transitions, then it seems clear that the pronoun **HIS** here refers to Jesus rather than to His Father.

Keeping in mind that this was a Jew writing to Jews, it makes perfect sense that the original phrase Paul used for **NAKED AND OPEN** brought to mind animal sacrifices. The word for **NAKED** reminded them of how the animal for sacrifice was stripped of its skin, and the word for **OPEN** reminded them of how its breast was then ripped open, its insides removed, and its backbones sliced lengthwise down the center (all of which corresponds to the "PIERCING" in v. 12). After that they were divided into quarters, so that outwardly and inwardly they were fully exposed to the priest for a comprehensive examination (Lev. 1:5-6).

The point here appears to have been that, if there were brethren among them who were fence-riding, they needed to pick a side and quickly—get in or get out—be hot or be cold, for if they didn't make up their own minds, they would soon be made up for them by the Lord and His Word once and for all!

(Side-note: In verse 14 the High Priest—the one who did the sacrificing—is brought up in the person of Jesus Christ who is the last, as well as the once-for-all, High Priest, for He's the One who permitted Himself to be thrust through by a Roman sword [John 19:32-34]; He was/is therefore worthy of all authority [Mat. 28:18].)

The word for **ACCOUNT** refers to a "reckoning"; there was a day of reckoning in the near future for the Jews, so Paul warned them that, if they didn't want to be part of the Jews whom Christ would reject and destroy (cf. Mat. 3:12), then they had better stop drifting and (as the next verse says) hold fast to their faith.

Hebrews 4:14–5:3

The last two sections, 3:7-19 & 4:1-13, concern the reward of spiritual/eternal rest that God was about to provide for those who were faithful to Him regardless of their circumstances. Beginning with 4:14 (which should probably be 5:1), Paul resumed the topic of Christ's priesthood that he began in 2:17, for the high priesthood of Jesus is the main subject of Hebrews: "THIS IS THE MAIN POINT OF THE THINGS WE ARE SAYING: WE HAVE SUCH A HIGH PRIEST WHO IS SEATED AT THE RIGHT HAND OF THE THRONE OF THE MAJESTY IN THE HEAVENS, A MINISTER OF THE SANCTUARY ... THE TRUE TABERNACLE WHICH THE LORD ERECTED AND NOT MAN" (8:1).

So, before going further, we should reread 2:17–3:2: "IN ALL THINGS JESUS HAD TO BE MADE LIKE HIS BRETHREN, THAT HE MIGHT BE A MERCIFUL AND FAITHFUL HIGH PRIEST IN THINGS PERTAINING TO GOD, TO MAKE PROPITIATION FOR THE SINS OF THE PEOPLE. FOR IN THAT HE HIMSELF HAS SUFFERED, BEING TEMPTED, HE IS ABLE ALSO TO AID THOSE WHO ARE TEMPTED. THEREFORE, HOLY BRETHREN, PARTAKERS OF THE HEAVENLY CALLING, CONSIDER THE APOSTLE AND HIGH PRIEST OF OUR CONFESSION, CHRIST JESUS."

After warning them to remain faithful, Paul here in 4:14-16 indicated that Jesus was willing—even eager—to aid them in all their troubles.

> **VERSE 14: SEEING THEN THAT WE HAVE A GREAT HIGH PRIEST WHO HAS PASSED THROUGH THE HEAVENS, JESUS THE SON OF GOD, LET US HOLD FAST OUR CONFESSION.**

So far Paul has demonstrated that Jesus is superior to the prophets, the angels, Moses, and Joshua; so at this point he proceeded to demonstrate that Jesus is superior to Aaron, the first high priest and father of the Levitical priesthood.

Note the ascending scale of importance: the prophets gave the Word to Israel; the Word was given to the prophets through angels; Moses led Israel out of Egypt; and Joshua led the nation into Canaan. But all this would've been in vain if Israel didn't have a high priest to mediate for them; so Aaron occupied the high point of importance among the servants of God in Israel.

Jesus being called **GREAT** here not only means that He's greater than the angels, the prophets, Moses, and Joshua, but that He's also a greater priest than Aaron, including his descendants—the Levites. While the Levites (who comprised the Levitical priesthood) were merely the sons of Aaron, Jesus was the Son of God!

By saying that Jesus **PASSED THROUGH THE HEAVENS** (the 1st & 2nd heavens, cf. 2 Cor. 12:1-4 & Acts 1:9-11), Paul was saying that Jesus was in the 3rd Heaven (at the very throne of God), which furnished Him the power to fulfill the divinely promised rest.

Unlike Aaron who could only go to the typical mercy seat in the holy of holies and offer the blood of animals, Jesus went straight to the real mercy seat in Heaven to offer His own blood. Later Paul wrote of Jesus that "WITH HIS OWN BLOOD HE ENTERED THE MOST HOLY PLACE ONCE FOR ALL, HAVING OBTAINED ETERNAL REDEMPTION" (Heb. 9:12).

Paul began Hebrews by referring to God's Son as having purged our sins and sat down at God's right hand (1:1-3). Then, for the first time in 2:9, he used the name "Jesus" in order to bring His humanity to their minds. Then in 2:17 he brought the high priesthood of this Son of God—this Jesus— into the picture. Now, so that there's no mistaking what all he had been driving at, Paul here put it all together by bringing up Christ's humanity by calling Him **JESUS** and His deity by calling Him **THE SON OF GOD**, meaning that He's the perfect **HIGH PRIEST** or Mediator between Heaven and Earth.

The phrase **HOLD FAST** means "to cling to tenaciously"; so (as mentioned back at 3:1) they were cautioned to cling ever so tightly to their initial confession of Jesus as their Messiah.

> **VERSE 15:** FOR WE DO NOT HAVE A HIGH PRIEST WHO CANNOT SYMPATHIZE WITH OUR WEAKNESSES, BUT WAS IN ALL POINTS TEMPTED AS WE ARE, YET WITHOUT SIN.

The word for **SYMPATHY** means "to suffer with," not just due to knowledge, but due also to His common experience with us in being human (the point Paul made in 2:17-18).

The word for **WEAKNESSES** refers to everything concerning our human susceptibility of being tempted to sin. So Paul was saying that, although Jesus didn't have the same susceptibility to commit sin that we do (else He would've sinned), He was still tempted in the same ways we are. In other words, He too was tempted with the lust of the flesh, the lust of the eyes, and the pride of life (1 John 2:16); and, because of who He was, He was very likely tempted in ways that we can't even imagine! Later in 7:26 Paul wrote, "SUCH A HIGH PRIEST WAS FITTING FOR US, WHO IS HOLY, HARMLESS, UNDEFILED, SEPARATE FROM SINNERS, AND HAS BECOME HIGHER THAN THE HEAVENS"; the sinlessness of Christ is illustrated at great length by Paul throughout chapters 7, 8, & 9.

For those who might say something like, "Well, if He never sinned, then He doesn't <u>really</u> understand and sympathize," think about this: One who has never been beaten in a fight knows more about the strength of his opponent than one who has experienced defeat. Why? Because he had to withstand the most the opponent could dish out. So Christ, having never fallen to temptation, knows more about the strength of the enemy than the vilest sinner, especially being tempted by the enemy personally and probably with more vigor than we ourselves have ever experienced since we aren't deity as He was/is. Thus Jesus is better qualified to understand our temptations than anyone else, as Westcott wrote, "Sympathy with the sinner in his trial does not depend on the experience of sin [itself], but on the experience of the strength of the temptation to sin which only the sinless can know in its full intensity.... [Besides] sin ... dulls sympathy by obscuring the idea of evil" (*The Epistle to the Hebrews*, 2:18).

(Side-note: There are myriads of scholars who believe in what's called, "The Impeccability of Christ"—the belief that, because He was 100% God as well as 100% man, He had not the ability to sin.)

> **VERSE 16:** LET US THEREFORE COME BOLDLY TO THE THRONE OF GRACE THAT WE MAY OBTAIN MERCY AND FIND GRACE TO HELP IN TIME OF NEED.

The original word for **LET US COME** literally means to "let us keep on coming" and is actually a reference to the idea of approaching God through a sin-sacrifice; under the <u>first</u> covenant the sin-sacrifice was an animal, while now under the ever-<u>last</u>-ing covenant (13:20) it's Jesus Christ (9:26).

The word **BOLDLY** doesn't mean "arrogantly," it means "with confidence," more confidence than with which they could have ever approached God via Old Testament high priests who were mere humans.

The **THRONE OF GRACE** is the real thing in Heaven typified by the ark of the mercy seat (cf. Jer. 3:16-17) in the most holy place of the tabernacle (1 Kgs. 8:6), that which only the high priest could approach (Heb. 9:25). Remember, in Old Testament life there were priests and people; in New Testament life there's no separation of priests and people, for all God's people <u>are</u> priests (1 Pet. 2:5 & 9), with Jesus as High Priest. This means that Christians aren't restricted access to God's throne through any human being; rather, we have free/direct access to the (divine) High Priest Himself who intercedes and mediates our case before God's throne of grace. (By joining the thoughts of Ephesians 2:18 & 3:12 one can find Paul teaching that we have access with confidence to the Father.)

The word **MERCY** is "aid related to past offenses," while the word **GRACE** is "aid related to future toil, trial, and temptation."

The phrase for **HELP IN TIME OF NEED** refers to "help before it's too late"; in this context it refers to help for them to avoid apostasy and enter God's rest while there's still time.

In 5:1-4 the two points Paul made are that a high priest must be sympathetic (5:1-3) and appointed by God (5:4).

> **VERSE 1:** FOR EVERY HIGH PRIEST TAKEN FROM AMONG MEN IS APPOINTED FOR MEN IN THINGS PERTAINING TO GOD THAT HE MAY OFFER BOTH GIFTS AND SACRIFICES FOR SINS.

The word **FOR** means "because"; Paul was here explaining why they could come to the throne for mercy and grace. So why could they? Because, though Jesus was <u>un</u>like the Levites in that He's the Son of God (4:14), He's like them in that He was also the Son of Man (2:14-17), someone who experienced temptation (4:15, cf. Jas. 1:13); the high priest, by God's design, was always **FROM AMONG MEN** and **FOR MEN**, not for God.

The phrase **THINGS PERTAINING TO GOD** is defined in this very statement as the offering of **GIFTS AND SACRIFICES FOR SINS**; in other words, those priests ministered in regard to man's relationship with God, that which Jesus does as well.

The word **GIFTS** refers to bloodless offerings; further, since this word doesn't appear to be connected to the phrase **FOR SINS**, then the gifts under consideration probably refer to voluntary offerings. The word **SACRIFICES**, however, **DOES** refer to bloody offerings that were **FOR SINS**.

> **VERSE 2:** HE CAN HAVE COMPASSION ON THOSE WHO ARE IGNORANT AND GOING ASTRAY, SINCE HE HIMSELF IS ALSO BESET BY WEAKNESSES.

While the word for "**SYMPATHY**" in 4:15 means "to suffer with someone," the word for **COMPASSION** here means "to suffer with someone to a limit." Thus, speaking of human high priests, this means that the emphasis is on how a morally weak priest (and each of them, being human, was morally weak) could have feelings for those like himself; but, because he was a high priest with a job to do, he had to restrain his emotions to be effective. Not only was he not to allow himself to be too tolerant, but he was also not to allow himself to be too severe toward the ignorant and erring.

Before considering the ignorant and erring, it seems that there were primarily three types of sin in the Old Testament times (and such may be the case today as well). There were sins committed in ignorance (Lev. 5:17-19), sins committed in passion (Lev. 6:1-7), and sins committed in rebellion (Num. 15:30-31). It also seems that, according to those passages, sins committed in ignorance or passion could be atoned for, but those committed in an attitude of rebellion could not (likely because rebellion is, by the nature of the beast, premeditated; cf. 1 Sam. 15:22-23 & Psa. 19:13). With this background, Paul probably had the sins of ignorance and passion in mind here in Hebrews 5:2.

Since the word **IGNORANT** is generally used in our day as an insult, it needs to be noted that Paul only meant it as a lack of knowledge; later in Hebrews 9:7 he wrote concerning sacrifices that were offered "FOR THE PEOPLE'S SINS COMMITTED IN IGNORANCE."

Whereas the phrase **THOSE ... GOING ASTRAY** seems to imply that they had not yet sinned, it actually comes from a word which refers to "erring ones" or "those committing error."

The word **BESET** comes from the same word as translated "SURROUNDED" in 12:1; but while there it's used positively, here it's used negatively. So the last part of 5:2 would be better understood today if "BESET" were translated as "plagued"; in other words, the high priests, being human, were plagued by the moral weaknesses of the flesh. This is also reminiscent of the idea that, while the prophet would cry out for the people to repent or be destroyed, the priests were to be sympathetic and help those who desired forgiveness.

Speaking of these priests as being plagued by sins, and speaking in the general context of Jesus as being superior to the first high priest, Aaron, it seems to be a good illustration to remember that Aaron was the one who took the lead in making the golden calf to worship at Mt. Sinai!

VERSE 3: BECAUSE OF THIS HE IS REQUIRED AS FOR THE PEOPLE, SO ALSO FOR HIMSELF, TO OFFER FOR SINS.

Leviticus 16:6 has God telling Moses to tell Aaron to "'OFFER THE BULL AS A SIN-OFFERING, WHICH IS FOR HIMSELF, AND MAKE ATONEMENT FOR HIMSELF AND FOR HIS HOUSE.'" And Leviticus 9:7 has Moses saying to his brother, Aaron, the high priest, "'GO TO THE ALTAR, OFFER YOUR SIN-OFFERING AND YOUR BURNT OFFERING, AND MAKE ATONEMENT FOR YOURSELF.'" Obviously this didn't apply to Jesus, because not only was He a High Priest, but He was also the Lamb, and the lamb had to be "WITHOUT BLEMISH" (i.e. without sin, Lev. 22:19; cf. Heb. 4:15).

IN SUMMARY: In 4:14-16 Paul taught these brethren that since they had such a Great High Priest in Jesus, the Son of God, who was tempted as a man, and who can therefore sympathize with man, they should have total confidence in coming to Father-God through His Son at any time and for any reason! Following that, in 5:1-3 Paul provided more reasons why Jesus is a High Priest by <u>comparing</u> Him with Aaron: {1} both were selected by God from among men; {2} both were appointed to represent man before God; {3} both experienced temptation; {4} both offered up sacrifices; and {5} both were to demonstrate compassion, which Jesus surely did and (unlike those dead priests) still does, as Paul went right on to discuss beginning in verse 6. Later, in 5:5-10, Paul, while further demonstrating Jesus' superiority, went on to <u>contrast</u> Jesus and Aaron (see next section.)

Hebrews 4:14

Hebrews 5:4-10

In 5:1-3 Paul concluded the prior paragraph (4:14—5:3) with reasons why Jesus qualifies as High Priest by <u>comparing</u> Him with Aaron, the first high priest: {1} both were selected by God from among men; {2} both were anointed to represent man before God; {3} both experienced temptation; {4} both offered sacrifices; and {5} both were to exhibit compassion.

Now in 5:4-10 Paul demonstrated that Jesus is a superior High Priest by <u>contrasting</u> Him with Aaron: {1} only Jesus is called God's Son; {2} only Jesus was given an everlasting priesthood; {3} only Jesus was made a priest after the order of Melchizedek; and {4} only Jesus cried out to God as the Lamb as well as the High Priest.

> **VERSE 4:** AND NO MAN TAKES THIS HONOR TO HIMSELF, BUT HE WHO IS CALLED BY GOD, JUST AS AARON WAS.

This verse repeats 5:1: "EVERY HIGH PRIEST ... IS APPOINTED BY GOD"; Paul reminded his readers of this in order to continue this topic with <u>contrasts</u> between Aaron—the head of the Old Covenant priesthood—and Jesus—the head of the New Covenant priesthood.

What's interesting in this verse is that, although the high priest was "FOR MAN" (5:1), man wasn't allowed to choose his own high priest—only God had that authority; so when anyone tried to usurp the position of high priest, there were severe penalties: First Samuel 13 relates how King Saul lost the kingdom due in part to presuming the work of a priest. (Side-note: There are many who believe that Paul spoke sarcastically of the high priest Ananias in Acts 23:5 because he was <u>not</u> authorized to be a high priest; and, according to history, he was one of—if not <u>the</u>—worst high priest to ever occupy the office.)

Other examples of the foregoing are as follows: First Kings 12 relates Jeroboam's institution of an unlawful priesthood, and the kingdom of Israel came to ruin; Second Chronicles 26 relates Uzziah's interference with the priestly office, and he became a leper; and Numbers 16 relates Korah's insurgence (aka a "REBELLION" per Jude 11) only to have the earth swallow him and his followers. (Interestingly, Paul also alluded to this Old Testament story in connection to the Hymenaen heresy which taught that—by AD 65—the resurrection had already occurred, 2 Tim. 2:17-19; in this passage Paul was proving to Timothy that this teaching would be clearly verified as erroneous once Jesus came [in just a few years at the actual time of the resurrection, AD 70] to condemn those who attempted to usurp Paul's authority as an inspired man of God; see http://eschatology.org for an article entitled *Covenant Eschatology and the Hymenaen Heresy*.)

> **VERSE 5: SO ALSO CHRIST DID NOT GLORIFY HIMSELF TO BECOME HIGH PRIEST, BUT IT WAS HE WHO SAID TO HIM, "YOU ARE MY SON, TODAY I HAVE BEGOTTEN YOU."**

The word **GLORIFY** would be better understood as "exalt"; in other words, Jesus didn't exalt Himself to the role of High Priest, but the One who claimed Jesus as His Son exalted Him to that position.

In this verse Paul again, as in 1:5, quoted from Psalm 2:7. The question becomes, "WHY GO THROUGH THE TROUBLE OF SAYING, 'IT WAS HE WHO SAID TO HIM, "YOU'RE MY SON, TODAY I'VE BEGOTTEN YOU,"'" instead of just saying, "It was God who appointed Him?" Well, there's a good reason for this: Recall from the study of 1:5 that the idea in Psalm 2:7 of Jesus being begotten and called God's Son has reference not to His birth via Mary, but to His resurrection from spiritual death. Thus Paul was implying that Jesus' resurrection/ascension to God's right hand (1:1-5) is directly connected to His being worthy of the once-for-all high priesthood. Why? Because He lives evermore to intercede for the saints, and because He, being the Lamb as well as the High Priest, endured the lowest depths of human suffering/death in order to be the perfected, just as 5:7-8 continues to discuss.

> **VERSE 6: AS HE ALSO SAYS IN ANOTHER PLACE** [PSA. 110:4], **"YOU ARE A PRIEST FOREVER ACCORDING TO THE ORDER OF MELCHIZEDEK."**

Although Paul brought up the priesthood of Christ being like that of Melchizedek, he strayed from this subject in verse 12, getting back to it in chapter 7; however, the point here for now is plain: unlike the Aaronic priesthood, the priesthood of Jesus is "FOREVER," just as that of Melchizedek who had no beginning or ending, as far as any record is concerned (7:3).

The word **FOREVER** here refers to the idea of "throughout the age"; in Exodus 40:15 God told Moses that the Levitical priesthood would be "AN EVERLASTING PRIESTHOOD," defined by God in the next phrase as "THROUGHOUT THEIR GENERATIONS"; and we know that their generations ended at the demise of Jerusalem (in large part due to the fact that all the genealogical records were destroyed). So, since Jesus will never cease to exist, His high priesthood will never cease to exist.

Unlike high priests such as the Acts 23 Ananias—who most are convinced usurped the office, Jesus (even though He wasn't of the lineage of Aaron) did _not_ usurp the office of high priest, because it was appointed by God that He would be High Priest hundreds of years before He was even born; in addition, His priesthood would be like that of Melchizedek who lived long before the Aaronic/Levitical priesthood came into existence.

Another interesting thought this verse brings up (discussed at length in chapter 7) is that Melchizedek, unlike Aaron, wasn't a mere priest; rather, he, like Joshua of Zechariah 6, was also a king (cf. Heb. 7:2). Jesus or Yeshua, therefore, as the clear anti-type of Melchizedek and the Zechariah 6 Joshua, is Priest _and_ King. Zechariah 6:13 says of the Messiah, "'HE ... SHALL ... RULE [from and] BE A PRIEST ON HIS THRONE.'" Remember what happened to king Uzziah when he attempted to fill the roles of both king and priest? He was judged by God and was cursed with leprosy, for that privilege was reserved for God's Messiah only.

> **VERSE 7: WHO** (JESUS, NOT MELCHIZEDEK, CF. V. 8), **IN THE DAYS OF HIS FLESH, WHEN HE HAD OFFERED UP PRAYERS AND SUPPLICATIONS, WITH VEHEMENT** (PASSIONATE) **CRIES AND TEARS TO HIM WHO WAS ABLE TO SAVE HIM FROM DEATH, WAS HEARD BECAUSE OF HIS GODLY FEAR.**

To most commentators and scholars, it seems obvious that this statement is an allusion to Jesus' prayers to the Father in the Garden of Gethsemane before He was betrayed by Judas; and it also seems obvious that Paul brought this up to emphasize his argument that, although Jesus didn't commit sin as other high priests, He did suffer as they did. (It would be appropriate at this point to read Matthew 26:36-44, while recalling Luke's record of help from an angel during this taxing time.)

The word for **OFFERED** was used of the priest who brought a sacrifice to the altar of God; hence, prayer is a sort of sacrifice—a sacrifice of the lips (cf. Heb. 13:15), which is why the prayer of a saint is referred to as an offering in Revelation 8:3-4.

When used separately, the words **PRAYERS** and **SUPPLICATIONS** are used interchangeably, but when used together they refer to a prayer prompted by a deep sense of helplessness.

Instead of the clause about the Father being **ABLE TO SAVE HIM FROM DEATH** meaning that God could save Jesus from dying, it actually means that God could (and did) bring Him out from the state of the 3-day death of their relationship that He had to suffer for sin (cf. Mat. 27:46 & Gal. 1:1); after all, certainly it wasn't physical death God's Son dreaded, but being separated or cut off from His Father.

The word for **FEAR** here isn't the word which means to be afraid of something; rather, this word highlights the idea of "respect," which is why the adjective **GODLY** is suitably supplied in the NKJV. Jesus' prayer was heard because of His respect for His Father, respect that wasn't only demonstrated in His prayer, but also throughout His entire life. And what was the result? Jesus was raised from the dead, taking us right back to the thought of Psalm 2:7 in 5:5 above.

> **VERSE 8: THOUGH HE WAS A SON, YET HE LEARNED OBEDIENCE BY THE THINGS WHICH HE SUFFERED.**

The word **SON** here isn't a referent to Jesus as a son of a man, but as a son of God, the indefinite article indicating His relational position to the Father.

The word **LEARNED** refers to an understanding that comes by experience, not merely by instinct or instruction; this is evident because it specifically states that He learned from the sufferings He experienced. (In fact, in the Greek there's a figure of speech called "paronomasia" which is used here to indicate that "He suffered–He learned" [cf. E. W. Bullinger's *Figures of Speech Used in the Bible*, p. 307].) The idea is that, even though Jesus as God knew what obedience was (in the sense of what we call "head-knowledge"), He didn't know what it was from experience; in other words, Jesus, as deity minus humanity, was never tempted to disobey the Father, which is why/how He learned obedience.

A good lesson this verse clearly teaches is that suffering is not always the consequence of one's personal sins; rather, adversity is meant to edify.

Questions to pose ourselves: If God's Son had to learn obedience, shouldn't His followers learn it as well? And if God's Son had to obey, should we expect special favors, such as the right to disobey?

> **VERSE 9: AND HAVING BEEN PERFECTED, HE BECAME THE AUTHOR OF ETERNAL SALVATION TO ALL WHO OBEY HIM.**

The basic idea behind the word for **PERFECTED** refers to a person's (or even a people's) attainment of God's goal for him; so this initial phrase points to how Jesus reached God's goal for Him concerning His eternal priesthood, a goal that was ultimately accomplished in His death. In Philippians 2:8 Paul wrote, "BEING FOUND IN APPEARANCE AS A MAN, JESUS HUMBLED HIMSELF AND BECAME OBEDIENT TO THE POINT OF DEATH, EVEN THE DEATH OF THE CROSS."

Just as Jesus was setting His face toward Jerusalem and His death, He told some Pharisees that He was headed there because that's where He would be "PERFECTED" (Luke 13:32).

The word **PERFECTED** here could also refer to "consecration"; in other words, just as Aaron and his sons were consecrated to the priestly office through sacrifices (Exo. 29), so Jesus was consecrated to the office by the sacrifice of Himself.

Before discussing the phrase **THE AUTHOR OF ETERNAL SALVATION**, recall 2:10 where, speaking of Jesus, Paul said that "IT WAS FITTING ... TO MAKE THE AUTHOR OF SALVATION PERFECT THROUGH SUFFERINGS." Although this is parallel to 5:7-9 in its primary thought and should therefore definitely be consulted when studying chapter 5, yet there's a slightly unnoticeable difference in the NKJV. As mentioned in the remarks at 2:10, the NKJV would've been better off in this case retaining the KJV translation of "CAPTAIN," because it refers to the idea of Jesus being the "leader" of man's salvation—the One who paved the way for US ("FORERUNNER" in 6:20). But the original word for **AUTHOR** here in 5:9 is a word which, although similar in meaning to the word in 2:10, actually refers to the idea of Jesus being the "cause" or "source" of salvation.

The salvation of Christ here is described as **ETERNAL**; neither the Law of Moses nor the Aaronic/Levitical priesthood provided for eternal salvation—the sins of the people were merely rolled forward till the "PERFECTED" Jesus could become "THE AUTHOR" and "THE CAPTAIN" of a flawless salvation. In fact, 7:19a reads, "THE LAW MADE NOTHING PERFECT." And 7:11a reads: "IF PERFECTION WERE THROUGH THE LEVITICAL PRIESTHOOD, ... WHAT FURTHER NEED WAS THERE THAT ANOTHER PRIEST SHOULD RISE ACCORDING TO THE ORDER OF MELCHIZEDEK?" Following that, 7:28 reads: "THE LAW APPOINTS AS HIGH PRIESTS MEN WHO HAVE WEAKNESS, BUT THE WORD OF THE OATH WHICH CAME AFTER THE LAW APPOINTS THE SON WHO HAS BEEN PERFECTED FOREVER." Then lastly, 9:12 & 15 read: "WITH HIS OWN BLOOD, JESUS ENTERED THE MOST HOLY PLACE ONCE FOR ALL, HAVING OBTAINED ETERNAL REDEMPTION.... FOR THIS REASON HE IS THE MEDIATOR OF THE NEW COVENANT ... FOR THE REDEMPTION OF THE TRANSGRESSIONS UNDER THE FIRST COVENANT, SO THAT THOSE WHO ARE CALLED MAY RECEIVE THE PROMISE OF THE ETERNAL INHERITANCE."

When Paul brought up **SALVATION TO ALL WHO OBEY HIM**, the thought behind verses 7-8 come to mind, meaning that, just as Jesus became Savior by obedience, we become saved by obedience. So since obedience was essential for Jesus to become Savior, why would anyone assume he could be saved without obedience/submission? Even faith toward God/Christ for salvation is a command (Acts 16:31).

> **VERSE 10:** [JESUS WAS] **CALLED BY GOD AS HIGH PRIEST "ACCORDING TO THE ORDER OF MELCHIZEDEK."**

The word **AS** was unnecessarily (perhaps even detrimentally) supplied, and the word for **CALLED** means "to dub or bestow a name upon," such as when parents-to-be ask each other, "What shall we call our baby?" meaning, "By what name should we choose to call him or her?" Thus this verse is simply saying that, because Jesus reached His Father's goal for Him as High Priest, God dubbed Him "High Priest after the likeness of Melchizedek." Actually, as the term "dubbed" suggests, the word for **CALLED** carries with it the idea of performing this dubbing publicly, meaning that, as He was pleased to call Jesus His Son at His baptism, God was pleased to call Him our High Priest. And how was this accomplished publicly? Through Jesus' resurrection/appearances/ascension to the heavenly mercy seat.

IN SUMMARY: As Paul began writing about in 2:17, there can be no doubt that, unlike Aaron, Jesus is perfectly qualified to be a merciful and faithful High Priest in things pertaining to God, because He learned obedience as a human through the experience of enduring toils, trials, and temptations that were even far greater than those endured by mere men ... and without succumbing to the pressure to sin. This is why {1} He was appointed High Priest directly by God Himself; {2} His appointment was after that of Melchizedek instead of Aaron, hence everlasting; {3} He's the Source of eternal salvation to all those who, like Him, obey; and {4} He's the Helper of the faithful while we're on this trying planet.

Hebrews 5:7

Hebrews 5:11–6:3

At this point in his epistle, Paul, apparently rather frustrated with his audience, broke off from his course of discussion concerning Jesus and the priesthood order of Melchizedek to warn them a fourth time.

As mentioned earlier, there are six warnings in Hebrews: the first three dealt primarily with their lack of faith leading to neglect, while this one, beginning with 5:11 and going all the way through 6:20, deals with their lack of spiritual growth.

> **VERSE 11:** OF WHOM WE HAVE MUCH TO SAY AND HARD TO EXPLAIN, SINCE YOU HAVE BECOME DULL OF HEARING.

Since the word for **WHOM** can be masculine or neuter, it falls to the interpreter to translate it as either "whom" or "which"; in this case the term "which" would be better, because the subject isn't Jesus or Melchizedek—it's actually the relationship of Jesus to the priestly order of Melchizedek.

The term **WE** could refer to Paul and his personal scribe (cf. Rom. 16:22, 1 Cor. 16:21, Gal. 6:11, Col. 4:18, & 2 The. 3:17), or it could have simply been a tactful way of saying, "We have lots to discuss."

Interestingly, the phrase **HARD TO EXPLAIN** is from one Greek word, the prefix of which means "difficult," while the root word means "interpretation," resulting in "explanation"; in fact, this is the term from which we get "hermeneutics." (See article on *Biblical Hermeneutics* at ASiteForTheLord.com/id4.html.)

By employing the phrase **SINCE YOU**, Paul blamed them for this being a difficult subject to explain, which indicates that the audience is what determines which parts of God's Word are milk and which parts are meat (cf. the next verse).

The phrase **HAVE BECOME** indicates that at one time these brethren weren't like this; but, due to their pulling away from the truths they once confessed, they had become (not were becoming) dull of hearing (cf. notes at 2:1-3 & 4:14).

The word for **DULL** is only found one other time in the New Testament—in 6:12 where it's translated as "sluggish"; the word for **HEARING** referred to their "understanding," an understanding that was drifting backward instead of pressing foreward (5:12b & 6:1a). Thus, due to backsliding into Judaism instead of advancing into Christianity (cf. 6:4-6), Paul had a difficult time figuring out how to get this important subject across to them.

Consider their immaturity: they Drifted from the Word (2:1-4); they Doubted the Word (3:7–4:13); and they were Dull in hearing the Word (5:11). Something we can learn from this then is that a symptom of spiritual problems is the attitude that Bible study/worship/preaching are "DULL."

VERSE 12: FOR THOUGH BY THIS TIME YOU OUGHT TO BE TEACHERS, YOU NEED SOMEONE TO TEACH YOU AGAIN THE FIRST PRINCIPLES OF THE ORACLES OF GOD; AND YOU HAVE COME TO NEED MILK AND NOT SOLID FOOD.

If this letter was written to Jewish Christians in Jerusalem, as seems to be the case, then that makes this first clause a very strong one; in other words, in saying **BY THIS TIME YOU OUGHT TO BE TEACHERS**, Paul was referring to the idea that the church had been established there for over 30 years!

Since the **FIRST PRINCIPLES** are **OF THE ORACLES OF GOD**, we should determine what these "ORACLES" are. The word for **ORACLES** (λογιον) is related to the term λογιας, the word translated "COLLECTION" in First Corinthians 16:1, but derived from the very familiar term λογος (logos) which is variously translated as "sayings" or "words" or even "teachings." However, while λογος could be used for something thought or stated, λογιον was only associated with divine thoughts/teachings. Thus, by combining all this, we discover that "THE ORACLES OF GOD" refer to the collection of teachings or sayings of God. So what was the only collection of God's sayings of which we know for sure they possessed at that time? The Old Testament. What else would people such as Paul use to convince Jews that Jesus was the promised Messiah?

Furthermore, the term λογιον was used of the Mosaical Law by Stephen (Acts 7:38) and Paul (Rom. 3:2), and since Hebrews deals so much with priesthood, it's also interesting to note that divine oracles were engraved on the high priest's breastplate in Old Testament times; in fact, *The Septuagint* (Greek) version of the Old Testament employs the term λογιον in Exodus 28:15 to describe that breastplate.

Now what of **THE FIRST PRINCIPLES**? What are principles? Some synonyms for "PRINCIPLES" are thoughts, truths, ingredients, and elements; applying it to this text, the phrase "FIRST PRINCIPLES" simply refers to the initial truths or first elements—of or about Christ (6:1)—found in "THE ORACLES OF GOD" (the Old Testament, something Jesus Himself affirmed in John 5:39). The original word for "PRINCIPLES" is also the term translated as "ELEMENTS" in Galatians 4:3 & 9 and Colossians 2:8 & 20 where the idea of that which is elementary/foundational is meant to describe the Old Testament—their present oracles of God. Notice, for instance, Galatians 3:24-25: "THE LAW WAS OUR TUTOR TO BRING US TO CHRIST.... [NOW] WE ARE NO LONGER UNDER A TUTOR." Then notice Galatians 4:1-3 & 9: "A CHILD ... IS UNDER GUARDIANS AND STEWARDS UNTIL THE TIME APPOINTED BY THE FATHER. EVEN SO WE, WHEN WE WERE CHILDREN, WERE IN BONDAGE UNDER THE ELEMENTS OF THE WORLD [the Law of the Jewish system].... BUT NOW ... HOW IS IT THAT YOU TURN AGAIN TO THE WEAK AND BEGGARLY ELEMENTS OF THE WORLD [this Jewish system and the law of sin and death], TO WHICH YOU DESIRE AGAIN TO BE IN BONDAGE?" Thus, if the oracles of God here in Hebrews 5 are a reference to the Law of Moses (which makes perfect sense in the context of this entire epistle), then what was Paul saying? If the Old Testament prophesied of Jesus, and if these Hebrews were headed back to that world (this letter was written before the Jewish world was destroyed), then they obviously needed to be retaught the very fundamentals of the Old Testament.

So for them to return to the world that foreshadowed Christ would be to completely miss the most basic point of the Old Testament (cf. Col. 2:16-17 & Heb. 10:1); Jesus being their High Priest is something that should've been fundamental to—of all people—those Jews who had become Christians!

The **MILK** of God's Word is equivalent to **THE FIRST PRINCIPLES OF THE ORACLES OF GOD** (or, as 6:1 puts it, "THE ELEMENTARY PRINCIPLES OF CHRIST" found in God's oracles), including that which he had already discussed—Jesus' fulfillment of the type/shadow of the Aaronic priesthood.

Thus meat or **SOLID FOOD** likely refers to the next step in the discussion of Jesus' priesthood that Paul was trying to take, for it was at the point of bringing up the priesthood of Jesus after the order of Melchizedek when he paused to scold them for making this more difficult on him than it should've been.

(Side-notes: {1} This verse implies that a person does <u>not</u> need to know everything or even a great deal about the Bible to be saved. {2} This verse implies that every Christian is [or at the very least "was"] expected to be a teacher of God's Word in one form or another. And {3} it's sad that many of those who complain about hearing the basics too often from the pulpit don't even know where to turn in the Bible to share with others the way to salvation.)

So why did Paul think they needed to be taught the first principles again?

> **VERSE 13: BECAUSE EVERYONE WHO PARTAKES ONLY OF MILK IS UNSKILLED IN THE WORD OF RIGHTEOUSNESS, FOR HE IS A BABE.**

The word for **UNSKILLED** means "inexperienced"; in other words, they needed to be taught so they could teach. And what were they expected to teach or share with the world? **THE WORD** [or teaching/good news] **OF** [or about] **RIGHTEOUSNESS**. This phrase is reminiscent of Romans 1:17 where Paul taught that through the Gospel (the New Testament) one learns how to gain God's righteousness by faith.

These brethren were so caught up in their return to the Old Covenant life or world that they were inexperienced in the good news teaching about the New Covenant and how to share it with others at this most important time in history.

Back in Paul's day, being called a "babe" as an adult wasn't a good thing as it is now; the word for **BABE** in this verse was used as a referent to someone who was ignorant, either due to a lack of being taught or to a lack of personal study and experience in teaching others.

Note an implied irony here: these brethren weren't unskilled because they were babes (which would be normal); they were babes because they were unskilled—and that by their own choice. Unlike normal children, they weren't learning and thus growing; so, because to not increase is to decrease, they were regressing instead of progressing.

> **VERSE 14:** BUT SOLID FOOD BELONGS TO THOSE WHO ARE OF FULL AGE, THAT IS, THOSE WHO BY REASON OF USE HAVE THEIR SENSES EXERCISED TO DISCERN BOTH GOOD AND EVIL.

The word for **USE** refers to that which has become second nature to someone. The old saying that "if you don't use it, you lose it" implies the axiom that one can't lose what he doesn't have; yet, in another irony to ponder, these brethren didn't have it because they didn't use it!

The phrase **FULL AGE** refers of course to maturity; and, unlike babies who will swallow nearly anything, mature people will be more careful about what they swallow.

The word **SENSES** refers to one's mental abilities here, not to the five senses we normally think of; and these exercised senses result in the ability to determine what's good or bad ... to swallow.

The phrase **GOOD AND EVIL** refers not to good and bad morals in this case, but to right and wrong doctrines, for that's what would've made them righteous in relation to this context.

Remember, these brethren were being severely pressured to return to Judaism, and this pressure (false teaching from Judaizers as well as persecution) was causing them to neglect —even renounce—what they had been taught and had previously accepted as true. This was why Paul indicated that such negligence leads to total apostasy (6:4-9).

There's something comforting in this verse that should be taken to heart: The implied general lesson here is that the more one exercises himself in reading, studying, meditating upon, and teaching God's Word, the more chance there is that he's correct in his interpretation; this is obviously why God expects respect among men in harmony with each one's amount of spiritual exercise (cf. notes at 13:7 & 17).

> **VERSE 1A: THEREFORE, LEAVING THE DISCUSSION OF THE ELEMENTARY PRINCIPLES OF CHRIST, LET US GO ON TO PERFECTION, NOT LAYING AGAIN [A] FOUNDATION OF...**

At this verse, Paul began to ease back into the subject of Jesus belonging to the Melchizedekian priesthood; and this "easing" actually encompasses the remainder of chapter 6.

It's important here to note that, when Paul used the phrase **LET US**, he didn't usually mean to include himself (cf. "let us" w/ "you" in 4:1)—it was (and is) merely a tactful way to motivate people; this is important because this phrase applies to both the "leaving" and the "going on" clauses in this verse. Thus, more literally, Paul was saying, "As mature Christians who have left behind them the first principles about the Messiah [found in the teachings as well as the types/shadows of the Old Testament, especially in relation to the Aaronic priesthood with its sacrifices/offerings], move on...."

So Paul went on to say, "LET'S GO ON TO PERFECTION." The word for **PERFECTION** refers to an "end," thus pointing to the purpose/goal/consummation/fulfillment of the Old Testament types/shadows/prophecies.

To **GO ON TO PERFECTION** then meant to leave behind them the Aaronic (temporary) priesthood while accepting the Melchizedekian (eternal) priesthood of Jesus which required their absolution from the old law (7:12). Since Melchizedek lived before Moses, Christ's priesthood wasn't meant to carry on the old law, but to supersede it. In fact, the clause "LET US GO ON" is passive in nature, meaning that this perfection—this end/goal—was coming, ready or not. Their wilderness wandering, their transition phase, their 40-year grace period was very near its end (10:37)! When referring to Jerusalem's demise in AD 70, Jesus said, "'THESE ARE THE DAYS OF VENGEANCE THAT ALL THINGS WHICH ARE WRITTEN MAY BE FULFILLED'" (Luke 21:22). The thing is, these brethren, instead of going backwards, needed all-the-more to seriously press forward, thinking about their future in relation to their present state.

Consider the six subjects Paul listed in verses 1b-2, keeping two things in mind: {1} They were being pressured to return to Judaism (the Scriptures that they had then), and {2} they didn't have much of the New Testament for their Christianity. So the result was that they were dwelling on what little they knew, apparently not growing by means of the resources at their disposal ... even after 30 years! They seemed to be content in drinking the milk of the Law (perhaps as a way to compromise with their persecutors). They just didn't seem to realize that they, <u>especially</u> in the 60s, didn't have the time to get stuck dabbling in the mere shadows of the substance which was unfolding right before their eyes!

> **VERSES 1B-2:** ...REPENTANCE FROM DEAD WORKS AND OF FAITH TOWARD GOD, OF THE DOCTRINE OF BAPTISMS [AND] OF LAYING ON OF HANDS, [AND] OF RESURRECTION FROM THE DEAD AND OF ETERNAL JUDGMENT.

Firstly it's probably worth mentioning that Paul wrote these six topics in three sets of two as can be seen in his use of the coordinating conjunction "AND." (As noted in brackets above, the NKJV left out two conjunctions.) So, for brevity's sake, let's succinctly paraphrase what Paul was likely saying here.

"Yes, studying, believing, and discussing the fact that men must turn from evil deeds (that lead to death) toward faith in God (that leads to life) is indeed good old first testament teaching that's brought to its fullness in the New Testament, but let's move on." (Notice that it's faith toward God instead of Jesus, indicating an Old Testament concept.)

And, "Yes, studying, believing, and discussing how the various ceremonial cleansings and laying hands on the sin-sacrifices beautifully picture our forgiveness and cleansing is indeed good old first testament teaching that's brought to its fullness in the New Testament, but let's move on."

And, "Yes, studying, believing, and discussing the wonders of resurrection and the terrors of eternal judgment is indeed good old first testament teaching that's brought to its fullness in the New Testament, but let's move on!" (Yes, both these ideas are taught in the Old Testament, e.g. Daniel 12.)

(Side-note: Not that I agree with every detail of his comments, but for a great and more in-depth study of 6:1-3, see Gary Workman's notes in *Studies in Hebrews: The Second Annual Denton Lectures*, ed. Dub McClish, 1983, p. 365.)

VERSE 3: AND THIS WE WILL DO IF GOD PERMITS.

As will become more clear in the comments of the next paragraph (6:4-12), since the hearts of these brethren could be too far gone already, Paul, by this statement, hinted at the possibility that God's nature may not permit the desired consequence of this teaching.

Because man has free-will, God will not, yea cannot, violate it; in other words, these brethren had to choose between returning to the first testament or pressing onward into New Testament—the actual goal of that foundational testament.

Hebrews 6:4-12

In 5:11–6:3 Paul toiled to wean a 30-year-old congregation from the milk of the Old Testament world of prophecies, types, and shadows of the coming Christ and propel them forward, deeper into the New Testament world of their fulfillment in Jesus, who would finish all things in the AD 70 destruction of Jerusalem/Judaism/Temple (Luke 21:22). Paul ended that section by saying, "AND THIS WE WILL DO IF GOD PERMITS," indicating that he hoped it wasn't too late for them—that they weren't already too far gone to get them turned around prior to the arrival of the perfection—the end, because they'd be destroyed (lost) right along with the rest of the Jews if they didn't get back on course.

In this section Paul continued his warning against apostasy.

> **VERSES 4A & 6: FOR IT IS IMPOSSIBLE ... IF THEY SHALL FALL AWAY, TO RENEW THEM AGAIN TO REPENTANCE, SINCE THEY CRUCIFY AGAIN FOR THEMSELVES THE SON OF GOD, AND PUT HIM TO AN OPEN SHAME.**

The word for **FALL AWAY** means "to deviate or turn aside from"; this term is related to the one Paul used in Galatians 5:4 when he told those Christians (who were having the same problem as these Hebrews), "YOU HAVE BECOME ESTRANGED FROM CHRIST, YOU WHO ATTEMPT TO BE JUSTIFIED BY LAW; YOU HAVE FALLEN FROM GRACE." In Hebrews 6:6 Paul wasn't talking about someone who fell into a moral sin and didn't want to repent of it (although that could perhaps be included); he was talking about the ominous subject of apostasy.

To apostatize means "to step away and stand aloof from something/someone," which is what Paul spoke of in 3:12 when he said, "BEWARE, BRETHREN, LEST THERE BE IN ANY OF YOU AN EVIL HEART OF UNBELIEF IN DEPARTING FROM THE LIVING GOD."

The word for **RENEW** is intriguing. There are two Greek words for "new": νεος refers to something "new in time," and καινος refers to something "new in condition"—to something that has been restored. The original word here is from καινος, with a prefix added for repetition; in other words, it refers to something that had been reconditioned once already, but would be reconditioned once again.

The way Paul used the word **REPENTANCE** here (viz. as a state or place) brings to mind the reality that repentance is a gift of God, a gift in the sense that He chose that He would allow repentance on the part of man in order to acquire salvation: in Acts 11:18 Peter spoke about how God has "GRANTED TO THE GENTILES REPENTANCE TO LIFE"; and in Second Timothy 2:25 Paul spoke of being patient with quarrelers just in case God "GRANT[ED] THEM REPENTANCE," which fits perfectly with Paul's "IF GOD PERMITS" clause in Hebrews 6:3. So the point for them in their time and under their circumstances is that, since only God could know the heart of a man concerning whether it was feasible to change him or not, they (with the possible exception of the principle in Mat. 7:6) were to merely do their duty, and let Him take care of the rest (cf. Mat. 13:24-30), something which would happen soon (Heb. 10:37).

According to the Greek scholars, the word for **IMPOSSIBLE** here cannot be toned down to mean "difficult"—it really does mean "impossible." Why would it have been impossible? Because God rejects those who reject Him and His teachings (cf. vv. 8-9); He could not, cannot, and will not save anyone against his/her will. Yes, a person on his own can choose to reassociate himself with what he had previously rejected, but God won't force him to do so; this is why Paul employed the pronoun "WE" (v. 3) and why it says that it's impossible to renew him/her, implying that it cannot be accomplished by someone else.

The question arises, Why did Paul speak of the impossibility of a return from falling away? Haven't we heard of people who "fell away" from the church and came back? Surely we have. So what's the deal here? Well, Paul said that this sort of people would be impossible to restore because **THEY CRUCIFY AGAIN FOR THEMSELVES THE SON OF GOD, AND PUT HIM TO AN OPEN SHAME.**

The phrase **FOR THEMSELVES** could either mean "as far as they were concerned" or that "they did it to their own detriment" because the cross would have no more value for them—to return to Judaism would be to renege on Jesus as being the Messiah, meaning that He was worthy of death for being a fraud. Besides, the putting **HIM TO AN OPEN SHAME** idea seems to contrast the **FOR THEMSELVES** idea; in other words, they wouldn't only (re)crucify Jesus to their own detriment, but by leaving what they once professed they would also bring blasphemy and shame on Him in the eyes of others. So, instead of bring-ing glory to the cross, they'd be encouraging people to see nothing in it but shame (cf. Gal. 3:13 & 5:11). Returning to verse 4, Paul described this sort of people:

> **VERSES 4B-5:** ...THOSE WHO WERE ONCE ENLIGHTENED, AND HAVE TASTED THE HEAVENLY GIFT, AND HAVE BECOME PARTAKERS OF THE HOLY SPIRIT, AND HAVE TASTED THE GOOD WORD OF GOD AND THE POWERS OF THE AGE TO COME...

Although all may not agree, it isn't difficult to perceive that {1} these five topics are depicted in a staircase fashion, and {2} the last four simultaneously describe the first one. So let's consider the first one, not just as the first in the series, but also as the first in contextual significance.

The word for **ENLIGHTENED** could mean a couple things, either separately or simultaneously: {1} it could refer to understand-ing in general (bringing in the generic idea that this word is described by the four topics that follow); or {2} it could refer to baptism, because this particular Greek word was used in the first few centuries to signify the result of one who came to understand (bringing in the more specific staircase idea with the first step—baptism); or {3} it could refer to both of these ideas simultaneously, which is the most acceptable expla-nation because the word **ONCE** means once for all, bringing up something such as baptism that's performed only once, while the last four, in the original, use the word "having," connecting them with the word "ENLIGHTENED." Now...

The concept of understanding brings to mind numerous passages such as the following: {1} of Jesus, Zacharias said, "'TO GIVE LIGHT TO THOSE WHO SIT IN DARKNESS'" (Luke 1:79), and {2} Paul wrote of "THE LIGHT OF ... KNOWLEDGE ... IN THE FACE OF JESUS CHRIST" (2 Cor. 4:6).

Concerning baptism, consider a parallel passage later in Hebrews: after speaking of receiving the knowledge of the truth in 10:26, Paul then said in verse 32, "RECALL THE FORMER DAYS IN WHICH, AFTER YOU WERE ILLUMINATED, YOU ENDURED GREAT STRUGGLE." When did they begin having their struggles? After their conversion of course.

The phrase **TASTED THE HEAVENLY GIFT** means that they had experienced Christ and His salvation in their lives (at least in an already-but-not-yet sense, for 9:28 indicates that salvation wouldn't be totally accomplished until Jesus returned from out of the most holy [the "SECOND"] place). This also brings to mind numerous passages such as the following: {1} Jesus said of Himself, "'IF YOU KNEW THE GIFT OF GOD AND WHO IT IS WHO SAYS TO YOU, "GIVE ME A DRINK," YOU WOULD HAVE ASKED HIM, AND HE WOULD HAVE GIVEN YOU LIVING WATER'" (John 4:10); {2} Jesus also said, "'I AM THE LIVING BREAD WHICH CAME DOWN FROM HEAVEN. IF ANYONE EATS OF THIS BREAD, HE WILL LIVE FOREVER'" (John 6:51); and {3}, speaking of Jesus, Peter wrote, "YOU HAVE TASTED THAT THE LORD IS GRACIOUS" (1 Pet. 2:3).

The phrase **PARTAKERS OF THE HOLY SPIRIT** probably refers to the idea found in First Corinthians 6:19 where Paul wrote, "DO YOU NOT KNOW THAT YOUR BODY IS THE TEMPLE OF THE HOLY SPIRIT?", reminiscent of Ephesians 1:13-14 which applied solely to Christians of that initial generation (a must read).

The phrase **THE GOOD WORD OF GOD** is interesting because it's suggestive of the various times just such a phrase was used in the Old Testament, referring to positive things. In Joshua 21:45 the promise of bringing the children of Israel into the land of Canaan was called "A GOOD WORD," and in Jeremiah 29:10 the bringing of God's people out of captivity was called a "GOOD WORD."

So it's no wonder that, when the writer of Psalm 45:1 wrote of the coming Messiah, he spoke of meditating on "A GOOD WORD," which corresponds perfectly here with people who were experiencing "THE GOOD WORD OF GOD"—the fulfilling of the pleasant promises of the Messianic age.

Now, taking note of the Greek term μελλω again (cf. 1:14 & 2:5), consider the phrase **THE POWERS OF THE AGE TO COME**. Such as when we speak of "the powers that be," the term for **POWERS** here was used in reference to other things besides supernatural intervention in the material universe (cf. Mat. 24:29, Titus 3:1, & 1 Pet. 3:22). Especially in the context of this letter in general (e.g. 11:35 & 12:22-28), and since Paul was referring to the following age—the New Covenant age, it seems obvious that he was alluding to those things which that dawning new age would bring, things such as reformation (Heb. 9:9-10), refreshing restoration (Acts 3:19-21), redemption (Eph. 1:13-14), and resurrection (Luke 20:35 & Php. 3:8-12 in which Paul again used the term "POWER"). Since revelation would be complete and Christ's enemies would be crushed, Paul may have also been including the future of the Gospel's increase (Isa. 9:7 & Rev. 21–22, esp. 22:17). The church was in its infancy during this transition period, so if it had "TASTED" the greatness of the dawning new age then (they were in the process of "RECEIVING" it after all, Heb. 12:28), how great it would be when it all finally arrived (cf. 1 Cor. 13:8-12)! Now on to Paul's illustration:

> **VERSES 7-8:** **FOR THE EARTH, WHICH DRINKS IN THE RAIN THAT OFTEN COMES UPON IT AND BEARS HERBS USEFUL FOR THOSE BY WHOM IT IS CULTIVATED, RECEIVES BLESSING FROM GOD; BUT IF IT BEARS THORNS AND BRIARS, IT IS REJECTED AND NEAR TO BEING CURSED, WHOSE END IS TO BE BURNED.**

The word for **EARTH** here means land, with primary reference to "a piece of ground," while the word for **HERBS** is the word from which we get "botany," the study of plants.

The word for **CULTIVATED** is the word from which we get the name "George," a name which means "a worker [not of the entire planet, but] of the land, a farmer, one who nurtures a piece of land for edible produce."

The word for **REJECTED** is the same as found in First Corinthians 9:27 where, in the KJV, Paul spoke of being "A CASTAWAY."

The **BURNING** is the curse, the result of rejection. The question is, Why did he say **NEAR TO BEING CURSED**, when the normal thing to say would've been, "it is rejected and will be burned"? Well, Paul obviously chose this particular time-statement because he had something in mind more general than just an individual who rejects Christ: that is, as the context has consistently upheld, he had in mind the "END" of Judaism that really was near its cursing at this time; so whoever among the Jews rejected Jesus shouldn't think they'd escape God's judgment or curse (fulfilling Isa. 5:1-7).

The **BLESSING FROM GOD** phrase corresponds to God being the Farmer (George); in other words, when the farmer sees that a piece of ground yields useful crops, he cares for it with more water and so on; but if it doesn't yield useful crops, he squanders no more time/energy/resources on it, moving on to other ground. This is reminiscent of both the general and the specific: The general would apply to how that God had tried and tried with the Jews and had reached the end of His patience; and, with this in mind, Jesus once said to them that "'THE KINGDOM OF GOD WILL BE TAKEN FROM YOU AND GIVEN TO A NATION BEARING THE FRUITS OF IT'" (Mat. 21:43). The specific would apply to how that Jewish Christians had plenty of time to bear fruit or be cursed; Jesus once said, "'I AM THE TRUE VINE, AND MY FATHER IS THE VINEDRESSER. EVERY BRANCH IN ME THAT DOES NOT BEAR FRUIT HE TAKES AWAY [He curses]; AND EVERY BRANCH THAT BEARS FRUIT HE PRUNES [He blesses], THAT IT MAY BEAR MORE FRUIT.... IF ANYONE DOES NOT ABIDE IN ME, HE IS CAST OUT AS A BRANCH AND IS WITHERED; AND THEY GATHER THEM AND THROW THEM INTO THE FIRE, AND THEY ARE BURNED'" (John 15:1-2 & 6). And surely one can also see that Paul had in mind the fulfillment of the prophecy of Isaiah 55:12-13 for those who tenaciously remained faithful to the Lord.

So, again, this could be an either/or situation, but the more contextual way to interpret this is as a both/and situation, especially if we keep in mind the audience and the times.

Now, just as a word of encouragement followed a solemn warning in 10:26-39, so the same is true here:

> **VERSE 9:** BUT, BELOVED, WE ARE CONFIDENT OF BETTER THINGS CONCERNING YOU, YES, THINGS THAT ACCOMPANY SALVATION, THOUGH WE SPEAK IN THIS MANNER.

By saying **WE ARE CONFIDENT OF BETTER THINGS CONCERNING YOU**, Paul made it clear that he wasn't saying that he believed they were presently in the position of being rejected; he was just trying to "head them off," as it were, to point them back in the right direction (cf. 3:12 & 4:1).

The phrase **THINGS THAT ACCOMPANY SALVATION** describe the "BETTER THINGS"; in other words, not only does this indicate that Paul believed them to still be in a saved condition, but it also—and primarily—indicates that they could bear a lot of good fruit, much like what he mentioned next in...

> **VERSE 10:** FOR GOD IS NOT UNJUST TO FORGET YOUR WORK AND LABOR OF LOVE WHICH YOU HAVE SHOWN TOWARD HIS NAME, IN THAT YOU HAVE MINISTERED TO THE SAINTS, AND DO MINISTER.

As other versions indicate, there's no word for "LABOR" in the original; so it reads more like this: "GOD IS NOT SO UNJUST AS TO OVERLOOK YOUR WORK AND THE LOVE WHICH YOU SHOWED FOR HIS SAKE IN SERVING THE SAINTS, AS YOU STILL DO" (RSV).

This verse demonstrates that just as Christ is persecuted when His people are persecuted (Acts 9:4), so God is served when the brethren are served (Mat. 25:40); and a personal example of this for Paul is found in 10:34: "YOU HAD COMPASSION ON ME IN MY CHAINS AND JOYFULLY ACCEPTED THE PLUNDERING OF YOUR GOODS." (Incidentally, if this is indeed the church in Jerusalem, Paul might even have had all the benevolent deeds of Acts 2:44-45, 4:32-37, & 6:1-6 in mind.)

> **VERSES 11-12:** AND WE DESIRE THAT EACH ONE OF YOU SHOW THE SAME DILIGENCE TO THE FULL ASSURANCE OF HOPE UNTIL THE END, THAT YOU DO NOT BECOME SLUGGISH, BUT IMITATE THOSE WHO THROUGH FAITH AND PATIENCE INHERIT THE PROMISES.

The word for **DESIRE** here is a very strong word, meaning that this is what Paul <u>greatly</u> wanted!

The phrase **SAME DILIGENCE** refers back to verse 10; in other words, Paul was encouraging them to work just as hard at securing their hope to the end as they had worked in serving their brethren.

The phrase **THE END** is equal to the time when they would **INHERIT THE PROMISES** (cf. 1:14 & notes at 3:6 concerning "THE END").

The word **SLUGGISH** is an antonym for **DILIGENCE**; to the Romans Paul once wrote, "DON'T BE SLOTHFUL IN DILIGENCE, BUT BE ZEALOUS IN SPIRIT, SERVING THE LORD" (12:11).

The word for **IMITATE** is the term from which we get the word "mimic" and is used in reference to imitating...

~ the Lord (Eph. 5:10 & 1 The. 1:6),

~ enduring brethren (1 Cor. 4:16, 11:1, Heb. 6:12, & 1 The. 1:6),

~ faithful congregations (1 The. 2:14), and...

~ that which is good (1 Pet. 3:13).

The word **PATIENCE** would probably be better translated here as "fortitude" or "determination" (cf. 10:32).

The last phrase literally reads, **THOSE WHO ... ARE INHERITING THE PROMISES** (cf. 12:28); in other words, they (unlike those of 11:13 & 39) had the privilege of living when the promises were being fulfilled. In 10:36 Paul similarly wrote that "YOU HAVE NEED OF ENDURANCE SO THAT, AFTER YOU HAVE DONE THE WILL OF GOD, YOU MAY RECEIVE THE PROMISE."

Hebrews 6:13-20

In 6:4-12 Paul wrote concerning the impossibility of being saved without Jesus, the very One who was the fulfillment of the old law to which they were returning, something which was obviously an illogical action for them to take.

Since Jesus was the hope of Israel, Paul in verse 12 brought up the idea of inheriting the promises made to Abraham—promises that could/would only be realized in Jesus, the One they had previously confessed as the Christ, but were now leaving behind.

Due to this "HABIT" of theirs (Heb. 10:25), Paul in 6:13-20 urged his weakening, first-generation, Jewish, Christian readers to imitate those who, through Abrahamic faith and perseverance, were experiencing the fulfillment of the promises.

VERSE 13: FOR WHEN GOD MADE A PROMISE TO ABRAHAM, BECAUSE HE COULD SWEAR BY NO ONE GREATER, HE SWORE BY HIMSELF...

Since they were becoming discouraged by the long delay of Christ's coming (for, as Peter indicated, He was expected to come in their generation, 2 Pet. 3:4), Paul alluded to their father Abraham's faith and perseverance (cf. 11:9-10 & 39). The emphasis of Hebrews 11, which has been dubbed "Faith's Hall of Fame," is the long outlook of true faith—involving patient waiting and endurance.

The example of Abraham demonstrates that the promise of God is certain; in other words, Paul was saying, "You think you've had a long wait—just think of father Abraham who has yet to receive the fulfillment of the promises that were made to him directly!"

The idea of God swearing means that He confirmed His promise (cf. v. 16); and this oath was made on Himself since He literally is the ultimate being: in Genesis 22:16 God said, "'BY MYSELF I HAVE SWORN,'" which would be for Him like saying, "I give you My word of honor."

(Side-note: It's interesting that this oath was made to Abraham *after* Isaac was ca. 25 years old, meaning that it didn't include the birth of Isaac, but all the blessings which would flow through him.)

> **VERSE 14:** ...SAYING, "SURELY BLESSING I WILL BLESS YOU, AND MULTIPLYING I WILL MULTIPLY YOU."

This type of repetitive wording is a figure of speech meant to emphasize; in other words, God was going to exceedingly bless and multiply Abraham and his seed! This same idea is found of Jesus when He is said to be the King of kings and Lord of lords (Rev. 19:16), meaning that Jesus is the kingliest king and the lordliest lord! It's also found in the phrase "HOLY OF HOLIES" (cf. both Darby's and Holman's versions of Heb. 9:3 & 12), meaning, as the NKJV puts it, "THE HOLIEST OF ALL" (Heb. 9:3) or "THE MOST HOLY PLACE" (Heb. 9:12).

The blessing of the promise was not only that Abraham's faith would be accounted to him for righteousness, but that the faith of his seed would likewise be accounted to them for righteousness: Paul wrote that "GOD, FORESEEING THAT HE WOULD BLESS THE NATIONS BY FAITH, PREACHED THE GOSPEL TO ABRAHAM BEFOREHAND, SAYING, 'IN YOU ALL THE NATIONS SHALL BE BLESSED'" (Gal. 3:8).

> **VERSE 15:** AND SO, AFTER ABRAHAM HAD PATIENTLY ENDURED, HE OBTAINED THE PROMISE.

The word for **ENDURED** is the same root translated "PATIENCE" in verse 12, actually referring to perseverance (something active), not mere patience (something passive, at least the way we usually understand it). (By the way, to "PATIENTLY ENDURE" is the opposite of being "SLUGGISH" per v. 12.)

Since the word for **OBTAINED** carries with it the idea of something merely lighting upon a person, it indicates that Abraham didn't personally receive the entire fulfillment of the promise, but only a touch/taste of it such as in the birth of Isaac and some of his descendants. But another way to look at it is this: Just as multiplying Abraham referred to his descendants, so his reception of the promise was fulfilled through his descendants. And still another way of looking at it can be found in John 8:56: Jesus said that "'YOUR FATHER ABRAHAM ... SAW [MY DAY] AND WAS GLAD'"; more than likely this means that Abraham saw the Messiah by the eye of faith (as referred to in 11:13).

> **VERSE 16: FOR MEN INDEED SWEAR BY THE GREATER, AND AN OATH FOR CONFIRMATION IS FOR THEM AN END OF ALL DISPUTE.**

Paul was illustrating the certainty/security of God's promise by alluding to His oath: God meant to put an end to any doubt by confirming His promise with an oath. Why bring this up? Because, since time immemorial, man has employed the use of oaths upon those greater than himself (usually God or His Word) in order to settle a matter; oaths, therefore, have become solemn. Oaths tend to cause people to think/say, "OK, as long as you swear, I trust you."

The point is this: If people feel like they can bank on what a man says under oath to God, surely he shouldn't only accept what God Himself says in oath, but he should also feel completely secure in so doing! Abraham did, and he didn't even live long enough to see the entirety of the promise fulfilled! Paul said that he "DIED IN FAITH, NOT HAVING RECEIVED THE PROMISES, BUT HAVING SEEN THEM AFAR OFF WAS ASSURED OF THEM" (11:13). But, unlike Abraham, these brethren were on the verge of finally experiencing the fulfillment of these long-awaited promises!

(Side-note: The difference between a promise and an oath is that in a promise a simple claim is made, while in an oath someone's character publicly/solemnly supports the claim; in a promise we look at words, while in an oath we look at the person, whether the oath-taker or the oath-supporter [cf. Rom. 1:9, 2 Cor. 1:23, etc.])

> **VERSE 17: THUS GOD, DETERMINING TO SHOW MORE ABUNDANTLY TO THE HEIRS OF [THE] PROMISE THE IMMUTABILITY OF HIS COUNSEL, CONFIRMED IT BY AN OATH...**

The clause **THUS GOD ... CONFIRMED IT BY AN OATH** means that—*think about this now*—God remarkably complied with His creation's own universal oath-taking custom!

By stating **TO SHOW MORE ABUNDANTLY ... THE IMMUTABILITY OF HIS COUNSEL**, Paul was saying that God disregarded the implied distrust in His Word alone and took the oath; He just could not make it on anyone other than Himself. See, a man makes an oath on someone greater than himself (such as God), because he's in essence saying that if he's lying he acknowledges the right of this "greater one" to punish him. But, since there's none above God to punish Him if He were to lie, He, to appease man, did all He could possibly do by taking an oath on the very same person men do—Himself; so if men trust themselves to make an oath on God, then surely men can trust God to make an oath on Himself!

The word **IMMUTABILITY** simply means "unchangeableness"; God wanted Abraham and all his physical and spiritual heirs to know that He's not a turncoat: to Timothy Paul succinctly said that God "CANNOT DENY HIMSELF" (2 Tim. 2:13), and James said of God that in Him "IS NO VARIATION OR [even a] SHADOW OR TURNING" (1:17).

The term for **COUNSEL** refers to a proposal based on one's desire; in other words, God proposed/promised certain things to Abraham based on His desires for mankind, then He took an oath to fulfill them.

The term for **CONFIRMED** here is different than the one for "CONFIRMATION" in verse 16: while the previous one merely means "to produce confidence," this one means "to pledge oneself as surety." In other words, since God couldn't take an oath on anyone greater, He, by swearing upon Himself, became the security-deposit for the sake of this promise. Similarly, Jesus (being the covenant Himself, Isa. 42:6 & 49:8), in a twist of irony, is the "SURETY" for the New Covenant (cf. 7:22).

Interestingly, since Paul here was headed back into his discussion of Christ's high priesthood according to the order of Melchizedek, there's a very distinct possibility that this verse about the oath of God to Abraham and his descendants includes His oath concerning Jesus' priesthood. In 6:20 Paul again brought up Psalm 110:4 where God spoke of swearing that Jesus will be a priest forever.

This is a very smooth transition. Moving from Melchizedek in 5:6-10 about Psalm 110:4, to a warning against apostasy in 5:11–6:12, to Abraham as an example of faithfulness due to his trust in God in 6:13-19, then back to Psalm 110:4 about Jesus and Melchizedek and Abraham's connection to him in 6:20–7:10 is a masterful piece of writing.

> **VERSE 18:** ...THAT BY TWO IMMUTABLE THINGS, IN WHICH IT IS IMPOSSIBLE FOR GOD TO LIE, WE MIGHT HAVE STRONG CONSOLATION WHO HAVE FLED FOR REFUGE TO LAY HOLD OF THE HOPE SET BEFORE US.

The phrase **TWO IMMUTABLE THINGS** either refers to two oaths (the one to Abraham and the one about Jesus' priesthood) or to God's promise and His oath (v. 17).

Regarding the idea that **IT'S IMPOSSIBLE FOR GOD TO LIE**, Numbers 23:19 reads, "GOD IS NOT A MAN THAT HE SHOULD LIE.... HAS HE EVER PROMISED AND NOT CARRIED IT THROUGH" (NLT)?

Since the word for **STRONG** refers to a barrier to resistance like an army or fortress, and since the word for **CONSOLATION** refers to encouragement resulting in solace, the phrase **STRONG CONSOLATION** might be better understood as "a fortress of encouragement." Peter once said, "THE LORD ISN'T REALLY BEING SLOW ABOUT HIS PROMISE AS SOME THINK" (2 Pet. 3:9, NLT), and this was right after he spoke about those who expected Him to come back and deliver them in their generation and were complaining that He wasn't fulfilling His promise (v. 4).

So, since God made a promise, took an oath, and cannot lie, they had no excuse for their lack of continuing to press onward, no matter what they were enduring (cf. Heb. 13:6).

The phrase **HAVE FLED FOR REFUGE** is the same as used in the Greek version of Deuteronomy 4:42 where it speaks of fleeing to a city of refuge (there were three on each side of River Jordan); these brethren had accepted Jesus as Messiah, so they were headed for God's eternal city of refuge, complying with John the Baptist's statement to "'FLEE FROM THE WRATH ABOUT TO [μελλω] COME'" (Mat. 3:7).

VERSE 19: THIS HOPE WE HAVE AS AN ANCHOR OF THE SOUL, BOTH SURE AND STEADFAST, AND WHICH ENTERS THE PRESENCE BEHIND THE VEIL...

The word **anchor** is from the term ανκυραν (anchuran); as one can see, "anchor," like "baptism," is actually a transliteration (a Greek word in English letters). Paul was telling them that their hope was their anchor—something that was found on ancient coins as an emblem of hope.

The anchor of their hope was **SURE AND STEADFAST**, meaning that it was totally secure in that the chain couldn't break, and the anchor couldn't slip off its mooring. And where did Paul say this chain and anchor—hope—extended into? **THE PRESENCE BEHIND THE VEIL**, or more literally, "the place behind the veil"—the most holy place. Consider this: the veil of the temple represented Jesus (Heb. 10:19-20), so when He died the veil of the temple was torn in two in order to signify His death (Luke 23:45); but not only that, for man through Jesus is now invited into the very presence of God (cf. 10:19-23 & John 14:6).

However, since the full glories of that invitation wouldn't be realized until Christ's high priestly work was completed, then the veil also signified the transition Christ was making from one covenant to another (from the covenant of sin and death to the covenant of reconciliation and life). In other words, by AD 70, after a generation of grace for the Jews, everything connected with the old law was totally/finally removed by Christ, thereby completing God's scheme of redemption.

Thus Paul was communicating to them that because their Messiah, through His death/resurrection, was in the Father's presence preparing their spiritual residence (cf. John 14:1ff), they, based on God's promises/oaths, had no good reason to forsake their confession of Jesus (4:14).

> **VERSE 20:** ...WHERE THE FORERUNNER HAS ENTERED FOR US, EVEN JESUS, HAVING BECOME HIGH PRIEST FOREVER ACCORDING TO THE ORDER OF MELCHIZEDEK.

There are two reasons indicated here as to why Jesus is a **HIGH PRIEST FOREVER ACCORDING TO THE ORDER OF MELCHIZEDEK**. Firstly, Melchizedek's priesthood (as opposed to Aaron's) has no end (implying that man has no end, for there's no reason for a priest if there are no humans [cf. Ecc. 1:4 and Psa. 148:3 & 6]); as Paul said in 7:3, Melchizedek, because there was no recorded genealogy for him, had no beginning or end to his days. Secondly, Levitical high priests were never thought of as "forerunners" (which is probably why, according to the original, Paul didn't place the definite article before "FORERUNNER"); rather, they (wearing 12 gems on their vests for the 12 tribes of Israel) were merely representatives of the individuals who couldn't even approach the tabernacle, much less enter its holy and holiest places! Even the priests weren't allowed to follow the high priest into the most holy place of God's presence, reminiscent of High Priest Jesus telling His disciples, "'WHERE I AM GOING YOU CANNOT COME'" (John 13:33), or "'WHERE I AM GOING YOU CANNOT FOLLOW ME NOW'" (John 13:36). Why? Because "THE NEW AND LIVING WAY" (Heb. 10:20) wouldn't be completely paved until AD 70. But once it was, then, as Jesus said, "'YOU SHALL FOLLOW ME AFTERWARD'" (John 13:36b), and they did.

Jesus went on to tell His disciples, "'SINCE I GO AND PREPARE A PLACE FOR YOU, I WILL COME AGAIN AND RECEIVE YOU TO MYSELF, THAT WHERE I AM YOU MAY BE ALSO'" (John 14:3). In other words, once His high priestly work was finished in the _real_ holy of holies, and once the old law of sin and death was totally and once-for-all removed, then they'd be fully accepted into God's presence as heavenly citizens. This helps us to understand that, at one time, if anyone besides the high priest entered the holy of holies, he'd _die_ (Exo. 28:35, cf. 28:43 & Num. 18:1ff); but now, because of Christ, we can _live_ in God's presence, meaning that, through forgiveness, our relationship to Him has been established in such a way as to provide us with reconciliation and therefore eternal life.

Hebrews 6.19

Hebrews 7:1-10

Paul began talking about the high priesthood of Jesus as being like that of Melchizedek back in chapter 5, but due to his frustration with the lack of growth among these brethren, he broke off from that subject to scold them for their immaturity. However...

While penning his thoughts in chapter 6, he masterfully led his audience directly back into the topic of Jesus' Melchizedekian priesthood—the primary topic of chapter 7. One might even envision 7:1-3 as a sermonette on 6:20.

> **VERSE 1:** F**OR THIS** M**ELCHIZEDEK** (**KING OF** S**ALEM, PRIEST OF THE** M**OST** H**IGH** G**OD, WHO MET** A**BRAHAM RETURNING FROM THE SLAUGHTER OF THE** K**INGS AND BLESSED HIM**...
> {I SUPPLIED THE PARENTHESES FROM V. 1 THRU V. 3.}

Melchizedek is only mentioned twice in the entirety of the Old Testament: once in Psalm 110:4 and once in Genesis 14:18-20, the record of his very brief encounter with Abram (Abraham's name till Gen. 17).

It's important to note that Melchizedek, unlike the Levites, but like Jesus (cf. Zec. 6:12-13), was both king and priest.

Because Jerusalem is called "S**ALEM**" in Psalm 76:2, it's pretty much indisputable that the city of **S**ALEM here is Jeru-Salem.

After Abram had slaughtered four evil kings in order to free his nephew Lot, he came to Salem where he met Melchizedek—God's "Gentile" priest—who blessed him. (Since Jews were of Abraham's lineage, there were no Jews yet [per se], which points to one of Paul's main points for comparing Jesus with Melchizedek—he existed before Jews came into existence!)

Abram recognized the superior office of Melchizedek and honored him in it, point being that though the Jews (including the Levites) made great claims of being related to Abraham, this verse indicates that Melchizedek blessed Abraham, and, as Paul said in verse 7, "THE INFERIOR IS BLESSED BY THE SUPERIOR" (RSV). And why did Melchizedek bless Lot's uncle? Because he knew that God was with Abram (Gen. 14:20), and also probably because Abram had rid the people of those evil kings. Now it was Abram's turn:

> **VERSE 2: ...TO WHOM ALSO ABRAHAM GAVE A TENTH PART OF ALL, FIRST BEING TRANSLATED "KING OF RIGHTEOUSNESS," AND THEN ALSO KING OF SALEM, MEANING "KING OF PEACE"...**

As mentioned earlier, Abraham acknowledged Melchizedek as God's high priest by giving him a tenth of the spoils he had taken from battle (v. 4).

It's interesting to note that not only did Melchizedek's priestly order exist long before Aaron's order, but also tithing was in existence long before the Law of Moses (cf. Jacob in Gen. 28:22); as God's priest, Melchizedek was entitled to a tenth of the income of God's people, and Abram knew this.

The idea of **FIRST BEING TRANSLATED** means that "righteous king" or "king of righteousness" is the literal meaning of the Hebrew term translated as "Melchizedek"; then, when it says **THEN ALSO ... "KING OF PEACE,"** it's merely referring to the meaning of "SALEM" (literally, "shalom") which means "peace."

Just as Melchizedek was a **KING OF RIGHTEOUSNESS** and a **KING OF PEACE**, so Jesus is a King of Righteousness (Jer. 23:5) and a Prince [or King] of Peace (Isa. 9:6). Peace and righteousness are found in combination at least ten times in Scripture (Psa. 72:3 & 7, 85:10, Isa. 32:17, 60:17, 62:1, Rom. 14:17, 2 Tim. 2:22, Heb. 12:10-11, & Jas. 3:17-18), implying that true peace can be experienced only in association with, or on the basis of, righteousness, which is why Paul taught that to enjoy peace with God, one must be declared righteous (Rom. 5:1).

> **VERSE 3:** ...WITHOUT FATHER, WITHOUT MOTHER, WITHOUT GENEALOGY, HAVING NEITHER BEGINNING OF DAYS NOR END OF LIFE, BUT MADE LIKE THE SON OF GOD) REMAINS A PRIEST CONTINUALLY.

Paul's main thought in 7:1-3 is that this Melchizedek remains a priest continuously; and he said this in connection to 6:20 in which he stated that Jesus is a High Priest forever according to the order of Melchizedek. Why? Because he "REMAINS A PRIEST CONTINUOUSLY" (and it should be translated as continuously, not continually). So if the Bible student will just mentally place a parenthesis after Melchizedek in verse 1, then one before "remains" here in verse 3 (as I've done), he'll see Paul's intended flow of thought from 6:20 all the way through 7:3.

It's important we keep in mind that Paul wasn't writing as much about Melchizedek's life as he was writing about Melchizedek's priesthood! And, if this is an accurate statement, then these three deductions follow: {1} When Paul spoke of Melchizedek as being without father and mother, he was referring to the idea that, unlike the Levites, he was without any priestly lineage; but, like Jesus, he was a priest by special appointment from God. {2} When Paul spoke of Melchizedek as being without genealogy, he was referring to the idea that, unlike the Levites, he was in no way related to Abraham. And {3} when Paul spoke of Melchizedek as being without beginning of days or ending of life, he was referring to his life as a priest. See, unlike the Levitical priests who could only serve from the age of 20 till death, God left no such revelation about Melchizedek's reign; rather, his priesthood was like that of God's Son—an eternal one (6:20). What this means is that as Melchizedek alone filled up the entirety of his priesthood, so Jesus fills up the entirety of His priesthood; each of them was/is uninterrupted in his duties. (In case someone is interested in pursuing the following: some scholars believe that Melchizedek was Jesus incarnate.)

And, to be sure the reader doesn't miss this, something that's clearly implied here (and perhaps also in Isa. 53:8 & Acts 8:33) is that Jesus has no posterity!

SUB-SUMMARY: Individual Levites couldn't claim to be specially ordained by God (i.e. they weren't lacking genealogy); they couldn't claim to have an endless ministry (i.e. they died); and they couldn't claim to be both kings and priests. But Jesus, like Melchizedek, could claim all of these, making Him a better priest than Aaron and his posterity.

> **VERSE 4: NOW CONSIDER HOW GREAT THIS MAN WAS, TO WHOM EVEN THE PATRIARCH ABRAHAM GAVE A TENTH OF THE SPOILS.**

In the eyes of the Jews, Abraham was the MIP (Most Important Person) among men ... period! Just before Abraham met Melchizedek, he had saved five kings, cleansed the land of four evil kings, and was returning home with a mother lode of possessions from the spoils of war! But <u>this man of God</u> paid homage to some virtually unknown man (at least he appears that way in the Bible) called Melchizedek! This is the point Paul built on from here through verse 10.

The original word for **SPOILS** here actually refers to the best of the plunder Abram took from his battles; in other words, he gave Melchizedek a tenth of all (v. 2), and it was a tenth of the best of all, thereby setting an example for generations to come.

> **VERSE 5: AND INDEED THOSE WHO ARE OF THE SONS OF LEVI, WHO RECEIVE THE PRIESTHOOD, HAVE A COMMANDMENT TO RECEIVE TITHES FROM THE PEOPLE ACCORDING TO THE LAW, THAT IS, FROM THEIR BRETHREN, THOUGH THEY HAVE COME FROM THE LOINS OF ABRAHAM.**

Paul said **THOSE WHO ARE OF THE SONS OF LEVI** because not every male Levite could be a priest, but only those of the family of Aaron; in other words, just remove the comma after "LEVI," and it makes sense. See, although <u>all</u> the tribes were children of Abraham, the Levites were commanded to exact tithes for themselves from all the <u>other</u> children of Abraham (at least from the standpoint of his grandson, Israel, the father of the twelve tribes).

The point is this: non-Levites paid tithes to their priests, not as an admission of inferiority, but because that's what they were commanded to do; however, in the case of Abraham and Melchizedek, there was no such command, meaning that Abraham voluntarily acknowledged his inferiority to God's High Priest, an attitude much more appreciated (cf. 2 Cor. 9:7).

So he who paid tithes was inferior to the one upon whom he bestowed them: Abram paid tithes to Melchizedek (meaning that Abraham was less important than Melchizedek), but the Levite priests (who descended from the eminent Abraham) took tithes from Abraham's descendants. So the argument is that although the Levitical priests were great enough to receive tithes from the people, yet their noble ancestor wasn't great enough to receive tithes from Melchizedek, but rather had to pay them!

> **VERSE 6: BUT HE WHOSE GENEALOGY IS NOT DERIVED FROM THEM RECEIVED TITHES FROM ABRAHAM AND BLESSED HIM WHO HAD THE PROMISES.**

Melchizedek, who had no part in the Levitical genealogy and therefore no legal right to exact tithes, took tithes from the patriarch himself! So, again, Melchizedek was greater than Abraham.

It could be that Paul mentioned Melchizedek blessing the one who had the promises—Abraham—for two reasons: {1} Paul could've mentioned it because one would think (and perhaps the Jews did) that Abraham—the one favored by God with **THE PROMISES**—should've been the one doing the blessing, but not so! And {2} he could've mentioned it because this scenario is a type of Jesus who blesses both Jew and Gentile. (Melchizedek was a priest over non-Abrahamic people, but he blessed Abraham.)

> **VERSE 7: NOW BEYOND ALL CONTRADICTION THE LESSER IS BLESSED BY THE BETTER.**

Everyone knows and agrees with this maxim, meaning that Melchizedek is greater than Abraham and his descendants because he gave the blessing, and Abraham, recognizing his place, received it. Melchizedek was a king and a priest, Abraham was neither. Just as Isaac blessed Jacob (Gen. 27:27-29) and Christ blessed the apostles (Luke 14:50-51), so Melchizedek blessed Abraham.

So what was this blessing? It's likely that this blessing wasn't some mere ritualistic prayer for good things to happen, but a reaffirming of the promise God had just made to Abraham. Here's the scenario: in Genesis 14 we find Abraham, who had recently received God's promise to bless the entire world through him (Gen. 12), meeting someone who had no earthly reason to know who Abram was (at least not personally), much less know about God's promise to him! But this man (Melchizedek) meets him (Abram) on the road to reaffirm that he (Abram) is God's chosen one, the one who would be the predecessor of the Messiah; now that's enough to make Abraham a believer that this fellow was indeed "THE [not 'a,' but 'the'] PRIEST OF THE MOST HIGH GOD" (Gen. 14:18).

> **VERSE 8: HERE MORTAL MEN RECEIVE TITHES, BUT THERE HE RECEIVES THEM, OF WHOM IT IS WITNESSED THAT HE LIVES.**

By the word **HERE** Paul was referring to what's often called the Mosaical Dispensation, the time of Moses and his Law.

The phrase **MORTAL MEN** means "dying men" and refers to the Levites who were constantly dying and being replaced in their priestly office under Moses' Law.

The word **THERE** refers to what's often called the Patriarchal Dispensation, the time of Melchizedek and his priestly reign prior to Moses and the laws about Aaron and his priestly reign. In other words, "Here (in the Mosaical era) mortal men (Levites) receive tithes, but there (in the Patriarchal era) he (Melchizedek) received them, of whom it is witnessed that he (Melchizedek) lives."

Paul's contrast was between dying men and an undying man who was therefore the greater of the two parties; this is important because the supplied present tense word **RECEIVES** should be the past tense "received," for it was obviously not his intention to teach that Melchizedek was still physically alive on Earth receiving tithes in Paul's time.

Thus <u>dying</u> priests were receiving tithes <u>under</u> Abraham, but an <u>undying</u> priest received tithes <u>from</u> Abraham. Since being of inferior Abraham rendered the Levites inferior, then their priesthood was inferior to Melchizedek's priesthood. So there should be no question why God ordained that His Son's priestly office be "ACCORDING TO THE ORDER OF MELCHIZEDEK" (6:20) instead of according to the order of Aaron.

Six times in the context of Paul's discussion about Melchizedek (5:6, 10, 6:20, 7:11, 17, & 21), he echoed God's words given through His servant David 500 years later concerning the Messiah's priesthood in Psalm 110:4: "'YOU ARE A PRIEST FOREVER ACCORDING TO THE ORDER OF MELCHIZEDEK.'" This is the inspired **WITNESS** to which Paul had reference. Concerning Jesus in 7:24-25 he wrote: "BECAUSE HE CONTINUES FOREVER, [HE] HAS AN UNCHANGEABLE PRIESTHOOD. THEREFORE HE IS ALSO ABLE TO SAVE TO THE UTTERMOST THOSE WHO COME TO GOD THROUGH HIM, SINCE HE EVER LIVES TO MAKE INTERCESSION FOR THEM."

> **VERSE 9:** EVEN LEVI, WHO RECEIVES TITHES, PAID TITHES THROUGH ABRAHAM, SO TO SPEAK.

This was Paul's first time to actually and directly contrast the Levitical/Aaronic priesthood with that of Melchizedek; prior to this, it was merely implied by allusions to Melchizedek's superiority to Abraham.

Another reason the Melchizedekian priesthood is greater than the Levitical priesthood is that not only did the highly esteemed Abraham pay tribute to Melchizedek, but Levi—and thus the Levites—also paid tithes to Melchizedek. And why would Paul say such a thing? Read the next verse:

> **VERSE 10:** FOR HE WAS STILL IN THE LOINS OF HIS FATHER WHEN MELCHIZEDEK MET HIM.

Although Levi wasn't yet born, he was to be a descendant of Abraham—the family representative; see, the Jews believed so strongly in the solidarity of their race that, even if they didn't like it, they no doubt perfectly understood Paul's unanswerable argument. The simple contention was this: Since Melchizedek is greater than Abraham, he's therefore also greater than Levi (the father of their present priesthood) <u>as well as</u> their present covenant that was inaugurated by Levi's great grandsons, Aaron and his brother Moses.

This is the premise of the book of Hebrews—Jesus and His covenant are better than that into which these Jewish Christians were regressing. Besides, to be consistent, the Jews (or Jewish Christians) couldn't claim the blessing of God that was confirmed by His priest (Melchizedek) to Abraham, then turn around and disagree with Paul's logic.

One last important point here is this: since Jesus was born without an earthly father, He, unlike Levi, was <u>not</u> of the loins of Abraham, indicating that Paul's argument about Abraham being inferior to Melchizedek does <u>not</u> apply to Jesus, meaning that Melchizedek is actually inferior to Jesus.

Hebrews 7:11-19

The apostle Paul's primary arguments in 7:1-10 concerned the eternal and therefore superior order of Melchizedek's priesthood over the temporal and therefore inferior order of Aaron's priesthood; and Jesus, not being of the lineage of Aaron but of God (who, like Melchizedek, has no beginning or ending), is therefore of Melchizedek's order.

In 7:11-19 Paul wrote concerning how the ultimate priesthood was/is realized in Christ, a notion which set the stage for his lengthy discussion to follow (in chapters 8-10) about how the Law of Christ (aka "THE LAW OF LIBERTY," Jam. 1:25) is greater than the Law of Moses (brother to the first high priest of the Levitical order—Aaron).

> **VERSE 11:** THEREFORE IF PERFECTION WERE THROUGH THE LEVITICAL PRIESTHOOD (FOR UNDER IT THE PEOPLE RECEIVED THE LAW), WHAT FURTHER NEED WAS THERE THAT ANOTHER PRIEST SHOULD RISE ACCORDING TO THE ORDER OF MELCHIZEDEK AND NOT BE CALLED ACCORDING TO THE ORDER OF AARON?

There are two Greek terms translated "if" in the New Testament: "εαν" which is almost <u>always</u> conditional (i.e. if that then this) and "ει" which is almost <u>never</u> conditional (i.e. since that, then this). The word for **IF** here is from "ει," meaning that <u>since</u> Jesus has become High Priest after the superior order of Melchizedek (6:20-7:10), <u>then</u> it's evident that the Levitical priesthood wasn't adequate to fulfill that which it foreshadowed.

The word for **PERFECTION** refers to the process or the act of completion, in this case the process or act of the completion of God's plan of man's restoration to His fellowship. See, the purpose of the priesthood was to remove the barrier of sin between God and man, so that man could have access to God; but, since the Levitical priesthood could only do that <u>typically</u>, a new priesthood had to be instituted which could do it <u>actually</u>, thereby providing man with salvation, which is why Paul later wrote in verse 25 that Jesus <u>saves</u> in a <u>completed</u> manner! Following that, in 9:9, he wrote of the Aaronic priesthood that "IT WAS SYMBOLIC OF THE PRESENT TIME [viz. *the not yet consummated Old Covenant time*]" and that it couldn't even "MAKE HIM WHO PERFORMED THE SERVICE PERFECT"; then, in 10:1, he said of the Law associated with that priesthood that it, "HAVING A SHADOW OF THE GOOD THINGS ABOUT TO [μελλω] COME, ... CAN NEVER ... MAKE THOSE WHO APPROACH PERFECT" (cf. 7:19 & Gal. 3:21).

The clause **UNDER** [the Levitical priesthood] **THE PEOPLE RECEIVED THE LAW** merely means that the two were inseparable: the Law and the Levitical priesthood were essentially given by God at the same point in time, each one reinforcing the other, meaning that they stand/fall together.

As with the word "if," so there are two Greek terms translated "another" in the New Testament: "αλλος" meaning "another of the same kind" and "ηετερος"—the one Paul chose here for **ANOTHER**—which means "another of a different kind"; so since the Levitical priesthood didn't bring anything to completion, there needed to be more than just another priest—there needed to be an entirely new priest<u>hood</u>, one after the order of Melchizedek instead of Aaron.

The response to the question of verse 11 of course is this: "There was no need." In other words, if the Levitical priesthood could've cleansed man of his sin, if it could've reconciled him with His Creator, if it could've provided for perfection, then there would've been no need for a priest of a different order, much less the death of the Son of God.

But since God <u>did</u> promise another priest after a different order from that of Aaron, and since the replaced priesthood found its authority in the Law of Moses (7:28), then it should be obvious that God never planned for man's salvation to be realized under the Levitical priesthood or its law. (What an argument! To deny this, they would've had to deny the inspiration of their favored King David and his 110th Psalm.)

> **VERSE 12: FOR THE PRIESTHOOD BEING CHANGED, OF NECESSITY THERE IS ALSO A CHANGE OF THE LAW.**

Just as may easily be noted in earlier statements (e.g. vv. 5, 8, & 9), take note of the present tense of this verse: The Jewish world was in the process of **BEING** supplanted by a new one (cf. 2:5)—a new world that would, of necessity, include a new law and a new priesthood.

The word for **CHANGED** means "to put one thing in the place of another," indicating that Paul wasn't merely teaching that the Melchizedekian priesthood was better than the Aaronic priesthood, but that it also superseded it! But, since the Law and Aaron's priesthood stand/fall together, this priesthood-substitution could only be accomplished by a substitution in the law which governed the priesthood; hence the Law of Christ superseded the Law of Moses.

So why did the Law need to change in order to change priesthoods?

> **VERSE 13: BECAUSE HE (JESUS) OF WHOM THESE THINGS ARE SPOKEN BELONGS TO ANOTHER TRIBE, FROM WHICH NO MAN HAS OFFICIATED AT THE ALTAR.**

The phrase **THINGS ... SPOKEN** refers to the words of Psalm 110:4—God's prophecy that there would arise One who would be a priest after the order of Melchizedek instead of after the order of Aaron.

It's interesting that the original word for **BELONGS TO** is the same word translated "SHARED IN THE SAME" in 2:14 where Paul wrote of Jesus taking part in humanity in order to destroy him who had the power of death—the devil. What makes this interesting is, as stated in the remarks for that verse, this word is active, meaning that Jesus "volunteered to become human" (something in which none of us had a choice), implying that Jesus was/is deity. So, in connection with this verse, such means that not only did Jesus choose to become human, but He also (obviously because it was His Father's will) chose to be born of the tribe of Judah instead of the tribe of Levi.

The word for **ANOTHER** here is the same as the one in verse 11 (see those comments); in other words, not only was Jesus not of the lineage of Aaron, He wasn't even a descendant of Levi! The prophets were very clear on this: speaking of the Messiah, Isaiah 11:10 prophesied that He "SHALL BE A ROOT OF JESSE." And who was Jesse's son? Jeremiah quoted God, saying, "'I WILL RAISE TO DAVID A BRANCH OF RIGHTEOUSNESS; A KING SHALL REIGN AND PROSPER AND EXECUTE JUDGMENT AND RIGHTEOUSNESS IN THE EARTH'" (Jer. 23:5).

Thus Jesus was a "BRANCH" of David from the "ROOT" of Jesse, meaning that the New Testament High Priest actually came through the kingly lineage, not the priestly lineage. And what lineage was that?

> **VERSE 14:** FOR IT IS EVIDENT THAT OUR LORD AROSE FROM JUDAH, OF WHICH TRIBE MOSES SPOKE NOTHING CONCERNING PRIESTHOOD.

Jesus was a successor of Levi's brother Judah, whose posterity—including Jesus—had no right in the least to fulfill the duty of a Levite, much less a priest or high priest! (Strongly suggested reading: Gen. 49:8-12, Mat. 2:1-6, & Rev. 5:5.)

Consider the irony: according to Matthew 27:1, the Levites were those who ultimately precipitated Jesus' crucifixion.

> **VERSES 15-16:** AND IT IS YET FAR MORE EVIDENT IF, IN THE LIKENESS OF MELCHIZEDEK, THERE ARISES ANOTHER PRIEST WHO HAS COME, NOT ACCORDING TO THE LAW OF A FLESHLY COMMANDMENT, BUT ACCORDING TO THE POWER OF AN ENDLESS LIFE.

What exactly is **FAR MORE EVIDENT**? Just backtrack momentarily. What's the point Paul was making? Verses 11-12 affirm that the Levitical priesthood and the Law had to be (and was being) superseded by a new priesthood and new law. To prove this, he presented two arguments: {1} He made a new argument in verse 14, namely that, according to the prophets as well as the common knowledge of these Hebrews, the Messiah, Jesus—the One they had accepted as God's new High Priest—was from the lineage of Judah not Levi; then {2} in verses 15-16 he recalled a previously established truth to further support his point, namely that Jesus, being God, is a priest who cannot, and therefore will not, die—a class of person/priest who the Law of Moses never took into consideration.

Incidentally, the apostle may have had the idea of Christ's resurrection in mind when he chose the term **ARISES**; in other words, since Jesus spoke of the power to raise Himself (John 10:17), and since He arose (as witnessed, 1 Cor. 15:3-7), then He proved His inherent virtue of indestructibility (i.e. His deity) which is what's meant by **THE POWER OF AN ENDLESS LIFE**.

Since the phrase "FLESHLY COMMANDMENT" is in contrast to the phrase "ENDLESS LIFE," and since the next two verses say what they say about the ending of the old law, the clause **NOT ACCORDING TO THE LAW OF A FLESHLY COMMANDMENT** means that High Priest Jesus was appointed to the office based not on His familial line, but based on His intrinsic superiority—His deity.

(Side-note: Romans 1:3-4 corresponds to this context, for in them Paul wrote of Jesus being born of David [giving Him the authority to be a king, Heb. 7:14] and of His being resurrected [giving Him the right to be, like Melchizedek, a priest forever, Heb. 7:1-3].)

> **VERSE 17: FOR... HE** (GOD) **TESTIFIES: "YOU** (JESUS) **ARE A PRIEST FOREVER ACCORDING TO THE ORDER OF MELCHIZEDEK."**

It's interesting that Paul quoted this Psalm (110:4) four times (5:6 & 10 and 7:17 & 21) and alluded to it at least three other times (6:20 and 7:11 & 15). It's interesting because many today claim that one cannot base a doctrine upon a single verse, but that's exactly what Paul did: Psalm 110:4 is the key verse, the hub around which the book of Hebrews revolves.

> **VERSE 18-19A:** FOR ON THE ONE HAND THERE IS AN ANNULLING OF THE FORMER COMMANDMENT BECAUSE OF ITS WEAKNESS AND UNPROFITABLENESS, FOR THE LAW MADE NOTHING PERFECT.

Verse 18 takes up the idea of verse 16 by speaking of the negative result of the power of an indestructible life taking over the fleshly ordinance. (The positive is noted below at 19b.)

The word for **ANNULLING** means "to make void or to do away with"; it's the same word as found in 9:26 where Paul said that Jesus "APPEARED TO PUT AWAY SIN BY THE SACRIFICE OF HIMSELF," indicating that the Law was to be and has been removed just as thoroughly as Jesus removes sin.

The phrase **THE FORMER COMMANDMENT** refers primarily to the law concerning priests being from Aaron's lineage, but the doing away with just that one rule voids the entire Law (cf. v. 11 & Gal. 5:3 inverted); this is true because of what Paul went on to say: the Law was weak and therefore unprofitable because it "MADE NOTHING PERFECT," meaning that it (as a mere shadow, 10:1) brought nothing to completion/conclusion; in other words, since it couldn't produce/offer a sacrifice that would pay for sin (10:4), it couldn't reconcile any one to his God. Paul commented on this idea in Romans 8:3 when he wrote: "WHAT THE LAW COULD NOT DO IN THAT IT WAS WEAK THROUGH THE FLESH, GOD DID BY SENDING HIS OWN SON."

Now as a disclaimer, Paul taught in Galatians 3 that, even though the Law was unprofitable for the purpose of pardoning sinners, it fulfilled its primary purpose which led up to the pardoning of sinners. In fact, the word for **FORMER** here carries with it the idea of "introducing": the Law, as Paul said in Galatians, brought man to Christ, introducing man to the new, eternal High Priest.

Thus it's important to remember that Paul said the Law was "WEAK," not completely powerless—it did what it was meant to do (cf. Rom. 7:12 & 14 where Paul said that the Law was holy/just/good/spiritual in nature).

> **VERSE 19B: ON THE OTHER HAND, THERE IS THE BRINGING IN OF A BETTER HOPE, THROUGH WHICH WE DRAW NEAR TO GOD.**

This is the positive result of the power of an indestructible life taking over the fleshly ordinance.

The phrase **BRINGING IN** actually carries with it the idea of "bringing in upon," which alludes back to the concept of replacement spoken of earlier, namely the Grace of the Gospel replacing the Works of the Law.

This is a **BETTER HOPE** because Christ's priesthood and gospel draw man near to God; 8:6 teaches that Jesus has received a ministry that's better than that of the Levites, by creating a better covenant based on better promises between God and man. The hope under the old law was for reconciliation to God later in the coming Messiah, but now, under the new law (of liberty), that restoration to God's fellowship is fulfilled in Christ (John 14:6).

Lastly, since God through His Son Jesus has accomplished everything possible on His part to open the door to man for forgiveness/reconciliation/salvation, the ball is in our court to draw near to Him, reminiscent of James 4:8: "DRAW NEAR TO GOD, AND HE WILL DRAW NEAR TO YOU."

128

Hebrews 7:20-28

In 7:1-10, based on the premise that Jesus is our High Priest after the order of Melchizedek (6:20), Paul wrote about the greatness of Melchizedek's priesthood, even over Aaron's priesthood that God Himself set up; yes, God established both priesthoods, but one was greater than the other. In 7:11-19 Paul wrote about how the priesthood of Christ Jesus superseded the priesthood of Levi. And now in verses 20-28 the reader finds Paul's explanation for this substitution.

In a nutshell, this passage of Scripture demonstrates that the priesthood of which Jesus is our High Priest is much superior to the priesthood of which Aaron was a priest because of what Jesus accomplished through it—redemption of man, that which the Levites could never do.

The two basic arguments are as follows: {1} unlike the Levites, Jesus was made High Priest by an oath from God, and {2} unlike the Levites, neither Jesus nor His priesthood will ever need to be replaced—they're timeless.

> **VERSES 20-21: INASMUCH AS HE WAS NOT MADE PRIEST WITHOUT AN OATH (FOR THEY HAVE BECOME PRIESTS WITHOUT AN OATH, BUT HE WITH AN OATH BY HIM WHO SAID TO HIM, "THE LORD HAS SWORN AND WILL NOT RELENT (OR 'RENEGE' ON IT): 'YOU ARE A PRIEST FOREVER ACCORDING TO THE ORDER OF MELCHIZEDEK'")...**

God took oaths in order to indicate the unchangeableness of things that He had set in order (Heb. 6:17, cf. Gen. 22:16-18, Deu. 1:34-36, 4:21-22, & Psa. 89:3-4) which teaches two things: {1} Since the Levites became priests apart from any oath by God at all, then God never meant for that priesthood to be everlasting; without an oath from God, it could be (and was) changed (cf. 7:12, the verse Paul built on thereafter); on the other hand, {2} since (as Paul wrote here as well as in 6:18-20) God <u>did</u> swear an oath concerning Christ's priesthood, then it, unlike the Levitical priesthood, is eternal/unchangeable.

Why did God swear concerning Jesus but not concerning Levi or his posterity? Because they weren't chosen based on their morality/spirituality, but merely on their lineage; Jesus and His priesthood, however, were established by an oath of God based on His character/nature (cf. 5:1-10).

> **VERSE 22:** ...**BY SO MUCH MORE** (OR "BY WHICH") **JESUS HAS BECOME** (OR "IS") **A SURETY OF A BETTER COVENANT.**

The word for **SURETY** (εγγυος) refers to "a guarantor"—one who makes <u>sure</u> the covenant is carried out on the part of both parties involved. In fact, here's an interesting fact about this term: all five Greek terms in *Strong's Exhaustive Concordance* that begin with "εγγ" are related to the <u>hand</u> —something close by. Notice the following:

Εγγιζω: to make near, to be at hand
Εγγραπηω: to engrave, inscribe, write with the hand
Εγγυος: (fr. limb e.g. *the hand*): pledged (e.g. by handshake)
Εγγυς: at hand, near, nigh, ready
Εγγυτερον: (comparative adj.) nearer, closer at hand

What's the point? It's obvious that the etymology of this term carries with it the idea that whatever was/is being guaranteed was/is something that would soon occur, at least within the lifetime of the recipient, implying of course that it was future, that it hadn't yet arrived. To bring it all together, it could read like this: "Because Jesus was made High Priest by an oath of God, He's the chosen Guarantor of a soon-to-arrive better covenant."

The word for **COVENANT** actually refers to an "arrangement" made by a superior for the benefit of an inferior; in other words, because of Jesus, God's people today are under a much better <u>arrangement</u> than the Jews were under Moses.

Speaking about Christ and His priesthood being established as endless and consistent by an oath from God, Paul went on in the next two verses to expand upon this thought.

> **VERSE 23: AND THERE WERE** (LIT. "ARE") **MANY PRIESTS, BECAUSE THEY WERE** (LIT. "ARE") **PREVENTED BY DEATH FROM CONTINUING.**

(Two initial *important* side-notes: {1} this statement is actually in the present tense in the original, indicating that the Levitical priesthood was still being practiced by the Jews at the time of Paul's writing; and {2} since it's the high priesthood of Jesus that's under consideration, Paul, by his use of the word PRIESTS here, was evidently alluding specifically to the high priests. So his point was this: whereas death kept any Aaronic high priest from remaining a priest forever, Jesus, who received His priesthood after His resurrection, is no longer subject to death.)

According to Robert Milligan in his 19th Century *Commentary on the Epistle to the Hebrews* (republished by the Gospel Advocate Co., 1984), Phannias Ben-Samuel was the 81st and last high priest (AD 67–70). Since "81" is the sacred number "3" squared then squared again, this suggests that the fullness of God's intention for the old priesthood system was completed at Jerusalem's destruction (AD 70).

Occasionally people hear about an illegal handling of a will, but because Jesus not only wrote and died for His will, but also rose from the dead to probate it Himself, He's without doubt the perfect High Priest!

> **VERSE 24: BUT HE, BECAUSE HE CONTINUES FOREVER, HAS AN UNCHANGEABLE PRIESTHOOD.**

In verse 8 Paul spoke of the Levitical priesthood as mortal, being yoked to ancestry/posterity; but in verse 16 he spoke of the Melchizedekian priesthood (Christ's priesthood) as immortal, having no yoke to ancestry/posterity.

The word for **UNCHANGEABLE** was used at the end of a legal contract and meant that it was "valid" and (unlike the contract with the Israelites through Moses) "unalterable," something that should've provided them a confidence unlike they had ever experienced. This word also carries with it the idea of "something that cannot be stepped across or into," meaning that it can neither be destroyed nor transferred. As Paul later said, "CHRIST IS THE SAME YESTERDAY, TODAY, AND FOREVER" (13:8), meaning that, while under the Levitical priesthood one might have a pleasant/moral priest one day and an unpleasant/immoral priest the next, Jesus was/is/always will be the same kind of priest.

> **VERSE 25:** THEREFORE HE IS ALSO ABLE TO SAVE TO THE UTTERMOST THOSE WHO COME TO GOD THROUGH HIM, SINCE HE EVER LIVES TO MAKE INTERCESSION FOR THEM.

The word for **UTTERMOST** means "completely or perfectly"; in other words, Jesus as our eternal High Priest doesn't just roll sins forward for a year as the Old Testament high priests did (cf. 10:1-3), He forgives them forever, remembering man's sins against him no more (10:17).

The drawing near to God in verse 19 is defined here by Paul as "coming to God through Christ"; as Jesus Himself said, "'NO ONE COMES TO THE FATHER EXCEPT THROUGH ME'" (John 14:6).

The word for **INTERCESSION** actually refers to everything Jesus has done and is doing even now as regards our salvation. (Today the word is pretty much limited to prayer, but this wasn't the case with the Greek word 2,000 years ago.)

> **VERSE 26:** FOR SUCH A HIGH PRIEST WAS FITTING FOR US, WHO IS HOLY, HARMLESS, UNDEFILED, SEPARATE FROM SINNERS, AND HAS BECOME HIGHER THAN THE HEAVENS.

Verses 26-28 provide a sketch of The Ideal Priest, a priest who isn't just better than Aaronic priests, but even better than Melchizedek (whom Paul left behind at this point, focusing on the perfection of Jesus/His priesthood/His covenant.)

Jesus, who "CONTINUES FOREVER" and "HAS AN UNCHANGEABLE PRIESTHOOD," is the fitting high priest for man because only He can therefore **SAVE TO THE UTTERMOST**. Besides, He's "HOLY, HARMLESS, [AND] UNDEFILED."

The Old Testament background for the original term for **HOLY** describes a person whose relationship to God was based on covenant faithfulness. It described one who genuinely fulfilled not only the external, but also the heart-expectations of the covenant; such a man was all who God wanted him to be. Jesus, having been perfectly loyal in obedience and having lived a life of perfect integrity, was all God wanted Him to be ... for man.

While the term for "HOLY" brings to mind Christ's relationship to God, the term for **HARMLESS** brings to mind the idea of Christ's relationship to His fellowman; for instance, even when He cleansed the temple and was wrongly executed, He harmed no one (cf. 1 Pet. 2:23).

While the active term for "HARMLESS" brings to mind Christ's relationship to His fellowman, the passive word for **UNDEFILED** brings to mind His relationship to evil; in other words, Jesus wasn't contaminated by His association with sinners.

Thus the phrase "HOLY, HARMLESS, [AND] UNDEFILED" describes Jesus spiritually/morally/religiously.

Further, Jesus is **SEPARATE** or distinct **FROM SINNERS**, not only because He's "WITHOUT SIN" (4:15)—"HOLY, HARMLESS, [AND] UNDEFILED," but also because He **HAS BECOME HIGHER THAN THE HEAVENS**, meaning that, unlike the Aaronic high priests, Jesus sits at the right hand of the very throne of God (cf. 8:1).

In 4:14 Paul said that Jesus had "PASSED THROUGH THE HEAVENS"; and in Ephesians 4:10 he wrote that Jesus is "FAR ABOVE ALL HEAVENS THAT HE MIGHT FILL ALL THINGS." (Eph. 4:10 was written in the subjunctive [future] tense because, by the time of Paul's letter to Ephesus, Jesus had yet to finish fulfilling all things.)

Even though Jesus came in the likeness of sinful flesh (Rom. 8:3), received and ate with sinners (Luke 15:1-2), and was a friend to sinners (Mat. 11:19), He remained separate/dissimilar from them in that He didn't participate in their evil deeds.

> **VERSE 27: JESUS DOES NOT NEED DAILY, AS THOSE HIGH PRIESTS, TO OFFER UP SACRIFICES, FIRST FOR HIS OWN SINS AND THEN FOR THE PEOPLE'S, FOR THIS HE DID ONCE FOR ALL WHEN HE OFFERED UP HIMSELF.**

The word for **DAILY** is from two terms which could literally be translated "day by day"; and since the word "day" was often used to denote any part of time (meaning that the phrase could mean "from time to time"), then it should be understood in relation to Paul's other statements about the high priestly sacrifices. Later in Hebrews Paul accurately spoke of how high priests offered sacrifices "ONCE A YEAR" (9:7) or "YEAR BY YEAR" (10:1); in fact, in Exodus 13:10 scholars are forced to see that "day by day" is a Jewish idiom (cf. Mat. 12:40) which should actually be translated as "YEAR BY YEAR." So one could read this to say that Jesus doesn't need—from time to time (whether daily/monthly/annually)—to offer up sacrifices.

This statement teaches at least three things: {1} Unlike the Aaronic priests (5:3), Jesus didn't/doesn't need to offer a sacrifice for Himself, but only for the people. {2} Unlike the Aaronic priests, Jesus doesn't offer a sacrifice annually, but did so <u>once</u> for <u>all</u> people for <u>all</u> time (9:28); in other words, He doesn't need to be resacrificed every week. (Speaking of Christ's sacrifice in 9:25-28, Paul wrote, "NOT THAT HE SHOULD OFFER HIMSELF OFTEN, AS THE HIGH PRIEST ENTERS THE MOST HOLY PLACE EVERY YEAR WITH BLOOD OF ANOTHER—HE THEN WOULD HAVE HAD TO SUFFER OFTEN SINCE THE FOUNDATION OF THE WORLD; BUT NOW, ONCE AT THE END OF THE AGES, HE HAS APPEARED TO PUT AWAY SIN BY THE SACRIFICE OF HIMSELF.... CHRIST WAS OFFERED ONCE TO BEAR THE SINS OF MANY.") And {3} unlike with the Aaronic priests, Jesus offered, not a calf or a goat, but <u>Himself</u> for the people (9:14).

The following verse sums up the last few verses and provides a transition for 8:1–10:18.

> **VERSE 28:** FOR THE LAW APPOINTS AS HIGH PRIESTS MEN WHO HAVE WEAKNESSES, BUT THE WORD OF THE OATH, WHICH CAME AFTER THE LAW, APPOINTS THE SON WHO HAS BEEN PERFECTED FOREVER.

Being human, Levitical/Aaronic high priests (and therefore their priesthood) were just weak in general; so while the Law constituted morally/spiritually/physically weak men (i.e. men subject to death) as high priests, God's declaration/oath (which followed the Law) constituted His perfected Son as High Priest.

(Note: This verse, again, connects Christ's priesthood with His sonship to God, that is, <u>to</u> <u>His</u> <u>deity</u>. So, unlike the Old Testament high priests, Jesus is the High Priest who suits man's needs perfectly.)

Preliminary Tabernacle Considerations: Hebrews 8–10

As will be discussed in 8:2, the tabernacle or temple of the Old Testament was a copy/shadow of the New Testament kingdom of God; however, as signified when the veil of the two-roomed tabernacle or temple was ripped down at the death of Christ (Mat. 27:51), the presence of God now fills the entirety of the REAL tabernacle, not just the one small room formerly known as the holy of holies or the most holy place.

God's Presence Before the Cross

Picture the now single-roomed, God-filled tabernacle as a spiritual building which embraces God's people in Heaven as well as His people on Earth—the entirety of His kingdom (**cf. Eph. 1:10**), bringing to mind the fulfillment of Christ's model prayer about the coming kingdom and things being done on Earth as in Heaven (cf. Mat. 6:10).

God's Presence After the Cross

As Christians—priests with Jesus as our High Priest (1 Pet. 2:9) —we're in God's presence now (i.e. in a face-to-face relationship with Him now [cf. 1 Cor. 13:12]), meaning that, due to our Redeemer's accomplishments, our sin has been completely removed, reconciling us to our Creator. (To reconcile means to make friends again with.) Hence the paradise of Eden—our relationship with God—has been restored through/in the Last Adam (aka Jesus, 1 Cor. 15:47).

In essence, this all means that Heaven has been expanded in order to encompass the saved of Earth—those who have chosen to enter into this tabernacle of salvation to become living sacrifices and priests of God.

Hear God's prophecy: "'I WILL MAKE A COVENANT OF PEACE WITH THEM [SPIRITUAL ISRAEL], AND IT SHALL BE AN EVERLASTING COVENANT WITH THEM; I WILL ESTABLISH THEM AND MULTIPLY THEM, AND I WILL SET MY SANCTUARY IN THEIR MIDST FOREVERMORE. MY TABERNACLE ALSO SHALL BE WITH THEM; INDEED I WILL BE THEIR GOD, AND THEY SHALL BE MY PEOPLE. THE NATIONS ALSO WILL KNOW THAT I, THE LORD, SANCTIFY [THEM] WHEN MY SANCTUARY IS IN THEIR MIDST FOREVERMORE'" (Eze. 37:26-28).

Compare those words with John's words: after alluding to the new heaven and earth (meaning the new administration, Isa. 65:17; 66:22; 2 Pet. 3:13; etc.) and the New Jerusalem (i.e. the church in its fulfilled kingdom state, Heb. 12:22-23) coming down out of Heaven to the Earth (not going up into Heaven, Rev. 21:2), John recorded a voice from Heaven, saying, "'BEHOLD, THE TABERNACLE OF GOD IS WITH MEN, AND HE WILL DWELL WITH THEM, AND THEY SHALL BE HIS PEOPLE. GOD HIMSELF WILL BE WITH THEM AND BE THEIR GOD.... HE WHO OVERCOMES SHALL INHERIT ALL THINGS, AND I WILL BE HIS GOD AND HE SHALL BE MY SON'" (Rev. 21:3 & 7).

Now since Ezekiel 37's New Covenant of peace obviously refers to the arrival of God's kingdom and covenant in the first century, who would take it upon himself to deny that Revelation 21 is about the fulfillment of Ezekiel 37? Not I! Why? Because the logical conclusion is that Revelation, which incidentally speaks profusely about the tabernacle, is speaking of the arrival of the new/eternal kingdom after Jerusalem's demise (found in chapters 18-19).

Here's the point as regards the Hebrew brethren: Yes, they were being persecuted, but they were within about 7 years of seeing the fulfillment of everything they had been looking for as a people for about 1,500 years! This is why Paul could say to them, "HAVE BOLDNESS TO ENTER THE HOLIEST BY THE BLOOD OF JESUS.... AND HAVING A HIGH PRIEST OVER THE HOUSE OF GOD, LET US DRAW NEAR WITH A TRUE HEART IN FULL ASSURANCE OF FAITH.... LET US HOLD FAST THE CONFESSION OF OUR HOPE WITHOUT WAVERING, FOR HE WHO PROMISED IS FAITHFUL. AND LET US CONSIDER ONE ANOTHER IN ORDER TO STIR UP LOVE AND GOOD WORKS, NOT FORSAKING THE ASSEMBLING OF OURSELVES TOGETHER AS IS THE MANNER OF SOME, BUT EXHORTING ONE ANOTHER, AND SO MUCH THE MORE AS YOU SEE THE DAY APPROACHING.... DO NOT CAST AWAY YOUR CONFIDENCE WHICH HAS GREAT REWARD, FOR YOU HAVE NEED OF ENDURANCE, SO THAT AFTER YOU HAVE DONE THE WILL OF GOD, YOU MAY RECEIVE THE PROMISE: 'FOR YET A LITTLE WHILE, AND HE WHO IS COMING WILL COME AND WILL NOT TARRY'" (Heb. 10:19-25 & 35-37).

So although one could say this about the entire letter, in chapters 8–10 of Hebrews, Paul should be perceived as trying his very best to encourage these brethren to stand firm until they could enjoy the fullness of the new/magnificent/spiritual tabernacle of God with men, resulting of course in their eternal life with God when they depart this earthly life.

Hebrews 8:1-5

According to the outline of the book of Hebrews found in the introduction of this commentary, so far Paul has discussed *The Superiority of Christ's Person* to that of prophets, angels, Moses, and Aaron in chapters 1–4 as well as *The Superiority of Christ's Priesthood* to that of Levi and Aaron, and (although of his priestly order) even that of Melchizedek in chapters 5–7.

Beginning in 8:1, Paul set out to discuss *The Superiority of Christ's Pact* or covenant to that of Moses; his first point is that *Christ's Pact Is Superior in Its Promises.*

> **VERSE 1: NOW THIS IS THE MAIN POINT OF THE THINGS WE ARE SAYING: WE HAVE SUCH A HIGH PRIEST, WHO IS SEATED AT THE RIGHT HAND OF THE THRONE OF THE MAJESTY IN THE HEAVENS,...**

By the phrase **SUCH A HIGH PRIEST** Paul meant "this kind of priest." What kind? A superior kind. After spending a lot of time in this letter listing numerous specific characteristics that make Jesus a superior High Priest, Paul here listed two other more generic attributes which bring them all together: put simply, Jesus is seated, and He's in Heaven.

The idea of His being **SEATED** is much more significant than most people in our culture would recognize. Why? Because there was no sitting in the Old Testament tabernacle: the furniture included no chairs, signifying that the work of those priests was never done (10:11-13). Each repeated sacrifice was only a reminder that none of the sacrifices ever provided complete forgiveness as Jesus has done "ONCE FOR ALL" (7:27).

The idea of Jesus being **IN HEAVEN** is also significant. This is because He was enthroned in and ministered from the real place that was only typified by the holy of holies. Besides,

139

no Levite priest ever sat on a throne; only a priest after the order of Melchizedek could be enthroned, for he was both priest _and_ king (reminiscent of the Joshua [Hebrew for Jesus] who became a living parable of the coming Messiah, Zec. 6:9-15).

As mentioned in the last section study, in all of this Paul was still building on 7:12 where he affirmed that, since the priesthood was changing, it was _necessary_ that the law change, for Jesus could no more probate an inferior will than the most gifted lawyer could probate an inadequate will.

> **VERSE 2: ...a Minister of the sanctuary and of the true tabernacle which the Lord erected and not man.**

The original word for **MINISTER** simply refers to a servant: Jesus serves or ministers to/for both God and man, much like the ideas found in the terms "intercessor" and "mediator."

The word for **SANCTUARY** (related to the term "saint") refers to a holy place. (Corresponding with "HEAVENS" in v. 1, the original word here is actually plural, thus "holy places.")

The word for **TABERNACLE** refers to a "tent," which is exactly what the tabernacle was—a tent that could be dismantled and reassembled whenever necessary; this lasted until King Solomon built the temple in its permanent place.

The word for **TRUE** refers to that which is "genuine," meaning Paul was contrasting that which is real with that which was merely a copy or shadow of it. If he hasn't already realized this, it's very important that the student of Hebrews (as well as the rest of the Bible) understand that what's _spiritual_ in nature is actually what's _real_, while that which was physical was _not_ real: the tabernacle was only a shadow pointing to the genuine article—the eternal kingdom of God. Since the real thing—the kingdom—is spiritual with its headquarters in Heaven, that explains how Jesus can serve those on Earth while at the same time be enthroned in Heaven. As John 1:17 teaches, whereas the shadows of the Law came through Moses, the reality came through Jesus (cf. Murdock, Moffatt, and the JMNT versions).

Thus, since Jesus serves in a superior sanctuary (one erected solely by deity), He's superior to Aaron; and since He's superior to Aaron, then the new law He inaugurated is superior to the law under which Aaron served—the point of the entire epistle to these Hebrew Christians.

> **VERSES 3-4A:** FOR EVERY HIGH PRIEST IS APPOINTED TO OFFER BOTH GIFTS AND SACRIFICES. THEREFORE IT IS NECESSARY THAT THIS ONE ALSO HAVE SOMETHING TO OFFER. FOR IF HE WERE ON EARTH, HE WOULD NOT BE A PRIEST.

Due to the contrast in verses 3 & 4, it's obvious Paul wasn't referring merely to the sacrifice Jesus had to make as a High Priest, but also to the place in which He offered the sacrifice—Heaven. In 9:24 Paul wrote that "CHRIST HAS NOT ENTERED THE HOLY PLACES MADE WITH HANDS WHICH ARE COPIES OF THE TRUE, BUT INTO HEAVEN ITSELF, NOW [in Paul's time] TO APPEAR IN THE PRESENCE OF GOD FOR US." And, as verse 25 goes on to indicate, this appearance in God's presence—the real sanctuary—is a reference to offering Himself to God on the heavenly mercy seat as our sacrifice.

Note another contrast here: while the phrase **GIFTS AND SACRIFICES** is plural, the word **SOMETHING** is singular, meaning that the once-for-all offering of Jesus satisfies forever. (Besides, the first word for **OFFER** is present tense [referring to that which is done continually], while the second word for **OFFER** is aorist tense [referring to that which was done once for all time].)

> **VERSE 4:** FOR IF HE WERE ON EARTH, HE WOULD NOT BE A PRIEST, SINCE THERE ARE PRIESTS WHO OFFER THE GIFTS ACCORDING TO THE LAW...

Besides the fact that offering a once-for-all-time sacrifice to God in His very presence in Heaven is obviously ideal, Jesus (especially prior to the demise of the Aaronic priesthood in AD 70) couldn't have been a priest on Earth because He wasn't of the lawful tribe; in other words, if He had tried to make an offering to God as a priest on Earth, He would've violated the Law, rendering Him worthy of death (cf. Num. 3:10).

God through David predicted that Jesus would be a priest (Psa. 110:4), and since Jesus was born into the tribe of Judah (the kingly tribe) instead of Aaron (the priestly tribe), then His priestly work, under the Law of Moses, couldn't be carried out on Earth. It had to be performed in Heaven!

> (Side-note: The word **OFFER** is present tense here as well, indicating that the temple was still standing and that this book was definitely penned before AD 70 [cf. 9:8].)

> **VERSE 5:** ...WHO SERVE THE COPY AND SHADOW OF THE HEAVENLY THINGS, AS MOSES WAS DIVINELY INSTRUCTED WHEN HE WAS ABOUT TO MAKE THE TABERNACLE. FOR HE SAID, "SEE THAT YOU MAKE ALL THINGS ACCORDING TO THE PATTERN SHOWN YOU ON THE MOUNTAIN."

For there to be a copy/shadow, there must be something real of which it's a copy/shadow; the tabernacle and its contents, as well as the priests and their work, were all modeled after—and therefore a copy of—something real. (Of interest is that the original term for **PATTERN** is the term from which we get our word "type.") So Paul was saying that Moses knew from the very beginning that the tabernacle was merely a copy or shadow of something more important and real, and these brethren were in the process of inheriting it!

Since Christ is ministering in the original tabernacle and not the copy, He's ministering in a better place. Hence Paul's question to them was this: "Why fellowship with priests who serve in a copied sanctuary when you can fellowship with Christ in the real thing?" To identify with those of the copy (when the real thing that it foreshadowed was within their grasp) would be like living on the blueprint instead of in the building itself!

Paul provided two evidences for the superiority of the New Covenant: {1} it's administered by a superior priest—Jesus, and {2} it's administered in/from a superior place—Heaven itself; the remainder of this chapter is devoted to how it's founded upon better promises.

Hebrews 8:6-13

As mentioned in the introduction to the comments on 8:1-5, in verse 1 Paul began discussing *The Superiority of Christ's Covenant*, a subject actually continued through 10:18.

In verses 1-5 Paul was setting the stage by talking about Christ's superior ministry through the New Covenant; now, in verses 6-13, the student will find Paul building upon that by showing how Christ's covenant is superior to that of Moses because it's founded upon better promises.

> **VERSE 6:** BUT NOW HE (JESUS) HAS OBTAINED A MORE EXCELLENT MINISTRY, INASMUCH AS HE IS ALSO MEDIATOR OF A BETTER COVENANT, WHICH WAS ESTABLISHED UPON BETTER PROMISES.

It could be said that this is the pivotal verse of this entire letter, because it was written to prove that the New Testament in Jesus' blood is superior to and takes the place of the first testament in animal's blood; Paul proved this to be true with pure logic and the Old Testament Scriptures.

The word **NOW** is a contrast term in relation to how Jesus couldn't have been a priest on Earth (v. 4); in other words, since He's "NOW" in Heaven, He can be and is our once-for-all-time High Priest.

The **MORE EXCELLENT MINISTRY** refers to Jesus' priestly ministry in Heaven as opposed to any priestly ministry of/by men on Earth. And, by virtue of this "MORE EXCELLENT MINISTRY," He's the **MEDIATOR OF A BETTER COVENANT**. A mediator is someone who operates as an intercessor between two parties; before Jesus, Moses and Aaron (and his priesthood, of course) were the go-betweens or mediators, but now there's only One Mediator—the Christ (1 Tim. 2:5).

We often hear in business how by-passing the middle man is a good thing, but this is neither true nor possible when it comes to Christianity and our salvation (John 14:6). As Job indicated in his time, it's necessary that man have just such a person: "'GOD IS NOT A MAN AS I AM THAT I MAY ANSWER HIM AND THAT WE SHOULD GO TO COURT TOGETHER. NOR IS THERE ANY MEDIATOR BETWEEN US WHO MAY LAY HIS HAND ON US BOTH'" (9:33).

A covenant is an agreement between two or more parties, the essence/purpose of which is to establish or re-establish a relationship between them; and this New Covenant is better than the Old Covenant because it was **ESTABLISHED UPON BETTER PROMISES**. The Law had numerous promises, all of which were either of a physical nature or pointed to something in the future that would be fulfilled in the next administration. Some of the "BETTER PROMISES" of the New Covenant are mentioned in the next few verses; in fact, the first promise alluded to is the implied promise of God's grace that would attend this covenant (vv. 7-9).

> **VERSE 7:** FOR IF THAT FIRST COVENANT HAD BEEN FAULTLESS, THEN NO PLACE WOULD HAVE BEEN SOUGHT FOR A SECOND.

As has already been stated various times in this commentary (cf. 7:18-19, etc.), the fault of the first covenant was found in that it couldn't bring about man's reconciliation to his Creator; it was fault*less*, however, for the purpose of which it was given—to point man to Christ and His New Covenant (cf. Gal. 3:19 & 24).

Due to prophecies such as the one in verse 8, the word **SOUGHT** here refers to how God was looking forward to the time when the New Covenant would be realized. Thus Paul was essentially saying the same thing here as in 7:11-12: "IF PERFECTION WERE THROUGH THE LEVITICAL PRIESTHOOD (FOR UNDER IT THE PEOPLE RECEIVED THE LAW), WHAT FURTHER NEED WAS THERE THAT ANOTHER PRIEST SHOULD RISE ACCORDING TO THE ORDER OF MELCHIZEDEK.... FOR THE PRIESTHOOD BEING CHANGED, OF NECESSITY THERE IS ALSO A CHANGE OF THE LAW." In fact, in Galatians 3:21 Paul said, "IF THERE HAD BEEN A LAW GIVEN WHICH COULD HAVE GIVEN LIFE, TRULY RIGHTEOUSNESS WOULD HAVE BEEN BY THE LAW." (Cf. Rom. 3:20, Gal. 2:16, & 3:11.)

> **VERSE 8:** BECAUSE FINDING FAULT WITH THEM, HE SAYS [In Jer. 31:31ff], "BEHOLD, THE DAYS ARE COMING, SAYS THE LORD, WHEN I WILL MAKE A NEW COVENANT WITH THE HOUSE OF ISRAEL AND WITH THE HOUSE OF JUDAH...

Paul again put his audience in a corner, because they either had to reject God's word through Jeremiah who prophesied of a new covenant, or they had to reject the New Covenant which they had already professed; either way, they had to admit that the Law was no more meant to continue forever than was the priesthood that Paul had already discussed based upon Psalm 110:4.

How to interpret the pronoun **THEM** here isn't easy, nor do I believe it's essential to know for certain how to interpret it, for either way it's interpreted does no injustice to this passage. The word "THEM" could refer to the numerous laws of the first testament, or it could refer to the people—all of God's people who were descendants of Jacob, that is. This verse could read, "Because He found fault with it, God said to them"—the people of the houses of Judah and Israel. Or, as most seem to believe and as is implied in the NKJV, it could mean "Because God found fault with the people," He promised a new covenant. If this is the correct interpretation, then not only was the Law faulty in that it couldn't provide total forgiveness, but the people were also faulty due to their defective character (cf. Gal. 3:10).

Paul chose a specific Greek word for the word **MAKE** here which doesn't merely refer to creating something, but also to finalizing that something, emphasizing the perfection of the New Testament.

> **VERSE 9:** "...NOT ACCORDING TO THE COVENANT THAT I MADE WITH THEIR FATHERS IN THE DAY WHEN I TOOK THEM BY THE HAND TO LEAD THEM OUT OF THE LAND OF EGYPT; BECAUSE THEY DID NOT CONTINUE IN MY COVENANT, AND I DISREGARDED THEM, SAYS THE LORD....

By saying **NOT ACCORDING TO THE OLD COVENANT**, the next few verses explain, in part, how the New Covenant is unlike the old one.

The word **DAY** here is used again in a generic sense, meaning that it isn't referring to a specific 24-hour period, but to a general period of time—a 40-year period in fact—from the time Moses first went to Pharaoh to free the Israelites until they entered Canaan.

The word for **CONTINUE** means "to be true to"; in other words, though the Israelites claimed that they would be loyal or true to God's covenant by Moses, they weren't.

The word for **DISREGARD** means "to not watch out for," meaning that, since the Israelites weren't loyal to God, He allowed them to endure various tragedies in life such as their many captivities which otherwise wouldn't have occurred. Or this word could have a broader reference to God's rejection of physical Israel for spiritual Israel. Either way, the meaning is that God gave them up for their disregard of Him and His laws (cf. Romans 1:24, 26, & 28).

Thus one of the "**BETTER PROMISES**" (v. 6) which can be derived from verses 7-9 is that God prophesied of and fulfilled the giving of a covenant of grace for salvation.

Now in verses 10-11 one will find the promise of being able to become children of God by choice; in other words, the New Covenant wouldn't be merely fleshly ordinances (9:10), but something that would work from the inside out to effect true change. (By the way, this is the idea that's found in *The Sermon on the Mount*.)

> **VERSE 10:** "**FOR THIS IS THE COVENANT THAT I WILL MAKE WITH THE HOUSE OF ISRAEL AFTER THOSE DAYS, SAYS THE LORD: I WILL PUT MY LAWS IN THEIR MIND AND WRITE THEM ON THEIR HEARTS; AND I WILL BE THEIR GOD, AND THEY SHALL BE MY PEOPLE....**

I believe the phrase **HOUSE OF ISRAEL** here has specific reference to physical Israel—the Jews, but an extended reference to spiritual Israel—the church, because it would be directed to the Jews first, then to the Gentiles, as the book of Acts indicates in connection with the work of Peter and Paul.

The idea here is that the New Covenant would be of a spiritual and eternal nature; in other words, by virtue of the fact that God would save man by grace, man would thereby have the ultimate motivation from within to obey God out of gratitude for being saved, not to be saved. Still another way to look at this is that, whereas people became part of the Old Covenant through birth (i.e. without the knowledge of what they were doing), people become part of the New Covenant by choice—by mind/heart, not by flesh. Interestingly, immediately preceding Psalm 110:4 about the coming of the Messianic High Priest to which Paul referred so often in Hebrews, David wrote to God in verse 3 saying, "YOUR PEOPLE SHALL BE <u>VOLUNTEERS</u> IN THE DAY OF YOUR POWER."

In the clause **I WILL BE THEIR GOD**, the "I" should be emphasized because the Israelites were constantly going after idols; the spiritual nature of the New Covenant would help keep them and us devoted only to God. So...

> **VERSE 11:** "**NONE OF THEM SHALL TEACH HIS NEIGHBOR AND NONE HIS BROTHER, SAYING, 'KNOW THE LORD,' FOR ALL SHALL KNOW ME, FROM THE LEAST OF THEM TO THE GREATEST OF THEM....**

The word for **NEIGHBOR** literally means "fellow-citizen," hence this statement has reference only to brethren—siblings in God's family; this means that, because people become part of the New Covenant family of God as adults and thus by <u>choice</u>, they won't have to utter: **KNOW THE LORD**. Again, because the ancient Jews became members of the Old Covenant people of God by birth, they had to be taught about the One who was their Lord, whereas first century Jews became members of the New Covenant people of God willingly, by faith, based on a <u>knowledge</u> of the Lord; as 11:6 says, "HE WHO COMES TO GOD MUST BELIEVE." This is likely why Jesus spoke of <u>Jews</u> as needing to be "BORN AGAIN."

The phrase **FROM THE LEAST TO THE GREATEST** no doubt refers to those from babes in Christ to the mature in Christ.

> **VERSE 12: "FOR I WILL BE MERCIFUL TO THEIR UNRIGHTEOUSNESS, AND THEIR SINS AND THEIR LAWLESS DEEDS I WILL REMEMBER NO MORE."**

The word translated as **FOR** here indicates that the blessings of the New Covenant would be based on one's decision to enter it.

For God to say **I WILL REMEMBER THEM NO MORE** was to them extremely significant because, whereas God remembered their sins again each year on the day of atonement under the Old Covenant (cf. 10:1-3), He forgets them forever under the New Covenant. (Incidentally, it's important to note that this clause about forgetting sin doesn't mean that God literally forgets, but that, as a <u>contrast</u> to the Mosaical age, He doesn't bring them up again.)

By doing this, God exemplifies for us what it means to forgive and forget: It means to treat one as though he never sinned against us in the first place. Why is this possible for God? Because of the cross whereon He treated His Son, instead of us, as if He had sinned against Him!

So the three promises seen in this passage, upon which the New Covenant is founded, are as follows: {1} the promise of grace due to the fault of the Old Covenant and people (7-9); {2} the promise of becoming children of God by choice (10-11); and {3} the promise of sins forgiven and forgotten (12).

> **VERSE 13: IN THAT HE SAYS, "A NEW COVENANT," HE HAS MADE THE FIRST OBSOLETE. NOW WHAT IS BECOMING OBSOLETE AND GROWING OLD IS READY TO VANISH AWAY.**

Instead of using the Greek word for **OBSOLETE** ("old" in the KJV) which means "old in age," Paul chose the word for "old in wear"; in other words, how old the Mosaical covenant was in years wasn't the point—the point was that it had served its purpose and was therefore to be replaced, meaning that the NKJV's translation is accurate (cf. additional & important notes at 1:1-2a). And to compliment this, instead of using the Greek word for **NEW** which means "new in time," Paul chose the word for "new in quality." There are two interesting points in this regard: {1} the New Covenant is of such quality that it cannot and will not grow old and die; and {2}, as this verse says, just by the fact that God created a covenant and called it "new," He necessarily implied, to the dismay of the Jews, that the first one became "old," meaning that God Himself (not some man or group of men) cancelled out the first covenant nearly 2,000 years ago.

The phrase **GROWING OLD** suggests that the Old Covenant—at the time Paul was writing, no less—was losing its strength and wasting away, even to the point that it would soon "VANISH AWAY." See, since Paul was expecting the old things to disappear, the conclusion is that, from his point in time (ca. AD 63), the Old Covenant would soon be gone (ca. AD 70), allowing for a covenant that was "NEW" in time (cf. Heb. 12:24 where we're taught that the old was being shaken loose, but the new would remain—yes, clearly implying an overlapping/trans-formational/transitional period of grace).

The same Greek word for "GROWING OLD" here was used in 1:11, a verse upon which many comments may be found concerning the passing away of the heavens and earth as being a reference to the passing away of the old administration, which of course fits perfectly here, the only other place Paul used this particular word in this letter. (Corresponding to this, see the following [last] page of this section-study.)

Second Corinthians 3:7-13 Annotated

If the ministry of death written and engraved on stones was glorious [*the two tablets of the Ten Commandments symbolized the Old Covenant as a whole*], so that the children of Israel couldn't look steadily at the face of Moses because of the glory of his countenance, which glory was passing away [*the original is present tense, meaning this shouldn't be translated as "was..." but as "is passing away" at the time Paul penned these words in AD 56*], how will the ministry of the Spirit not be much more glorious [*the giving of the Spirit to the first generation Christians symbolized the New Covenant which the Spirit revealed*]? For if the ministry of condemnation had glory [*the Old Covenant, based on Law, could only provide condemnation, not reconciliation*], the ministry of righteousness exceeds much more in glory [*the New Covenant, in which man finds righteousness, provides reconciliation to God*]. For even what was made glorious [*the Old Covenant*] had no glory in this respect, because of the glory that excels [*because the glory of the New is so much greater than that of the Old, it's almost as if the Old had **no** glory*]. For if what is passing away was glorious [Question: *Why was the verb translated correctly here, but not in verses 7 & 13?*], what remains is much more glorious [cf. Heb. 12:27]. Therefore, since we have such hope, we use great boldness of speech—unlike Moses who put a veil over his face so that the children of Israel couldn't look steadily at the end of what was passing away [*"was" here should be "is" as well*]. [*Noting that the phrase "glory to glory" means from the Old Covenant age to the New Covenant age, observe it's present tense in Paul's time as well!*]

Hebrews 9:1-10

After writing about Christ being a superior person and a superior priest in chapters 1-7, Paul began chapter 8 writing about Christ having a superior pact or covenant, a study that continues through 10:18.

Since Paul has proven in chapter 8 that Christ's covenant is founded upon better promises than that of Moses, he proceeded to prove in chapter 9 that Christ's covenant also includes a better sanctuary than that of Aaron.

> **VERSE 1: THEN INDEED EVEN THE FIRST COVENANT HAD ORDINANCES OF DIVINE SERVICE AND THE EARTHLY SANCTUARY.**

The phrase **ORDINANCES OF DIVINE SERVICE** refers to the rules and rites of worship tailored for service to God, some of which are discussed in verses 6-10.

The word for **EARTHLY** is from the Greek term κοσμος and likely has reference to another of its accepted meanings besides "world" and "earth": here it probably refers to that which is ornamental or beautiful due to its arrangement and orderliness (cf. 1 Pet. 3:3). So here it could refer to the sanctuary as being decked out with the furniture used in worship to Yahweh. After all, Paul did continue in verses 2-5 to describe the inside of this God-designed tabernacle (8:5).

Therefore, keeping in mind that Paul was addressing Jewish Christians who still had some affinity to the Law, 9:1 fits perfectly between 8:13 and 9:11 when read as follows: "Yes, you're right: the first covenant had rules of worship and a beautifully decked out place of worship designed by God Himself.... But Christ came as High Priest of the good things to come, with the greater and more perfect tabernacle not made with hands, that is, not of this creation."

> **VERSE 2:** FOR A TABERNACLE WAS PREPARED: THE FIRST PART, IN WHICH WAS THE LAMPSTAND, THE TABLE, AND THE SHOWBREAD, WHICH IS CALLED THE SANCTUARY...

Paul recalled the original tabernacle referred to in 8:5. The bread is called **SHOWBREAD** because the original terminology for it referred to "the bread of the presence," the presence of God, that is. There were twelve unleavened loaves of this bread—one for each tribe, and they were eaten by the priests every Saturday (Lev. 24:5-9).

The **LAMPSTAND** was made up of seven oil-lamps; these lamps were to be kept lighted all night, every night, from evening till morning (Lev. 24:2-4).

As with the term "saint," the word for **SANCTUARY** is the word for "holy," often referred to by teachers as merely "the holy place" as opposed to "the most holy place."

> **VERSE 3:** ...**AND BEHIND THE SECOND VEIL, THE PART OF THE TABERNACLE WHICH IS CALLED THE HOLIEST OF ALL**...

There were actually two veils, entryways, or doors: one on the east side exterior of the tabernacle to separate the outer court from the interior of the tabernacle (Exo. 26:36-37) and one in the interior near the west side to separate the most holy place from the holy place (Exo. 26:31-33).

The phrase **THE HOLIEST OF ALL** could be literally translated as "holy of holies," for there were two holy places, one being considered more sacred than the other: only the high priest could enter the holy of holies or the most holy place or the holiest of all.

Unlike the holy place that was rectangular, it isn't an insignificant matter that the holiest of all (taking up one-third of the tabernacle's interior) was a perfect square. Notice what John wrote about the New Jerusalem in this regard: "THE CITY IS LAID OUT AS A SQUARE.... ITS LENGTH, BREADTH, AND HEIGHT ARE EQUAL"—a perfect cube (Rev. 21:16). Besides that, he said of this city, "I, JOHN, SAW THE HOLY CITY, NEW JERUSALEM, COMING DOWN OUT OF HEAVEN FROM GOD.... AND I HEARD A LOUD VOICE FROM HEAVEN SAYING, 'BEHOLD, THE TABERNACLE OF GOD IS WITH MEN, AND HE WILL DWELL WITH THEM, AND THEY SHALL BE HIS PEOPLE, AND GOD HIMSELF WILL BE WITH THEM AND BE THEIR GOD" (Rev. 21:2-3). It was in the most holy place where God was said to dwell.

Therefore, since Paul associated the Old Covenant with old Jerusalem and the New Covenant with New Jerusalem (Gal. 4:22-26), then one may conclude that in AD 70, when old Jerusalem was annihilated once and for all (taking all its Old Covenant vestiges with it), the coming of New Jerusalem arrived with the fullness of the New Covenant, bringing with it restoration to God's presence (cf. 9:10 & Acts 3:19-21).

VERSE 4: ...WHICH HAD THE GOLDEN ALTAR OF INCENSE AND THE ARK OF THE COVENANT OVERLAID ON ALL SIDES WITH GOLD, IN WHICH WERE THE GOLDEN POT THAT HAD THE MANNA [Exo. 16:32-33], **AARON'S ROD THAT BUDDED** [Num. 17:1-10], **AND THE TABLETS OF THE COVENANT** [Exo. 25:16]...

Actually, the altar of incense was in the holy place (Exo. 30:6-8), not the most holy place. So why did Paul apparently place it in the most holy place here? Because, although upon this altar incense was burned twice a day (Exo. 30:7-8), that wasn't its primary purpose.

Its primary purpose was to provide burning coals for the high priest to take <u>into</u> the holiest of all and place on the mercy seat of the ark with incense on the annual Day of Atonement (Lev. 16:12-13); this is why it was positioned immediately in front of the interior veil to the holiest of all.

VERSE 5: ...AND ABOVE IT (THE ARK OF THE COVENANT) **WERE THE CHERUBIM OF GLORY OVERSHADOWING THE MERCY SEAT. OF THESE THINGS WE CANNOT NOW SPEAK IN DETAIL.**

CHERUBIM is the plural form of "CHERUB," a heavenly or angelic creature depicted, like the sphinx, as a being made up of differing parts of various animals of Earth, including humans (cf. Ezekiel chap. 1 w/ chap. 10).

They're called cherubim **OF GLORY** here probably because of their position by the place of God's presence or glory, then and now (cf. 1 Sam. 4:21-22).

(Side-note: Aside from the fact that they're described slightly differently [cf. Isa. 6 w/ Eze. 10], the only difference between seraphim and cherubim appears to be in regard to their angelic rank.)

The phrase **MERCY SEAT** (rendered "PROPITIATION" in Rom. 3:25) is from a word meaning "reconciliation by means of covering." This ark-covering symbolized God's throne where mercy is offered on the basis of justice satisfied—something of course achieved later in Christ ... once for all time. God once said to Moses about this ark and mercy seat, "'THERE I WILL MEET WITH YOU, AND I WILL SPEAK WITH YOU FROM ABOVE THE MERCY SEAT, FROM BETWEEN THE TWO CHERUBIM WHICH ARE ON THE ARK OF THE TESTIMONY...'" (Exo. 25:22), which is exactly what He did (Num. 7:89).

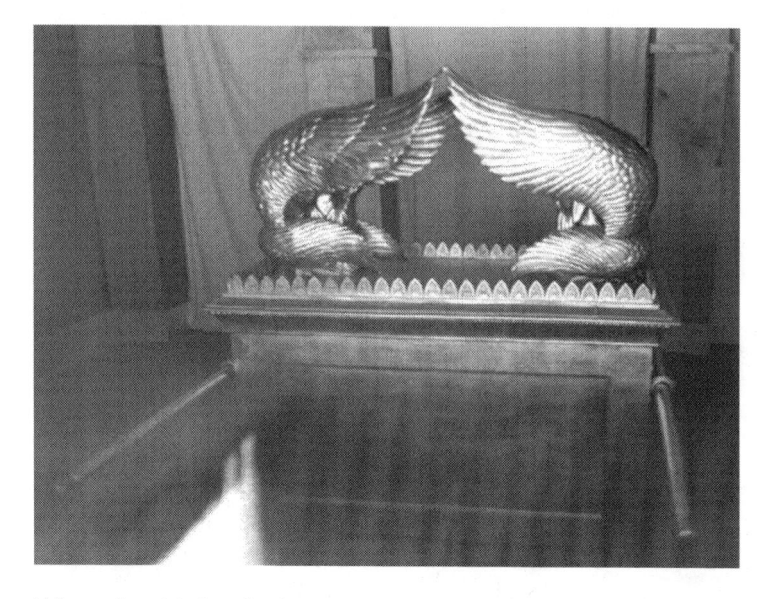

When the high priest smeared the blood on the mercy seat (Lev. 16:14), it depicted God seeing only the blood-sacrifice and not the broken covenant covered by the mercy seat, implying that man couldn't and wouldn't be saved by law. Some reading this will likely recall the Indiana Jones film,

The Raiders of the Lost Ark, in which everyone who looked into the ark died. This was based on the story of how God once struck over 50,000 people dead for peering into the ark (1 Sam. 6:19-20). And why would this be? Because they had to remove the mercy seat in order to look in at the Law. The point seems very clear that God was saying—even in ancient days—"Apart from My mercy, the Law is death."

> **VERSE 6: NOW WHEN THESE THINGS HAD BEEN THUS PREPARED, THE PRIESTS ALWAYS WENT INTO THE FIRST PART OF THE TABERNACLE, PERFORMING THE SERVICES.**

After Paul had dealt sufficiently with the tabernacle, he proceeded in verses 6-10 to discuss some of the services performed in it and how that the new system is superior to the old one.

His main point here seems to have been to emphasize their inaccessibility to the holy of holies. Since Paul was writing about the first part of the tabernacle—the holy place, then the **PRIESTS** he had in mind here were obviously the ordinary priests, not the high priests who he discussed in verse 7.

The word **ALWAYS** here is a contrast word, meaning that, while the high priests went into the most holy place twice on <u>one day</u> a year, the priests went into the holy place at least twice <u>every day</u>.

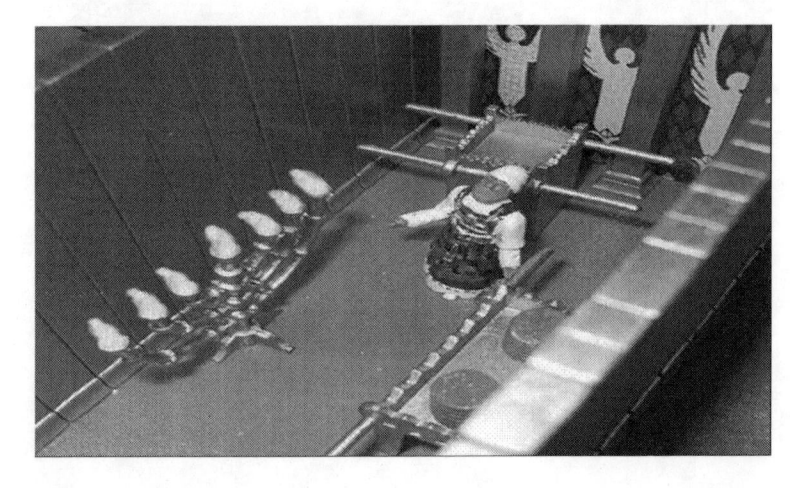

It's also noteworthy that, once again, as also in the following statement, Paul was writing in the present tense: the word for **WENT** here should be rendered "are going" or "go" ("is going" or "goes" in v. 7), just as the word for **OFFERED** in verse 7 should be rendered "is offering" or "offers."

> **VERSE 7:** BUT INTO THE SECOND PART THE HIGH PRIEST WENT ALONE ONCE A YEAR, NOT WITHOUT BLOOD, WHICH HE OFFERED FOR HIMSELF AND FOR THE PEOPLE'S SINS COMMITTED IN IGNORANCE...

Unlike the ordinary priests, it appears that the high priest could only enter the tabernacle one day of the year—the Day of Atonement (Lev. 16:2 & 34), the 10th of Tishri (Lev. 16:29, falling on or near Oct. 1st); this is the day known as "Yom Kippur."

On that day he entered **THE SECOND PART** of the tabernacle, the holy of holies, twice: firstly with incense and bull's blood for his sins (something which didn't apply to our High Priest Jesus, 7:26), then secondly with goat's blood for the people's sins.

There are three different Greek terms translated as **FOR**: one that meant "in order to" (Acts 2:38), another that meant "in place of" (1 Cor. 11:15), and the one used here that means "on behalf of."

Although **SINS COMMITTED IN IGNORANCE** is an accurate translation, many scholars believe that these Jewish readers knew Paul was referring to all sin (except maybe the "high-handed" sins mentioned in Num. 15:30-31), including those committed in ignorance. Why? For two reasons: {1} If sins of ignorance are included, then logic dictates that the others would be as well! And {2} it's difficult to read Leviticus 16 and come away with any other belief, especially verse 16: God said of the high priest, "'HE SHALL MAKE ATONEMENT ... BECAUSE OF THE UNCLEANNESS OF THE CHILDREN OF ISRAEL, AND BECAUSE OF THEIR TRANSGRESSIONS, FOR ALL THEIR SINS.'" (For more information on this, cf. *Synonyms of the New Testament* by Richard Trench, p. 260.)

> **VERSE 8:** ...THE HOLY SPIRIT INDICATING THIS, THAT THE WAY INTO THE HOLIEST OF ALL WAS NOT YET MADE MANIFEST WHILE THE FIRST TABERNACLE WAS STILL STANDING.

By saying **THE HOLY SPIRIT INDICATING THIS**, Paul was saying that the tabernacle, with all of its assorted services, symbolized something (v. 9a): the main thing it symbolized is that, before Christ came, God's presence was inaccessible. Here are the facts of the matter: Instead of being out in the open among the people like a politician vying for office, God sat on a small throne, in a small room into which only one person, one day a year, could enter. And even that seemed to be "a necessary evil" in order to depict how God was finally going to work out man's reconciliation to Him once and for all through His Messiah/Son.

The phrase **WAS NOT YET MADE** literally reads, "has not yet been made," denoting present tense (as in AD 63), not past (as in AD 30 or prior).

The phrase **THE FIRST TABERNACLE** is from the exact same original phrase as has been found throughout this passage when Paul wrote about **THE FIRST PART**—the holy place of the tabernacle. And the phrase **WAS STILL STANDING** actually reads, "has a standing," referring to its status/position of some eminence in the eyes of God (for only He could/would impose its symbolic [v. 9] services until a very specifically set time [v. 10]). So, especially with reference to verses 9-10 in which Paul listed several works that had to be constantly executed within the holy place, consider this: It appears Paul was implying that the first part of the tabernacle (the holy place) represented works, all of which couldn't/didn't make the priests (much less ordinary people) worthy of God's presence. (Even the high priest had to make an offering for himself prior to making one for the people.)

When His Son died, God (prefiguring what would soon be accomplished in Christ at AD 70) tore down the veil that separated the ordinary priests from His presence (Mark 15:38), denoting that the necessity of all these works of law were going to be removed once and for all time and people; any position of eminence that the holy place once had before God would be eliminated, and the two places would become one, manifesting the way into the eternal presence of God by grace (cf. Eph. 1:10). (Cf. pictures on p. 136.)

> **VERSE 9:** IT WAS SYMBOLIC FOR THE PRESENT TIME IN WHICH BOTH GIFTS AND SACRIFICES ARE OFFERED WHICH CANNOT MAKE HIM WHO PERFORMED THE SERVICE PERFECT IN REGARD TO THE CONSCIENCE...

Throughout the remarks in this volume, I've tried to consistently point out the numerous places in which most versions have chosen to translate present tense verbs in either the past or future tense; in case there's any misunderstanding about the tense of this context, Paul, in unmistakable terms here, wrote **FOR THE PRESENT TIME** or "for the time now present."

The term for **SYMBOLIC** is the word for "parable," an illustration used to explain something by comparison; in other words, the tabernacle (and later the temple) was never meant to be the real thing, but only to portray and point to the real thing —reconciliation to God by means of the Kingdom of Heaven. (One could actually say that Hebrews 9 is Christ's last parable.)

Concerning the verb **ARE**, it appears to be one of the present tense verbs that the translators missed while altering their tenses from what Paul originally wrote by inspiration (or they realized that it, being so close to the "present time" phrase, would be too conspicuous to change); regardless of the reason why this verb was left in the correct tense, this verb supports Paul's usage of the present tense in relation to the then-current Judaic sacrifices which would be once-and-for-all removed from God's sight in AD 70.

The phrase **PERFECT IN REGARD TO CONSCIENCE** means that the Old Testament saint could never have the sense of forgiveness that you and I can have today, because he was constantly reminded of past sins that kept catching up with him (cf. 10:3). The Old Covenant simply couldn't provide an internal/eternal cleansing and perfection because it was...

> **VERSE 10:** ...CONCERNED ONLY WITH FOODS AND DRINKS, VARIOUS WASHINGS, AND FLESHLY ORDINANCES IMPOSED UNTIL THE TIME OF REFORMATION.

The Torah, especially the ceremonial portion of it (which is probably actually the bulk of it), just concerned itself with things related to that which was physical in nature. Why? In order to symbolize that which would be much more significant and of a spiritual nature in the future.

Since the term **UNTIL** indicates purpose, then it's clear that God was the One behind the **IMPOSITION**.

The phrase **THE TIME OF REFORMATION** means exactly what it sounds like it means: that which was originally created or formed straight had become warped, so Jesus came to re-form or re-straighten it.

Related phrases are "THE REGENERATION" (Mat. 19:28) and "THE TIMES OF RESTORATION" (Acts 3:21), all three referring to the age-changing events between AD 30 & 70, especially the consummation of those changes at AD 70 when Jerusalem and its temple met their demise. This time was only 5 to 7 years from the writing of Hebrews. (Once again, note the present tense of verses 9 & 10: "ARE ... CONCERNED.")

In Eden God and Adam had fellowship (Gen. 3:8), then sin entered (3:1-5), separating the two (Isa. 59:2); so Jesus (the Last Adam, 1 Cor. 15:45) came and restored that relationship for all who desire it (Rom. 5:10 & 2 Cor. 5:18).

Let's end this section by reading one version which did decide to retain the present tense throughout Hebrews 9:8-10. *The New American Standard Bible: Updated Edition*, published in 1997 by The Lockman Foundation reads, "THE HOLY SPIRIT IS SIGNIFYING THIS, THAT THE WAY INTO THE HOLY PLACE HAS NOT YET BECOME DISCLOSED WHILE THE OUTER TABERNACLE IS STILL STANDING, WHICH IS A SYMBOL FOR THE PRESENT TIME. ACCORDINGLY BOTH GIFTS AND SACRIFICES ARE OFFERED WHICH CANNOT MAKE THE WORSHIPPER PERFECT IN CONSCIENCE, SINCE THEY RELATE ONLY TO FOOD AND DRINK AND VARIOUS WASHINGS, REGULATIONS FOR THE BODY IMPOSED UNTIL A TIME OF REFORMATION."

Hebrews 9:11-15

At the outset of chapter 9, Paul began to demonstrate that Christ's covenant is better than that of Moses, not just because it's founded upon better promises (chap. 8), but also because it includes a better tabernacle than that of Aaron.

In 9:1-5 Paul pictured the sanctuary and its furnishings for his audience; then in verses 6-10 he explained that all of those literal/physical things were merely symbols pointing to the real thing; and now, upon that basis, in verses 11-14 Paul wrote about some of the things that those items symbolized.

> **VERSE 11: BUT CHRIST CAME AS HIGH PRIEST OF THE GOOD THINGS TO COME, WITH THE GREATER AND MORE PERFECT TABERNACLE NOT MADE WITH HANDS, THAT IS, NOT OF THIS CREATION.**

The word for **CAME** means "to make one's appearance" (cf. other versions such as the NASB in which it's translated as "appeared"). And when did Jesus make His appearance as High Priest? According to Hebrews 5:5-10, it was after His resurrection; and, according to verse 12 below, it occurred within the most holy place—Heaven.

The word for the phrase **TO COME** means "about to come" (see a more in-depth consideration of this Greek term at 2:5). It's the same term found in 8:5 where it speaks of when Moses "WAS ABOUT TO MAKE THE TABERNACLE"; in other words, it wasn't something thousands of years in the future, but something on the verge of occurring. (A good reason to accept *The Received Text* here is because it's the exact same word and phrase found in 10:1 in either text.)

These **GOOD THINGS TO COME** have reference to everything that would/did accomplish the reformation spoken of in verse 10—redemption, regeneration, reconciliation, restoration, resurrection, etc.; put succinctly, this means that through or because of Jesus, man now has access to God.

The original term for **WITH** here is διa; being genitive, it would be better translated as "through."

The phrase **THE GREATER AND MORE PERFECT TABERNACLE** refers of course to the real spiritual entity to which the physical symbolic entity merely pointed—the single-room tabernacle or kingdom wherein all of God's people are united as one reconciled body. Ephesians 1:10 (very slightly paraphrased to fit our time after the consummation of all things) says that "IN THE ... FULLNESS OF THE TIMES [in the 1st century] [GOD] ... GATHER[ED] TOGETHER IN ONE ALL THINGS IN CHRIST [the temple, REV. 21:22], BOTH WHICH ARE IN HEAVEN AND WHICH ARE ON EARTH." (Cf. 2 The. 2:1, Mat. 24:31, Luke 13:29, & even Heb. 10:25 [esp. in connection w/ 2 The. 2:1].)

This one-roomed tabernacle is also called by a few other names in Hebrews: "THE CITY ... WHOSE BUILDER ... IS GOD ... [and] A HEAVENLY COUNTRY" in 11:9 & 16, and "MOUNT ZION," "THE CITY OF THE LIVING GOD," "THE HEAVENLY JERUSALEM," "THE CHURCH OF THE FIRSTBORN ONES," "THE GENERAL ASSEMBLY," as well as simply "A KINGDOM" in 12:22-23 & 28 (cf. chart on p. 35). So it was/is through/by means of this tabernacle that Jesus did/does fulfill His high priestly profession.

The phrase **NOT MADE WITH HANDS** refers to the same idea as found in 8:2 where it speaks of "THE TRUE TABERNACLE WHICH THE LORD ERECTED AND NOT MAN." (Consider 2 Cor. 4:18–5:8 as a commentary on Rom. 8:18-23; also see web link at bottom of p. 43.)

The phrase **NOT OF THIS CREATION** means of course that this true/genuine/real tabernacle is of a spiritual/heavenly nature, not a physical/temporal nature: Jesus Himself said, "'MY KINGDOM IS NOT OF THIS WORLD'" (John 18:36).

VERSE 12: NOT WITH THE BLOOD OF GOATS AND CALVES, BUT WITH HIS OWN BLOOD HE ENTERED THE MOST HOLY PLACE ONCE FOR ALL, HAVING OBTAINED ETERNAL REDEMPTION. (CF. 6:19-20 & 9:24.)

The phrase **HIS OWN** is not from the usual personal pronoun αυτος; it's from the more specific term ιδιος, meaning that this blood was unique to Jesus. Here's an example: ιδιος is the word used in John 5:18 where it speaks of the Jews wanting to kill Jesus because He claimed Yahweh as His Father. Since all the Jews claimed Yahweh to be their Father, why would this be a problem? Well, according to John 5:18, Jesus didn't use the idea behind αυτος which would've indicated that He was a child of God just as other Jews were; rather, He used the idea behind ιδιος which indicated that Yahweh was His Father in a unique way, meaning that He was/is deity just as Yahweh is deity.

So what made the blood of Jesus unique? It flowed in the veins of One who was sinless in regard to His humanity and deity in regard to His person, the combination of which made His blood the only blood that could be acceptably sprinkled on the mercy seat in the true holy of holies (at least that's the picture God meant for us to see, not Jesus conveying His literal/physical blood into the spiritual/heavenly realm and smearing it on a literal/physical seat).

The phrase **ONCE FOR ALL** means (as the context indicates in 9:25–10:10) "once for all time," meaning it wasn't done over and over again every year as with the Old Testament high priests (see the *New Living Translation* & the *New Century Version*, as well as other translations, e.g. Wycliffe's, Webster's, & Young's). In fact, this is the notion behind the word "ETERNAL" here: instead of referring to the doctrine of eternal security (aka "once saved, always saved"), it's actually just a synonym for the once-for-all-time concept.

The word **REDEMPTION** refers to "a release by payment of a ransom," such as when money was paid in order to free a slave; sinners are slaves of sin, and "THE WAGES OF SIN IS DEATH" (Rom. 6:23), a debt Jesus paid for those who want freedom from sin and its consequential eternal death.

Contrasts to note: {1} there was animal blood under the Old Testament, while Jesus' blood is under the New Testament; {2} high priests entered the holiest by means of/with animal blood, while Jesus' entered by means of/with His own blood; {3} animal blood was given involuntarily, while Jesus' blood was given voluntarily; {4} animals were offered repeatedly, while Jesus was offered once; and {5} animal blood covered sins briefly, while Jesus' blood removes sin eternally.

The NASB rendered verses 11-12 more accurately: "WHEN CHRIST APPEARED AS A HIGH PRIEST OF THE GOOD THINGS TO COME, HE ENTERED THROUGH THE GREATER AND MORE PERFECT TABERNACLE NOT MADE WITH HANDS, THAT IS TO SAY, NOT OF THIS CREATION; AND NOT THROUGH THE BLOOD OF GOATS AND CALVES, BUT THROUGH HIS OWN BLOOD HE ENTERED THE HOLY PLACE ONCE FOR ALL [time], HAVING OBTAINED ETERNAL REDEMPTION."

VERSE 13: FOR IF [LIT. ει SINCE] **THE BLOOD OF BULLS AND GOATS AND THE ASHES OF A HEIFER, SPRINKLING THE UNCLEAN, SANCTIFIES FOR THE PURIFYING OF THE FLESH...**

Here Paul added the heifer-sacrifice and the sprinkling of her ashes with water over people who became ceremonially unclean as a result of some sort of contact with a dead body; see, if a Jew had any such contact and then entered the tabernacle area, he was cut off from Israel (Num. 19:1-10). Ceremonial defilement was not in and of itself sin, but (like leavening) it was a <u>type</u> or picture of sin; this is why it's said that the blood of animals could cleanse this defilement. It was only the flesh that was defiled by contact with the dead, so it was only the flesh that was cleansed, meaning that defilement and cleansing were both symbolic; this ceremony didn't make anyone morally or spiritually better, just physically. In fact, recall verse 9: such things were "SYMBOLIC FOR THE PRESENT TIME IN WHICH BOTH GIFTS AND SACRIFICES ARE OFFERED WHICH CANNOT MAKE HIM WHO PERFORMED THE SERVICE PERFECT IN REGARD TO CONSCIENCE."

The word **UNCLEAN** here refers to that which is "unhallowed or not related to or associated with God," while **SANCTIFIES** means "set apart to/for God." So the unclean Israelite was "out of bounds" when it came to participating in any service or worship to God; but when he fulfilled the Levitical ritual in relation to this uncleanness, then he was sanctified or set apart to and for God once again. So if animal sacrifices could do these things, then...

> **VERSE 14:** ...HOW MUCH MORE SHALL THE BLOOD OF CHRIST, WHO THROUGH THE ETERNAL SPIRIT OFFERED HIMSELF WITHOUT SPOT TO GOD, PURGE YOUR CONSCIENCE FROM DEAD WORKS TO SERVE THE LIVING GOD?

While the sacrifice of a heifer sanctified one physically in order to serve God acceptably under the Old Testament, the sacrifice of Jesus sanctifies one spiritually in order to serve God acceptably under the New Testament. Christ's sacrifice is greater because He (as a human) was **WITHOUT SPOT** or sinless and because He (as deity) offered Himself for mankind.

The phrase **ETERNAL SPIRIT** has no definite article before it, indicating that it is <u>not</u> a reference to the Holy Spirit as the *New King James Version* indicates with the capital "s." Rather, it's probably (due to context) a reference to the eternal nature (or deity) of Jesus Himself; the *Contemporary English Version* says, "HE OFFERED HIMSELF AS AN ETERNAL AND SPIRITUAL SACRIFICE." Besides, *just as it requires that which is physical to affect that which is physical, so it requires that which is spiritual to affect that which is spiritual*, which also signifies that this entire scenario here is spiritual in nature; in other words, as indicated earlier, Jesus didn't take His literal/physical blood to Heaven with Him (cf. notes at 8:10-11).

A cleansed conscience (cf. 1 Pet. 3:21) occurs when one is assured of absolute forgiveness, that which those under the Old Testament didn't possess until Christ came and fulfilled the righteousness of the Law (Rom. 8:3-4); still another way to put it is that a cleansed conscience equals access to and reconciliation with **THE LIVING GOD**.

The phrase **DEAD WORKS** probably has reference to how that attempts to be saved by works (as in Old Testament times) are dead in the sense of being effective, while now, through Christ, man can be saved by grace; since dead works for a living God are worthless, our works through Christ are living (Rom. 12:1-2), because they're performed out of appreciation instead of as an attempt to merit salvation. Now to Paul's point in this context:

> **VERSE 15:** AND FOR THIS REASON HE IS THE MEDIATOR OF THE NEW COVENANT BY MEANS OF DEATH FOR THE REDEMPTION OF THE TRANSGRESSIONS UNDER THE FIRST COVENANT, THAT THOSE WHO ARE CALLED MAY RECEIVE THE PROMISE OF THE ETERNAL INHERITANCE.

The phrase **FOR THIS REASON** refers to the fact that, while animal blood merely cleansed from ceremonial defilements (cf. notes at v. 13), Jesus' blood cleanses from actual sin, making Him the Mediator of the New Covenant.

The word **MEDIATOR** refers to one who intervenes between two parties, either to make or restore peace by forming a compact or ratifying a covenant: by His death on the cross, Jesus removed the barrier and penalty of sin between God and man.

Notice that Jesus wasn't here called the Testator but the Mediator, reminiscent of the idea brought up in 7:23 that Jesus not only died to ratify, but rose to mediate as well.

The phrase **REDEMPTION OF THE TRANSGRESSIONS UNDER THE FIRST COVENANT** means that even the faithful under the Old Covenant were saved by virtue of Christ's atoning work in His creation of the New Covenant. Why? Again, because the first covenant made no provisions for the complete removal of sin. It's believed by many that this is what's meant by the prophecy of Zechariah 14:8: "IN THAT DAY IT WILL BE THAT LIVING WATERS SHALL FLOW FROM JERUSALEM, HALF OF THEM TOWARD THE EASTERN SEA AND HALF OF THEM TOWARD THE WESTERN SEA." In other words, the salvation of Messiah would extend in both directions in time from His cross: into the past and into the future, making His cross the pivotal point in history. (This may be what's meant by Jesus being slain from the foundation of the world, Rev. 13:8.) Paul said it this way in Romans 3:24-25: "BEING JUSTIFIED FREELY BY HIS GRACE THROUGH THE REDEMPTION THAT IS IN CHRIST JESUS, WHOM GOD SET FORTH TO BE A PROPITIATION ... BECAUSE IN HIS FORBEARANCE GOD HAD PASSED OVER THE SINS THAT WERE PREVIOUSLY COMMITTED" (cf. Acts 17:30). How did He "pass over them"? By "forbearing" or holding their sins in a "book of remembrance" until Jesus' blood removed them in order for God to forget them for good (Heb. 10:17). (Thus the book of Rev. 3:5, etc. is no more.)

The phrase **THOSE WHO ARE CALLED** refers of course to any and all who were called by and accepted the Gospel: at another time, Paul, speaking of <u>salvation</u>, wrote, "TO WHICH GOD CALLED YOU BY OUR GOSPEL, FOR THE OBTAINING OF THE GLORY OF OUR LORD JESUS CHRIST" (2 The. 2:13-14).

The phrase **ETERNAL INHERITANCE** is a contrast to the temporary inheritance of Canaan; this "ETERNAL INHERITANCE" was available to those who accepted Jesus as their Messiah because His blood "OBTAINED ETERNAL REDEMPTION" (v. 12). (Cf. Heb. 3 & 4.)

Hebrews 9:14

Hebrews 9:16-28

At least four things were gleaned from the study of 9:11-15:

1} Verse 11 teaches that the resurrected Jesus became the new High Priest between men and God, and that (at the time of Hebrews) He was building a spiritual/eternal replacement tabernacle for the one in Jerusalem that He would destroy at His AD 70 coming. (The new one would have room for any and everyone [cf. John 14:2-3, unless one interprets the "dwellings" as individuals in which deity would dwell].)

2} Verse 12 teaches that this greater tabernacle was established upon the unique blood of Jesus—the only blood that could/did result in the eternal redemption of any/all who desire it (cf. Rev. 22:17).

3} Verses 13-14 teach that Christ's blood made it possible for mankind to come into possession of a clear conscience, a conscience that couldn't be achieved by any works of any sort.

4} Verse 15 teaches that Jesus' blood had to be shed (i.e., He had to die, Lev. 17:11) to ratify the New Covenant and that He had to be resurrected to mediate this covenant which had come along with the new priesthood (cf. 7:12).

Now in 9:16-23 the student discovers more concerning why Jesus had to die and shed His blood. After writing about "ETERNAL INHERITANCE" in verse 15, Paul wrote the following in...

> **VERSES 16-17:** FOR WHERE THERE IS A TESTAMENT, THERE MUST ALSO OF NECESSITY BE THE DEATH OF A TESTATOR. FOR A TESTAMENT IS IN FORCE AFTER MEN ARE DEAD, SINCE IT HAS NO POWER AT ALL WHILE THE TESTATOR LIVES.

The word for **TESTAMENT** refers to stipulations or an agreement between two parties; obviously here it specifically refers to a will of conditions left by the dead, a will that must be agreed upon and submitted to by the living before any rewards in it may be claimed.

A testament **HAS NO POWER AT ALL WHILE THE TESTATOR LIVES**; in other words, no one, even today, can, for example, obtain his father's will and force the courts into executing it as long as his father is still alive. Of course the father (like the one in Luke 15) can go ahead and distribute whatever he wishes while he's alive; however, it must be remembered in such a case that this father isn't executing a ratified will, something which can only transpire by means of his demise—while alive he's merely doing what he wishes with what he has. In Matthew 9:1-6 Jesus forgave a paralytic, and when the scribes got irritated with Him, Jesus said, "'THE SON OF MAN HAS POWER ON EARTH TO FORGIVE SINS.'" (The recognized "already-but-not-yet" principle must also be kept in mind; i.e., forgiveness for anyone by Jesus was predicated upon His death, burial, and resurrection, meaning that if Jesus hadn't died, then the fellow in Matthew 9 actually wouldn't have been forgiven.)

> **VERSE 18:** THEREFORE NOT EVEN THE FIRST COVENANT WAS DEDICATED WITHOUT BLOOD.

Since all this is true in the case of a will, it's also true of all the covenants of God—they all required ratification and establishment by means of death and the sprinkling of blood.

Thus even the Old Covenant, which was but a type of the New, was not established **WITHOUT BLOOD**.

> **VERSES 19-20:** FOR WHEN MOSES HAD SPOKEN EVERY PRECEPT [RULE] TO ALL THE PEOPLE ACCORDING TO THE LAW, HE TOOK THE BLOOD OF CALVES AND GOATS, WITH WATER, SCARLET WOOL, AND [OR ON] HYSSOP [BRANCHES], **AND SPRINKLED BOTH THE BOOK ITSELF AND ALL THE PEOPLE, SAYING, "THIS IS THE BLOOD OF THE COVENANT WHICH GOD HAS COMMANDED** [OR BETTER, 'ENJOINED TO'] **YOU."** (CF. EXO. 24:1-6.)

The Testator of the Old Covenant was God, for it was God who was the source of salvation for those in Old Testament times. But God wasn't yet ready to come in the person of His Son and die for mankind, so He provided a substitute which would typify Him in death, a death that would make the first testament effective; this substitution was of course an animal.

Thus the emphasis in verses 19-20 is that everything connected with the testament bears the mark of blood, the shedding of which resulted in death; as seen here, blood is that which seals not only a covenant, but also the people to that covenant.

(Interesting side-note: Consider how these verses correspond to the Lord's Supper: the loaf = the people [1 Cor. 10:17], the juice = the blood [Matt. 26:26], and the cup = the covenant [1 Cor. 11:25]; as those first generation Christians drank from the cup of blessing [1 Cor. 10:16]—the drinking vessel containing grape juice [cf. Isa. 65:8], they, at that point, could see the clear connection among all three: people → blood ← covenant.)

Since **HYSSOP** isn't described in the Bible, and since there were at least three different plants to which this could refer, then we must conclude that Bible hyssop must have been the only one of the three that had long enough and strong enough stems to use in Bible ways, and that would be the caper plant.

> **VERSE 21:** THEN LIKEWISE HE SPRINKLED WITH BLOOD BOTH THE TABERNACLE AND ALL THE VESSELS OF THE MINISTRY.

Sprinkling all these things with blood seemed to express the exceeding sinfulness of man; in other words, man is so sinful and sin itself is so bad that it spilled over onto the things he used to worship and serve a holy God! So those things needed to be cleansed as well (cf. Rom. 8:18-23).

Again, as has been the case throughout this context, this is all symbolic for us to comprehend just how God sees sin.

> **VERSE 22:** AND ACCORDING TO THE LAW ALMOST ALL THINGS ARE PURGED WITH BLOOD, AND WITHOUT SHEDDING OF BLOOD THERE IS NO REMISSION.

Since he said that **ALMOST ALL THINGS ARE PURGED WITH BLOOD**, what was left out? Things that were symbolically cleansed with water and/or fire (cf. Num. 31:22-24).

Paul's point was simply that there just wasn't/isn't any sin that could/can be annulled without bloodshed/death (cf. Lev. 17:11 & Rom. 6:23); that has just always and admittedly been the requirement of the nature of deity (cf. Isa. 55:8-9 & 2 Cor. 5:7), whether or not man understands why such was chosen to be the case.

The word for **REMISSION** means "to send away" (reminiscent of the scapegoat of Lev. 16), so it came to mean "to pardon a wrong or to cancel an obligation or a punishment," making it related to the concept of mercy.

> **VERSE 23:** THEREFORE IT WAS NECESSARY THAT THE COPIES OF THE THINGS IN THE HEAVENS SHOULD BE PURIFIED WITH THESE, BUT THE HEAVENLY THINGS THEMSELVES WITH BETTER SACRIFICES THAN THESE.

The phrase **THE COPIES OF THE THINGS IN THE HEAVENS SHOULD BE PURIFIED WITH THESE** refers back to the Aaronic priesthood and the tabernacle; and since the tabernacle of God was situated in the midst of a sinful nation, it (and everything belonging to it) was cleansed by the blood of animal sacrifices.

Concerning the phrase **HEAVENLY THINGS**, there's actually no word in the original for "things"; the word **HEAVENLY** is what's plural, meaning that logic/context must determine to what "heavenlies" refers. Since Paul was discussing the cleansing of sin and the ceremonial impurities of/due to the people, then the seemingly logical/contextual meaning of "heavenlies" would be that this term alludes back to the consciences of men (v. 14).

The Old Testament priesthood foreshadowed New Testament Christians, and the Old Testament tabernacle typified the New Testament kingdom in which Christians serve God. So **THE HEAVENLY THINGS** here could be translated as "the heavenly ones"; in other words, those of the heavenly kingdom are those who've been purified by the blood of Christ.

The phrase **BETTER SACRIFICES** obviously refers to the sacrifice of Christ. But since Paul often claimed that there was only the one sacrifice of Christ (v. 26), why did he say "sacrifices" plural? Perhaps he did such merely to retain the parallel: it was because Jesus' one sacrifice equaled, yea surpassed, all the previous sacrifices!

> **VERSE 24: FOR CHRIST HAS NOT ENTERED THE HOLY PLACES MADE WITH HANDS WHICH ARE COPIES OF THE TRUE, BUT INTO HEAVEN ITSELF, NOW TO APPEAR IN THE PRESENCE OF GOD FOR US...**

Not only do verses 24-28 contrast verses 19-23, but they also cite three appearances of Christ. As Paul already stated a few times, instead of entering the literal/physical/man-made tabernacle with His blood, Jesus went into that which the tabernacle in part pictured—Heaven itself! (The tabernacle also pictured the kingdom.)

Unlike the earthly high priests who could only appear before God once a year, Jesus appears before God on a continuous/eternal basis. Also, unlike the earthly high priests who had to conceal themselves in smoke while in the presence of God in the holy of holies, Jesus appears face to face with God in Heaven; since Jesus died sinless, there's no need for anything to hide Him from God.

He does this **FOR US**: on behalf of those cleansed, Jesus stands in the presence of God, meaning that we have access to God because and only because of Jesus. So if these Jewish brethren were to return to their old ways, they would be rejecting the One whom God provided as their substitution!

> **VERSES 25-26A: ...NOT THAT HE SHOULD OFFER HIMSELF OFTEN, AS THE HIGH PRIEST ENTERS THE MOST HOLY PLACE EVERY YEAR WITH THE BLOOD OF ANOTHER—HE THEN WOULD HAVE HAD TO SUFFER OFTEN SINCE THE FOUNDATION OF THE WORLD...**

This offering of Himself refers to His <u>second appearance</u>—His appearance before God's throne as the Old Testament high priests appeared before the mercy seat in the holy of holies with the blood of the lamb.

If the sacrificial service of Christ was exactly like that of the Old Testament, then He would've been required to begin His sacrificing immediately after Adam's sin; however, since only once was necessary, and since it's God's general rule that men die only once (v. 27), Jesus could and did wait until the perfect timing of God to offer Himself one time for all time (Eph. 1:7-12, Gal. 4:4-5, etc.). In other words...

> **VERSE 26B: ...BUT NOW, ONCE AT THE END OF THE AGES, HE HAS APPEARED TO PUT AWAY SIN BY THE SACRIFICE OF HIMSELF.**

The phrase **THE END OF THE AGES** simply refers to the last generation of time in the Mosaical age (which of course came after the Patriarchal age, making plural **AGES**); and it was at this time in the Mosaical age ("the climax of history," per the *New English Bible*) that Christ came in His <u>first appearance</u> and sacrificed Himself for man. (It's interesting also to note that the phrase **NOW, AT/IN THE END OF THE AGES** implies that Paul and these Hebrew brethren were still <u>in</u> the Mosaical age [cf. 1:2; 1 Pet. 1:20; Heb. 8:13; 2 Cor. 3:11; etc.].)

(Side-note: unlike the KJV, the NKJV has this verse correct: "world" is from κοσμος while **AGES** is from αιον. Something else interesting is that the Bible <u>never</u> uses κοσμος when speaking of the end of the "world" [our physical universe]; that's *King James* language.)

Some scholars believe that the original term concerning **SIN** here actually has reference to sin-offerings, fulfilling Daniel 9:27 (the context of which concerns Jerusalem's AD 70 destruction);

in other words, Christ's one sacrifice put an end to all sacrifices. On the other hand, if Paul merely meant **SIN**, then that works just as well, fulfilling Daniel 9:24 (the context of which, again, concerns Jerusalem's AD 70 destruction).

> **VERSE 27-28A:** AND AS IT IS APPOINTED FOR MEN TO DIE ONCE, BUT AFTER THIS THE JUDGMENT, SO CHRIST WAS OFFERED ONCE TO BEAR THE SINS OF MANY.

Christ was a man, and as a man He lived and died never to come to Earth and live and die again; in Romans Paul put it this way: "CHRIST, HAVING BEEN RAISED FROM THE DEAD, DIES NO MORE. DEATH NO LONGER HAS DOMINION OVER HIM. FOR THE DEATH THAT HE DIED, HE DIED TO SIN ONCE FOR ALL" (6:9-10a).

The word **BUT** here denotes a contrast; in other words, the difference is that Jesus, instead of dying and being judged for His sin, died in order to provide forgiveness for our sin, thus making our individual judgments favorable.

There's no definite article before **JUDGMENT**, meaning that the judgment wasn't under consideration here; rather, at the time of one's death, he's already judged (regardless if he believes in a separate time of sentencing, i.e. whether he believes he goes directly to Heaven or not). Besides, *if Paul had the judgment in mind, why would that have any dependence upon the appointment of death upon men/mankind? Doesn't the Bible speak of men still being alive at the Lord's judgment?* (At the end of this section, there will be fifteen other versions of this verse quoted for consideration. Also the student might find it interesting that translators not only decided to supply the definite article in this passage, but they further decided to omit it from 1 Pet. 4:17. Chew upon that for a while. ☺)

Paul's indisputable point here is that Jesus' death for our reconciliation to God would no more be repeated than our individual deaths/judgments, implying no reincarnation!

The phrase **TO BEAR THE SINS OF MANY** may be another reference to the Old Testament scapegoat (Lev. 16, cf. Isa. 53:6).

> **VERSE 28B: TO THOSE WHO EAGERLY WAIT FOR HIM HE WILL APPEAR A SECOND TIME, APART FROM SIN FOR SALVATION.**

The phrase **EAGERLY WAIT FOR HIM** carries with it the idea of "intense yearning." And why would that be, especially in relation to these Hebrews? Because of their suffering of persecution by their Jewish brethren. But there's more.

Since the original of the phrase **A SECOND TIME** literally means "out of (εκ) a/the second" (*no word for "time" being found in the original*), this phrase (in this context of Jesus entering the most holy place with His blood, v. 24) obviously means that He was expected to reappear *out of the second place*—the most holy place (cf. 9:3). In other words, just as Aaron entered the most holy place with sin then reappeared without sin resulting in glory (Lev. 9:22-23), so Jesus entered Heaven with our sin and His cleansing blood, then reappeared without sin resulting in glory (salvation); in fact, the *Jonathan Mitchell New Testament* (JMNT), which takes great care in translating the original, renders the part of this verse about Jesus' reappearance as His coming "FORTH FROM OUT OF THE MIDST OF THE SECOND PLACE." Bingo!

This is the second appearance to people, but the third appearance of this passage: In chronological order and like the high priest on the Day of Atonement, Jesus first appeared to put away sin (v. 26), then He appeared before God with the sin-offering (v. 24), and lastly Paul referred to His appearance in glory (Col. 3:4) with salvation (v. 28). (Cf. Lev. 16:15-24.)

So what coming of Jesus is under consideration here? Well, in context it has reference to Christ's coming in AD 70. Why? Because Jesus' Day of Atonement work was completed within a generation—at the time of the end of the Old Covenant and the fully established New Covenant. (Essentially, one way to view this is that the old wife, Hagar, died at the cross when Deity became engaged to Sarah, Gal. 4:21-31; then Deity married Sarah ca. AD 70.)

When the work of High Priest Jesus was accomplished in the true holiest of all and God had accepted His sacrifice on behalf of mankind, He returned to once and for all time put an end to the Old Testament economy with all its remaining vestiges: Jerusalem, its temple, and its unacceptable sin-offerings which merely spit in the face of God's Son (cf. Heb. 10:29); this AD 70 coming of Messiah brought to fruition the redemption of mankind in all its totality.

In fact, isn't this exactly what Jesus promised His disciples when He foretold of these very times in Luke 21:28? "'NOW WHEN THESE THINGS BEGIN TO HAPPEN, LOOK UP AND LIFT YOUR HEADS, BECAUSE YOUR REDEMPTION DRAWS NEAR.'" Now let's consult some other words by Paul from Ephesians 1:13a-14. After speaking in verse 10 of how God was in the process of gathering all in Heaven and Earth together in Christ, he went on to write of the soon-to-arrive time of the fulfillment of that gathering and of what had been provided for them in the interim: "IN CHRIST YOU ALSO TRUSTED AFTER YOU HEARD ... THE GOSPEL OF YOUR SALVATION; IN WHOM ALSO, HAVING BELIEVED, YOU WERE SEALED WITH THE HOLY SPIRIT OF PROMISE, WHO IS THE GUARANTEE OF OUR INHERITANCE UNTIL THE REDEMPTION OF THE PURCHASED POSSESSION."

Even Peter used this idea to encourage suffering brethren: In First Peter 1:5 he wrote to them about "SALVATION READY TO BE REVEALED IN THE LAST TIME" or, as Paul put it here in Hebrews, "AT THE CONSUMMATION OF THE AGES" (v. 26). The thing is, if Christ did _not_ return or reappear from out of Heaven (Heb. 9:28), then the logical conclusion is that there's still, even today, no redemption or salvation for us! And who will admit to that?

One other issue of import: The original term translated as **FOR** here is the same as in Acts 2:38; in other words, it's εις which means "in order to attain." So here this tells us that Jesus didn't return because/after salvation was already attained, but _in order to attain_ completed salvation for us.

Hebrews 9:27 in Fifteen Versions
(From http://studybible.info/compare/Hebrews%209:27)

YLT: "As it is laid up to men once to die, and after this—judgment."

Darby: "Forasmuch as it is the portion of men once to die, and after this judgment."

Rotherham: "Inasmuch as it is in store for men—once for all to die, but after this, judgment."

20th Century: "As it is ordained for men to die but once (death being followed by judgment)."

WNT: "Since it is reserved for all mankind once to die, and afterwards to be judged."

Moffatt: "Just as it is appointed for men to die once and after that to be judged."

Goodspeed: "Just as men are destined to die once and after that to be judged."

Williams: "Just as men must die but once and after that be judged."

BBE: "Because by God's law death comes to men once, and after that they are judged."

LITV: "As it is reserved to men once to die, and after this judgment."

AUV: "Just as it is destined for people to die one time, and [then] after that to be judged."

ACV: "Inasmuch as it is reserved to men once to die, and after this, judgment."

WEB: "Inasmuch as it is appointed for men to die once, and after this, judgment."

CAB: "Just as it is appointed for men once to die, and after this judgment."

ISV: "Just as people are destined to die once and after that to be judged."

Hebrews 10:1-18

Beginning with chapter 8:1, Paul started dealing with the superiority of Christ's Law or covenant over that of Moses: chapter 8 concerned the better promises of Christ's covenant, while chapter 9 concerned the better sanctuary and sacrifice of Christ's covenant.

Here in chapter 10 Paul wrote of the superior results of that greater sacrifice and sanctuary. The first paragraph (vv. 1-10) teaches that, unlike Old Testament sacrifices, Christ's sacrifice actually/eternally removes sin, producing clear consciences, alluding back to the point found in 9:14.

> **VERSE 1:** FOR THE LAW, HAVING A SHADOW OF THE GOOD THINGS TO COME, AND NOT THE VERY IMAGE OF THOSE THINGS, CAN NEVER WITH THESE SAME SACRIFICES, WHICH THEY OFFER CONTINUALLY YEAR BY YEAR, MAKE THOSE WHO APPROACH PERFECT.

At the end of chapter 9 Paul was speaking specifically about the finality of Christ's single sacrifice—one that made His sacrifice better; that's why Paul began this verse with the word **FOR** or "because."

The word for **SHADOW** refers to something very general in nature, something lacking the details necessary to obtain a clear comprehension. On the other hand, the phrase for **VERY IMAGE** refers to something specific in nature, something possessing the details necessary to obtain a clear comprehension. So instead of Moses' Law portraying a very specific outline of **THE GOOD THINGS TO COME**, it merely provided a very generic outline of them.

This is reminiscent of the blind man of Bethsaida: after Jesus touched him the first time, he said that people looked like trees; then, after Jesus touched him the second time, he saw them clearly (Mark 8:22-25). (Perhaps this incident was meant to picture the very point we're making here.) Peter wrote that Moses' Law was so vague in its foreshadowings that even the angels couldn't comprehend exactly what God had in mind (1 Pet. 1:12; cf. Jesus' words in Mat. 13:16-17).

The idea that the Law was only "A SHADOW"—an abstract of something real—is the primary thing which made the Law of Moses and its sacrifices inferior to the Law of Christ and His sacrifice; in fact, the word "SHADOW" is emphatic in the original here (cf. Col. 2:14-17 & John 1:17 where "TRUTH" = "reality").

Saying that the Law possessed **A SHADOW OF THE GOOD THINGS TO COME** implies that the Law did <u>not</u> consist of those "GOOD THINGS," such as the salvation of 9:28 (cf. 8:4-5 & 9:9)!

The phrase **TO COME** is from μελλω which, as mentioned three times before (2:5, 6:5, & 9:11), refers to something "about to come, on the verge of transpiring." Why "on the verge"? Because the law hadn't yet been fulfilled (cf. Mat. 5:18); note the present tense verb "having" here and the present tense in Colossians 2:16-17 where Paul wrote that Old Testament things "<u>ARE</u>" shadows of things about to come.

The very idea that sacrifices were offered continually indicated that the Law was comprised of nothing but shadows or types of something real/eternal, needing no repetition.

The word for **PERFECT** simply refers to forgiveness (see "ONCE PURGED" in the next verse), the primary "GOOD THING" that the Law couldn't provide (cf. 7:19).

VERSES 2-4: FOR THEN WOULD THEY NOT HAVE CEASED TO BE OFFERED? FOR THE WORSHIPPERS, ONCE PURGED, WOULD HAVE HAD NO MORE CONSCIOUSNESS OF SINS. BUT IN THOSE SACRIFICES THERE IS A REMINDER OF SINS EVERY YEAR. FOR IT IS NOT POSSIBLE THAT THE BLOOD OF BULLS AND GOATS COULD TAKE AWAY SINS.

In other words, if Moses' Law could've resolved the fellowship problem between God and man, wouldn't those priests have ceased offering those sacrifices? This is a rhetorical question demanding a "Yes" response: once something is paid for, one doesn't continue paying for it; besides, repetition conflicts with finality.

The response would also logically be "Yes" because, if the people had been once-for-all forgiven, they wouldn't be reminded of those past sins. But, as verse 3 goes on to say, in those sacrifices they _were_ reminded of those sins that hadn't yet—before Christ—been forgiven forever, never to be remembered again (more about this at v. 17).

It's interesting that Paul, instead of saying "in those sacrifices there's remission of sins every year," said "IN THOSE SACRIFICES THERE'S A REMINDER OF SINS EVERY YEAR." (His employment of "SINS" plural indicates that he really was referring to the bringing-back-up of the sins they had committed in the past, not just to the idea that they were sinners in general.)

How sad it would've been to have lived under the Law: whereas they could have _no_ genuine clear/cleansed/good conscience, we today _do_ (or at least _can_) have such via a submissive faith (1 Pet. 3:21), followed by an uncondemning walk with God (1 John 1:7, 9, & 3:18-21).

The reason sins weren't removed under the Old Covenant is simply because the blood of animals couldn't effect the removal of sin. The question arises, however, "Why _can't_ animal blood effect the removal of sin?" The following are some possible answers:

1. To offer something _for_ _our_ _sin_ that doesn't belong to us (Psa. 50:10), that's of a lower order than we are (Gen. 1:26-28), and that isn't even accountable for its own actions is clearly unreasonable! So, and let's consider this as number...

2. There's no relation of any kind between our moral defilement and material sacrifices, animals, or otherwise (cf. Psa. 51:16-17 & Mic. 6:7). Now, although this sounds rational, I personally lean toward answer number...

3. The same reason that getting dipped in water can't eliminate sin is the same reason that animal blood can't eliminate it: they both depend on or point toward the only object that can ultimately eradicate it—the blood of Christ!

Nevertheless, it seems that all we can know for sure is that the nature of God's justice could only be satisfied with a perfect sacrifice—a sacrifice of course that could only be supplied by deity!

> **VERSES 5-7:** THEREFORE, WHEN HE CAME INTO THE WORLD, HE SAID: "SACRIFICE AND OFFERING YOU DID NOT DESIRE, BUT A BODY YOU HAVE PREPARED FOR ME. IN BURNT OFFERINGS AND SACRIFICES FOR SIN YOU HAD NO PLEASURE. THEN I SAID, 'BEHOLD, I HAVE COME—IN THE VOLUME OF THE BOOK IT IS WRITTEN OF ME—TO DO YOUR WILL, O GOD.'"

This is from Psalm 40:7-9, the theme of which is that deliverance from sin is not procured by animal sacrifices, but by one who would perfectly discharge/satisfy the will of God.

The **SACRIFICE AND OFFERING** and the **BURNT OFFERINGS AND SACRIFICES** phrases refer to the work of the Levitical priesthood.

When it says that God **HAD NO PLEASURE** in them, it didn't mean that they weren't part of His will for His Old Covenant people, for it was (cf. v. 8); it rather meant that there was no satisfaction for sin found in those shadows/types. (The tenses in this passage don't allow for it to refer only to God's displeasure of Levitical offerings between AD 30 & 70.)

The clause **I HAVE COME ... TO DO YOUR WILL** implies two things: {1} unlike animals, Jesus obeyed God's will, and, unlike humans, did so perfectly (even unto death, Php. 2:8); and {2} His incarnation and sacrifice were accomplished voluntarily.

The phrase **A BODY ... PREPARED FOR ME** clearly indicates {1} that, unlike you and I, Jesus existed before this incarnation, and {2} that God Himself supplied the sacrifice.

Our word **VOLUME** (which, by the way, is the correct translation of the original term here) is from the Latin "volvo" (yes, like the car) which means "to roll"; thus "volume" came to refer to a large _scroll_, in this case probably the volume of the five books of Moses, since very little else had yet been written by the time of David.

The Torah not only included prophecies, but also shadows/types of the coming Messiah. The reason Paul used this Old Testament prophecy was the same reason he used such all through Hebrews (e.g. vv. 16-17)—to demonstrate that even their own Scriptures proved what he affirmed.

> **VERSES 8-9:** PREVIOUSLY SAYING, "SACRIFICE AND OFFERING, BURNT OFFERINGS, AND OFFERINGS FOR SIN YOU DID NOT DESIRE, NOR HAD PLEASURE IN THEM" (WHICH ARE OFFERED ACCORDING TO THE LAW), THEN HE SAID, "BEHOLD, I HAVE COME TO DO YOUR WILL, O GOD." HE TAKES AWAY THE FIRST THAT HE MAY ESTABLISH THE SECOND.

Paul merely repeated himself in order to demonstrate that the Messiah (who was a Jew, a son of David who wrote Psalm 40) acknowledged that God's ultimate pleasure was not to be found in all those Old Testament sacrifices/offerings. So the Messiah willingly accomplished that which would provide ultimate pleasure to God—He'd live the perfect human life, then become the once-for-all perfect sacrifice and High Priest between God and men, reconciling them by means of a new priesthood and covenant (cf. 7:18-19).

Let's not fail to see in this connection that not only was Paul contrasting a perfect sacrifice with imperfect sacrifices, but that he was also contrasting all those _numerous_ sacrifices with Christ's _one_ sacrifice.

One other thing of note is that this is yet another place in which Paul employed the present tense to indicate something transpiring when he wrote: literally it reads, "He _is_ taking away the first" to "establish the second."

> **VERSE 10:** BY THAT WILL WE HAVE BEEN SANCTIFIED THROUGH THE OFFERING OF THE BODY OF JESUS CHRIST ONCE FOR ALL.

The phrase **THAT WILL** refers to the will of God to have Jesus perfectly take the place of the Old Testament sacrifices; by His fulfillment of God's will in this manner, Jesus has indeed set the bar high, compelling us to obey, for obedience is preferable to every (imperfect) sacrifice imaginable (1 Sam. 15:22).

The word for **SANCTIFIED** means "to be cleansed, thus set apart to and for God" (more about this at v. 14).

Just as one sacrifice was contrasted to numerous sacrifices in verse 9, so here the once-for-all-time sacrifice of Jesus is contrasted to the repeated sacrifices of the Old Testament. Thus Paul has demonstrated that the divine authority which instituted the Levitical priesthood and sacrifices is the same authority which abolished them; in other words, it's by God's will that the first covenant was taken away in order that the second may be established—only Jesus' single sacrifice is now acceptable.

> **VERSES 11-12:** AND EVERY PRIEST STANDS MINISTERING DAILY AND OFFERING REPEATEDLY THE SAME SACRIFICES WHICH CAN NEVER TAKE AWAY SINS. BUT THIS MAN, AFTER HE HAD OFFERED ONE SACRIFICE FOR SINS FOREVER, SAT DOWN AT THE RIGHT HAND OF GOD...

Similar to many other passages already noted in these studies on Hebrews, this one indicates that the temple was still open for business at the time of this epistle; this means that the Aaronic priests refused to accept the sign of the temple's soon coming conclusion when, at Jesus' death, the veil of the temple was torn from top to bottom. So they continued offering sacrifices according to the Law of Moses, even though their Messiah had come to take their places.

These sacrifices were offered repeatedly precisely because they were imperfect; so imperfect, in fact, that, no matter how many times they were repeated, they'd never reach the desired goal—true atonement of the soul, that which the single sacrifice of Christ accomplished forevermore.

Note the Parallels Between...

Verse 1	& Verse 11
The Law	The Priests
Yearly	Daily
Sacrifices	Sacrifices
Can Never Perfect	Can Never Remove

It seems impossible for one to <u>not</u> notice that, whereas the Old Testament priests stood as restless servants, Jesus was pictured in verse 12 as sitting at rest.

By the way, there's no word here in the original for **MAN**; the word that evidently should've been supplied here is "Priest": in other words, while <u>those</u> priests do that, <u>this</u> Priest did this!

> **VERSE 13:** ...FROM THAT TIME WAITING TILL HIS ENEMIES ARE MADE HIS FOOTSTOOL (CF. 1:13).

The idea of verses 12 & 13 are taken directly from Psalm 110:1. The question is, Who are/were these **ENEMIES**? According to Jesus Himself, His enemies (plural) at least included the Jews who rejected Him. Speaking in a prophetic parable about them, He said, "'BRING HERE THOSE ENEMIES OF MINE WHO DID NOT WANT ME TO REIGN OVER THEM, AND SLAY THEM BEFORE ME'" (Luke 19:27, cf. Luke 20:17-19). In Romans 11:28 and Philippians 3:18 Paul said that unbelieving Jews were the enemies; and in Revelation 2:9 and 3:9 Jesus called Judaism the synagogue of του σατανα (the satanas)—the enemy.

The only other thing that might be included in the category of "ENEMIES" here would be found in First Corinthians 15:26: "THE LAST ENEMY THAT SHALL BE DESTROYED IS DEATH"; and what's interesting about this statement is that Paul, later in that same chapter, said that "THE STING OF DEATH IS SIN, AND THE STRENGTH OF SIN IS" ... What? ... "THE LAW" (v. 56), an idea of course which fits right into these studies in Hebrews from what's often referred to as "a preterist (an in-the-past or fulfilled) perspective."

As far as the **FOOTSTOOL** motif here is concerned, it's an allusion to the ancient custom of placing one's foot on the neck of a defeated enemy (cf. Jsh. 10:22-25); some of the more haughty victors used their defeated enemies as footstools from which to mount their horses. (Cf. notes at 1:13.)

> **VERSE 14: FOR BY ONE OFFERING HE HAS PERFECTED FOREVER THOSE WHO ARE BEING SANCTIFIED.**

Again, as mentioned various times before in these studies, the word **PERFECTED** refers to "a state of consummation or completion," in this letter often with reference to once-for-all forgiveness of sin.

When this verse (as with 2:11) speaks of **BEING SANCTIFIED**, it isn't referring to individuals being sanctified over a period of time (as many teach, contradicting Paul's immediate point); rather, Paul here meant that the **ONE** [single] **OFFERING** of Jesus (as opposed to the repeated offerings of animals) completes or finalizes forgiveness/redemption/reconciliation/eternal life, thus saints with "NO MORE CONSCIOUSNESS OF SINS" (v. 2)!

> **VERSES 15-17: AND THE HOLY SPIRIT ALSO WITNESSES TO US, FOR AFTER HE HAD SAID BEFORE, "THIS IS THE COVENANT THAT I WILL MAKE WITH THEM AFTER THOSE DAYS, SAYS THE LORD: I WILL PUT MY LAWS INTO THEIR HEARTS, AND IN THEIR MINDS I WILL WRITE THEM," THEN HE ADDS, "THEIR SINS AND THEIR LAWLESS DEEDS I WILL REMEMBER NO MORE."**

Before he quoted from Jeremiah here, Paul, as he knew his Jewish brethren would agree, affirmed the inspiration of this prophet. Why? Because he was clinching his argument on the finality of the New Covenant by challenging them to accept Jeremiah's prophecy and thus the New Testament, or reject the New Testament and so also their own prophet.

As discussed at 8:10, the idea here is that the New Covenant is of a spiritual/eternal nature; hence, by virtue of the fact that God saves man by grace, man thereby has the ultimate motivation from within to obey out of <u>gratitude</u> for this gift, instead of in an attempt to <u>merit</u> this gift.

Still another way to look at this is that, while people became part of the Old Covenant through birth (not knowing what they were doing), people become part of the New Covenant by choice—by mind and heart, not by flesh. In fact, right after Psalm 110:1 (to which Paul just alluded in verses 12 & 13), David wrote/said to God in verse 3 that "YOUR PEOPLE SHALL BE <u>VOLUNTEERS</u> IN THE DAY OF YOUR POWER"—in the Messianic age.

The main point of Paul here in verse 17 is about how sin, unlike in the Old Testament times, is remembered **NO MORE** in the New Testament era, supporting of course the point of verse 14 earlier.

> **VERSE 18: NOW WHERE THERE IS REMISSION OF THESE, THERE IS NO LONGER AN OFFERING FOR SIN** (CF. 10:26).

In other words, there's no other offering necessary, nor should there be another offering made, for that would express misgivings in God's new arrangement.

The consequences of sin are threefold: {1} debt requiring forgiveness, {2} bondage requiring redemption, and {3} alienation requiring reconciliation; and all of these—forgiveness/redemption/reconciliation—are found only in the Christ!

IN SUMMARY OF 10:1-18

Verses 1-4 deal with the _inadequacy_ of the Law's necessity for repeated sacrifices for sins.

>Verses 5-10 deal with the repeated sacrifices being superseded by the single sacrifice of the Christ.

>Verses 11-14 deal with the Levitical priests being superseded by the single Priest who's enthroned at God's right hand.

Verses 15-18 deal with the _adequacy_ of the New Covenant which makes repeated sacrifices unnecessary.

Hebrews 10:19-31

Paul began this grand epistle in chapters 1–7 by discussing *The Superiority of Christ's Person* (1:1–4:13) and *Priesthood* (4:14–7:28). Then in chapter 8:1–10:18 he focused on *The Superiority of Christ's Pact*. At this point the reader comes upon the last main division of Hebrews, chapter 10:19–13:25, in which he encounters Paul's dissertation concerning *The Superiority of Christ's Principle*.

Paul's initial point here (as noted in the outline) is that *Christ's Faith-Principle Is the Response to Superior Things* (10:19-39, verses that lead into the famous faith-discussion of chapter 11). However, since to deal with the 10:19-39 all at once would make for too lengthy a chapter, we'll begin analyzing this section by considering only verses 19-31.

> **VERSES 19-21:** [THESE VERSES SUMMARIZE ALL OF HEBREWS 1:1–10:18.] **THEREFORE, BRETHREN, HAVING BOLDNESS TO ENTER THE HOLIEST BY THE BLOOD OF JESUS, BY A NEW AND LIVING WAY WHICH HE CONSECRATED FOR US, THROUGH THE VEIL, THAT IS, HIS FLESH, AND HAVING A HIGH PRIEST OVER THE HOUSE OF GOD...**

Because death was the penalty, Old Testament worshippers weren't bold enough to enter into the holy of holies—into God's presence, but after Christ's sacrifice they could and did have **BOLDNESS** to enter into God's presence (cf. Eph. 3:11b-12).

The word for **NEW** literally means "freshly-slain," and the word for **WAY** is the term for "road." So while in Old Testament times the high priest sprinkled the blood of sacrifice on the ground seven times on his way to the earthly dwelling place of God (Lev. 16:14), today we have Jesus' blood leading us into reconciliation and the presence of God (cf. notes on 2:10).

This passage is saying essentially the same thing that Jesus Himself said: "'I AM THE WAY'" (John 14:6); in other words, He's the freshly-slain road, who (unlike the Old Testament slain) still lives! And since He's a **LIVING** sacrifice (being always "freshly-slain," so to speak), no other sacrifice is necessary.

The word for **CONSECRATED** here refers to the fact that (as in 9:18) Christ's blood has "set apart" or "dedicated" this road for us, implying that this way is "THE WAY" that He established or opened up for business on our behalf.

By the phrase **THROUGH THE VEIL, THAT IS, HIS FLESH** Paul reminded his readers of the veil that barred man's access to God, the veil that the high priest *pushed aside* as He entered the holy of holies. Similarly, until Jesus' humanity was *put aside* on the cross, man was barred from access to God—an uncrucified savior would've been no savior at all; so when His body was destroyed, His Father destroyed the temple's inner veil (Mat. 27:51), indicating the imminent demise of the entire temple and its standing in the eyes of God (cf. remarks at 9:8-10).

Paul seemed to be saying the same thing here that he said in verses 5-10; in other words, by Jesus taking upon Himself a human form, He could/did sacrifice Himself that He—through His shed blood/death/resurrection/ascension—might eradicate the first way (the old/dead way) in order to establish the second way (the new/living way).

Concerning the phrase **A HIGH PRIEST** here, this is actually the one place where Paul used the phrase "a great priest" instead of a High Priest, apparently to describe/contrast Jesus' priesthood with all who had gone before Him; interestingly, Paul called Jesus all of the following: priest (7:11), high priest (9:11), great priest (10:21), and great high priest (4:14).

Earlier Paul spoke of how that, while Moses was merely part of God's house (3:5), Jesus is "OVER HIS OWN HOUSE" (3:1 & 6). I bring this up because it's noteworthy that Paul repeats that idea here, but instead of calling it the house of Jesus as in 3:6, he called it **THE HOUSE OF GOD**, paralleling the term "GOD" with Jesus (for those who claim Jesus wasn't/isn't deity)!

Something else of import is this: although one could say that "THE HOUSE OF GOD" here is "THE CHURCH OF THE LIVING GOD" (per 1 Tim. 3:15), Paul obviously had more than the saints living on Earth in mind (cf. 8:1-2). Therefore, based on this acceptable boldness, based on this great high priest, and based on everything Paul had written thus far, he launched into a series of exhortations concerning their <u>faith</u> (v. 22 & chapter 11), <u>hope</u> (v. 23 & chapter 12), and <u>love</u> (vv. 24-25 & chapter 13), that which he also touched on in First Corinthians 13:13.

> **VERSE 22:** ...LET US DRAW NEAR WITH A TRUE HEART IN FULL ASSURANCE OF FAITH, HAVING OUR HEARTS SPRINKLED FROM AN EVIL CONSCIENCE AND OUR BODIES WASHED WITH PURE WATER.

In some cases in the Bible the phrase **LET US** is in the imperative mood, meaning that it's a direct command; but here it's in the subjunctive mood, meaning that Paul was arguing for something that they should logically do: "Because we did that, we should also do this!" In fact, the next three "LET US" phrases literally mean "we should," indicating that Paul was saying this because his readers had the faith/boldness to enter into God's presence (i.e. become Christians) in the first place, and because they had the Messiah as their great eternal high priest, they should likewise do this (v. 22), that (v. 23), and the other (vv. 24-25). (Cf. Luke 14:28-31.)

The idea of "A GREAT PRIEST" corresponds to how they could (or why they should) **DRAW NEAR** to God, while the idea of "BOLDNESS" corresponds to the phrase **FULL ASSURANCE OF FAITH**—the boldness that faith prompts; in other words, they were being provoked to draw near to God via the springboard of confidence in the work of Christ that was about to be completed.

Why is this drawing near a drawing near <u>to God</u>? Because this context is parallel to 4:14-16. The main point of this passage is continuing to draw near, instead of drawing back (v. 39).

Remembering that Paul was writing to Christians here (v. 19), the idea of drawing near with a true heart corresponds to John 4:24 where Jesus said that God's people must worship Him in truth.

The last clause of this verse expands on the first part of verses 19-20. In other words, **HAVING THEIR HEARTS SPRINKLED FROM AN EVIL CONSCIENCE AND THEIR BODIES WASHED WITH PURE WATER** is how they entered into the presence of God by the blood of Jesus; it's also what occurred when they chose that freshly-slain and living way that Jesus consecrated.

The word for **SPRINKLED** refers not to water but to the blood of Christ, meaning that just as priests sprinkled blood on items to be purified in the Old Testament (9:13 & 22), so Jesus' blood purifies the conscience now (9:14). (Consider Jesus' shed blood, baptism, and the conscience relative to the following passages: John 19:31-34, Rom. 6:3-6, & 1 Pet. 3:21.)

The phrase **EVIL CONSCIENCE** doesn't refer to a wicked conscience, but to a consciousness of evil/sin.

The phrase **PURE WATER** refers to unmixed water; in the Old Testament the water used for purification was mixed with ashes (9:13 & Num. 19:1-10), while such isn't necessary in New Testament baptism.

(Side-note: Since Paul was evidently echoing Ezekiel 36:25, the serious Bible student should consider how the Jewish prophecy of Ezekiel 36–37 applies here.)

Just as the Old Testament priests undergo various washings and apply blood on Atonement Day (Lev. 16), and just as Jesus shed water and blood on the cross (John 19:34), so it takes both water and blood to reconcile (to make "at-one") a person, rendering him a Christian, someone who belongs to God in body and spirit (1 Cor. 6:20); as Jesus said, "'BLESSED ARE THE PURE IN HEART, FOR THEY SHALL SEE [AS IN 'KNOW'] GOD.'"

VERSE 23: LET US HOLD FAST THE CONFESSION OF OUR HOPE WITHOUT WAVERING, FOR HE WHO PROMISED IS FAITHFUL.

While the previous verse speaks of what God did, this verse speaks of what they were to do: **HOLD FAST**.

It's interesting that, after speaking of faith and baptism, Paul also brought up the concept of **CONFESSION**—obviously their confession of Jesus as the promised Messiah who would make all things new.

The word **WAVERING** is from a term meaning "to lean backwards," thus, since hope is always ahead, they needed to continuously lean or press forward; so the point was that, if they went back to the old Law, they'd be forsaking their previous confession of the Messiah and His mission.

Probably writing to some of the very people who had left Christ because they lost hope in His ever coming (perhaps even people who were leading others away), Peter wrote, "THE LORD IS NOT SLACK CONCERNING HIS PROMISE" (2 Pet. 3:9). (For an in-depth study of 2 Pet. 3, see ASiteForTheLord.com/id15.html.)

> **VERSES 24-25:** AND LET US CONSIDER ONE ANOTHER IN ORDER TO STIR UP LOVE AND GOOD WORKS, NOT FORSAKING THE ASSEMBLING OF OURSELVES TOGETHER AS IS THE MANNER OF SOME, BUT EXHORTING ONE ANOTHER, AND SO MUCH THE MORE AS YOU SEE THE DAY APPROACHING.

To **CONSIDER** means "to perceive clearly and fully," meaning that the best way for them to help ward off apostasy for themselves and others was to give a lot of serious thought to each brother's/sister's individual circumstances, tendencies, abilities, etc.

The phrase **TO STIR UP** [excite/incite] **LOVE AND GOOD WORKS** would be the best way to prevent apostasy because, by helping others in their various situations, they'd keep their minds off themselves and their own problems. (Such is an axiom which always works, even in our day and time.)

The phrase **NOT FORSAKING** simply means not giving up on their gathering together.

THE ASSEMBLING is a verbal noun (a gerund), a phrase depicting an action as if it were a noun (the end-result of an action in such a case as this one).

Note two other significant points: {1} "THE ASSEMBLING" is singular, not plural as is usually implied by the way this verse is applied to weekly meetings of corporate worship; and {2} "ASSEMBLING" has a definite article preceding it. So, due to what we've just noted, and due to the context having reference to their forsaking their confession and hope, and due to the fact that the only other place this exact phrase is found (and by the same writer) is in Second Thessalonians 2:1 where Paul was speaking about the gathering together of the saints at the coming of Christ, it would be dishonest of me to avoid taking the position that such is what Paul was also talking about here. Notice: In that Thessalonian passage Paul said, "CONCERNING THE COMING OF OUR LORD ... AND OUR GATHERING (or "assembling" [note the "ing"]) TOGETHER TO HIM...." And this corresponds very well of course to Jesus' own words when in Matthew 24:31 He spoke of how at His coming His messengers would "GATHER TOGETHER HIS ELECT," a statement He made, by the way, before He went on to say that "THIS GENERATION WILL BY NO MEANS PASS AWAY UNTIL ALL THESE THINGS ARE FULFILLED" (v. 34). Luke's parallel to this has Jesus saying, "'WHEN THESE THINGS BEGIN TO HAPPEN, LOOK UP AND LIFT UP YOUR HEADS, BECAUSE YOUR REDEMPTION [AND THE KINGDOM] DRAWS NEAR'" or "is approaching" (21:28 & 31). (Cf. Eze. 11:17 for the background promise of God.)

The word for **EXHORTING** means to motivate someone by whatever means necessary, whether it be comforting/instructing/warning/rebuking or even begging ... just about anything to excite/inspire someone to move or keep moving in the right direction (cf. *Greek-English Lexicon of the New Testament* by Joseph Thayer).

So what's **THE DAY APPROACHING**? Whatever day this is, it obviously must correspond to the following criteria: {1} it must fit the context; {2} due to the definite article "THE" [an article of antecedent] it must have already been mentioned; {3} it must have been a day common to all of them; {4} it must have been a day they could "SEE ... APPROACHING"; and {5} it must have been the kind of a day that would cause them to be more diligent in exhortation as it drew near.

So what day would fit all of this criteria? The day of their deaths? No (cf. nos. 1-4). The first day of the week? No (cf. nos. 2 & 5). An end-of-time judgment day? No (cf. nos. 2 & 4). So the only appropriate answer appears to be the day of the Lord AD 70 (cf. 8:13, 9:28b, 10:13, 27, & 37-38; also Mat. 24:15 & 33). After all, not only did this day alleviate Christian persecution (cf. no. 1), but it also totally removed any vestiges of the Old Covenant associated with sin/death so that the New Covenant associated with the kingdom of righteousness/life could appear in its fullness (cf. no. 1).

In summary of verse 25, surely it's impossible for one <u>not</u> to see that Paul had in mind the fulfillment of the prophecy of Jeremiah 4:5-6! The honest student must read and consider.

VERSES 26-27: For if we sin willfully after we have received the knowledge of the truth, there no longer remains a sacrifice for sins, but a certain fearful expectation of judgment and fiery indignation which will devour the adversaries.

The initial **FOR** here was apparently chosen to motivate the reader to believe that Paul was basing this statement on the entirety of the previous paragraph wherein he spoke of what they should do: instead of deserting the Christ, they should draw near to God by holding fast to their first love and by keeping each other motivated in that direction.

To **SIN WILLFULLY** is to sin knowing full well what one is doing; it isn't being "OVERTAKEN" in a fault (per Gal. 6:1) or committing a sin in "IGNORANCE" (per Heb. 9:7)—it's a deliberate <u>persistency</u> in a sin, here the sin of apostasy.

The original for **KNOWLEDGE** is a term for profuse or complete knowledge, not sparse or partial knowledge.

If this **JUDGMENT** is kept in context, it's obvious that it has reference to <u>the</u> judgment of <u>the</u> day (or the judgment day) of verse 25; in fact, everything in the rest of this chapter finds its basis in the day of verse 25. Due to that day that they could see approaching, Paul cautioned them to not forsake their assembling together to Him (cf. 2 The. 2:1). The next statement then begins with the explanatory term "BECAUSE," going on to speak of the fear to be experienced (v. 31) in God's punishment (v. 30) of fiery indignation (v. 27) upon the enemy.

Then, to top it off, Paul recautioned them to remain confident and faithful, for that day was to come upon their world in a very, very little while (v. 37). Besides, verse 27 is an obvious quote of Zephaniah 1:8, a prophecy of Jerusalem's demise. Before quoting that, keep in mind that **INDIGNATION** here may be translated as "jealousy." "NEITHER THEIR SILVER NOR THEIR GOLD SHALL BE ABLE TO DELIVER THEM IN THE DAY OF THE LORD'S WRATH; BUT THE WHOLE LAND SHALL BE DEVOURED BY THE FIRE OF HIS JEALOUSY (i.e. indignation), FOR HE WILL MAKE A SPEEDY RIDDANCE OF ALL THOSE WHO DWELL IN THE LAND." One more evidence is this: as is used ten other times in Hebrews, the word **WILL** is again from μελλω which means "about to," making it even more obvious that Paul had in mind the demise of Judaism in AD 70. (Paul McReynold's *Word Study Greek-English New Testament* translates μελλω as "about to" <u>all</u> 109 times.)

Although it very well could refer to literal fire in reference to Jerusalem's destruction (and its attendant gehenna), **FIERY** here doesn't necessarily have to be interpreted literally; it could rather refer merely to "intensity," such as in the statement that "Fred has a fiery or hot temper."

Continuing the idea behind the word "FIERY," the word **DEVOUR** means to "eat up"; in other words, just as a literal fire eats up practically everything in its path, so the wrath of God would annihilate pretty much everything Jewish.

THE ADVERSARIES (plural) are primarily the Christ-rejecting Jews and persecutors of God's true-blue Jews (cf. 1:13 & 10:13 for more thoughts on this).

So since they knew full well what was right, Paul was merely making sure they understood the consequence of deserting Christ, especially at this ominous point in time, for they'd be forsaking the only sacrifice capable of reconciling them to

God, meaning that the only thing they'd have to look forward to was the same indictment and condemnation that their Christ-rejecting Jewish brethren would receive, and perhaps even worse (vv. 28ff, cf. Luke 12:42-48).

Thus they needed to choose who they'd be more afraid of: those who could throw sticks and stones at them or He who could forever destroy them in gehenna (Mat. 10:28)?

> **VERSE 28:** ANYONE WHO HAS REJECTED MOSES' LAW DIES WITHOUT MERCY ON THE TESTIMONY OF TWO OR THREE WITNESSES.

In other words, if Moses had the right to attach the sentence of death to apostasy from his inferior law (forsaking Yahweh for other gods, Deu. 13:6-11 & 17:2-7), how much more of a right does God have to attach such a sentence to apostasy from His superior law (forsaking His Son for Moses)?

(Note the present tense here, again indicating that the Law was still considered in effect in AD 63; cf. 8:13 & 9:8-10.)

> **VERSE 29:** OF HOW MUCH WORSE PUNISHMENT, DO YOU SUPPOSE, WILL HE BE THOUGHT WORTHY WHO HAS TRAMPLED THE SON OF GOD UNDERFOOT, COUNTED THE BLOOD OF THE COVENANT BY WHICH HE WAS SANCTIFIED A COMMON THING, AND INSULTED THE SPIRIT OF GRACE?

To trample Jesus underfoot (as pigs trample pearls, Mat. 7:6) means to treat Him with the same contempt as those who stripped Him, slapped Him, whipped Him, spat on Him, and finally crucified Him (cf. 1 Cor. 11:27)!

Corresponding to "KNOWLEDGE" in verse 26, **COUNTED** refers to a conscious judgment resting on a deliberate weighing of the facts, implying an intentional rejection of Jesus' sacrifice and essentially saying that His blood is no more significant than the blood of the thieves crucified with Him.

The Spirit was the source of the miraculous gifts bestowed on the first generation Christians as further proof of Christ's claims and His New Covenant (cf. 6:4-6); so to turn back to Moses and his covenant was to blaspheme the Spirit—to commit the unforgivable sin. Why? Because without Christ, sin cannot be forgiven.

> **VERSES 30-31: FOR WE KNOW HIM WHO SAID, "VENGEANCE IS MINE, I WILL REPAY," SAYS THE LORD. AND AGAIN, "THE LORD WILL JUDGE HIS PEOPLE." [SO] IT IS A FEARFUL THING TO FALL INTO THE HANDS OF THE LIVING GOD.**

Paul was again alluding to an Old Covenant promise of God found in Deuteronomy 32 (specifically verses 35-36), a chapter which includes the foretelling of Jerusalem's end-of-the-age destruction (cf. verses 18, 21, & 32, as well as 35-36).

Paul also echoed this in Romans 12:19 where he taught those recipients not to take revenge on their enemies, for God claimed that right; in other words, Paul was implying that God's vengeance wouldn't be so much for Himself as for the maltreatment of His people. But here in Hebrews he added the warning that, even if they had become part of God's people, they'd still have to answer to Him if they renounced Him, His ways, and His people (especially to the point of causing trouble for them).

The phrase **LIVING GOD** is used in the Bible in opposition to (dead) idols, corresponding perfectly to the usual manner of apostasy in the Old Testament—leaving Yahweh for idols, that which God considered (spiritual) adultery (cf. notes at v. 28).

Hebrews 10:32-39

Back in 10:19 is where Paul began applying all his preceding thoughts, as well as where he began heading toward his conclusion by writing about *Christ's Superior Principle of Faith.*

Hebrews 10:19-39 concern Christ's faith-principle being the only appropriate response to all those superior matters about which Paul had previously written; in fact, verses 19-21 sum up everything from 1:1–10:18.

Then in verses 22-25 Paul essentially outlined the next three chapters by encouraging faith, hope, and love in his audience of those who were—one by one—deserting Christ, while in verses 26-31 he warned them about the consequences of such a decision.

Now in verses 32-39 we find a call to perseverance based on God's faithfulness (something Paul actually brought to mind in verse 23).

One other thing worthy of note here is that Paul was still repeating himself some: Just as it was previously indicated that verses 26-31 are parallel to 6:4-8, so now we'll see how verses 32-39 are clearly parallel to 6:9-12. This means that after he warned them he attempted to encourage them by expressing the faith in them that they could still turn things around. And it's interesting that this expression of faith in them wasn't based on the fact that other saints had persevered or were persevering (as he went on to deal with later in chapter 11), but on the fact that they themselves had once done well under great persecution for Christ.

> **VERSE 32: BUT RECALL THE FORMER DAYS IN WHICH, AFTER YOU WERE ILLUMINATED, YOU ENDURED A GREAT STRUGGLE WITH SUFFERINGS...**

The word **RECALL** is in the present not aorist tense, indicating that they were to keep their earlier days as energetic, dynamic Christians ever before them.

The term **ILLUMINATED** simply means that they were made aware of the Christ and had accepted Him, which in turn means that Paul was referring to a time immediately after they became Christians, a time when they had that initial zeal for Christ (cf. 6:4).

The phrase **GREAT STRUGGLE** is from the Greek term for the English word "athletic"; the verb form originally meant "to contend in games." So Paul was talking about a fierce conflict with the forces of evil; in fact, according to 12:4 it seems that what they had suffered earlier was as much as could be suffered short of bloodshed. Perhaps they had come through the same difficult circumstances to which Paul alluded in First Thessalonians 2:14-16 (cf. Acts 8:1-3).

> **VERSE 33: ...PARTLY WHILE YOU WERE MADE A SPECTACLE BOTH BY REPROACHES AND TRIBULATIONS, AND PARTLY WHILE YOU BECAME COMPANIONS OF THOSE WHO WERE SO TREATED...**

The word for **SPECTACLE** is from the Greek term for the English expression "theater," yes, as in the Roman amphitheater; however, while the Romans usually used wild beasts against Christians in this public place, the Jews (the chief persecutors of *Jewish* Christians at this time) publicly brought "REPROACHES AND TRIBULATIONS" of other sorts against them.

TRIBULATIONS referred to the physical suffering which included imprisonments (cf. 2 Cor. 11:22-33), while **REPROACHES** referred to the emotional suffering that included false charges (cf. Rev. 16:13-14), reminiscent of how "devil" means "false accuser."

Not only were they personally harassed for accepting Jesus as the Messiah, but they were also harassed for emotionally supporting, physically harboring, and even financially aiding others who were being persecuted for accepting Jesus as the Christ (cf. 6:10).

> **VERSE 34:** ...**FOR YOU HAD COMPASSION ON ME IN MY CHAINS, AND JOYFULLY ACCEPTED THE PLUNDERING OF YOUR GOODS, KNOWING THAT YOU HAVE A BETTER AND AN ENDURING POSSESSION FOR YOURSELVES IN HEAVEN.**

As most other versions support, the best manuscripts omit the personal pronouns, reading, "YOU HAD COMPASSION ON THOSE IN PRISON," which actually corresponds better to the context: Paul was reminding them of the early days of their Christianity, likely a reference to a time thirty years earlier, and a time when the Apostle Paul was still the Pharisee Saul.

The word **COMPASSION** here, like the word "VISIT" in James 1:27, carries with it some type of action, perhaps even the same action as the word "VISIT" in James; in other words, the word "VISIT" doesn't mean to merely pop in on people, but to actually physically help those in need with food, medicine, clothing, etc. In fact, it appears that at that time/place in history, the needs of prisoners weren't provided by the government, meaning that prisoner-provisions were made by family/friends.

The term **PLUNDERING** brings to mind a "seizure" or a "confiscation," implying two motives: it could refer to a mere form of persecution, or it could (and likely does) refer to disinheritance as a Jew. See, in the eyes of apostate Israel, when a Jew forsook Moses for Jesus, his share of the property was withheld from him, and his credit and every source of gain was withdrawn (cf. Rev. 13:16-17). (Such makes one wonder if this could've been the reason for the event in Acts 4:34-35 & 6:1-3.)

(Actually, non-Christian Jews were considered "apostate" Israel because they were the ones who forsook Moses. Why? Because if they truly believed Moses, they would've accepted Jesus, for Moses wrote of Him [John 5:46]! Besides, isn't this why Jesus called apostate Jews "THE SYNAGOGUE [or church] OF SATAN," Rev. 2:9 & 3:9?)

Getting back to the motives, surely it's also possible that Paul meant to include both motives: to persecute them and to confiscate their possessions in order to disinherit them. The question is, How could they endure these **JOYFULLY**? Because they knew they had a superior/eternal possession on its way from Heaven (Rev. 21:2). Jesus once said, "'Do NOT LAY UP FOR YOURSELVES TREASURES ON EARTH, WHERE MOTH AND RUST DESTROY, AND WHERE THIEVES BREAK IN AND STEAL; BUT LAY UP FOR YOURSELVES TREASURES IN HEAVEN, WHERE NEITHER MOTH NOR RUST DESTROYS AND WHERE THIEVES DO NOT BREAK IN AND STEAL'" (Mat. 6:19-20). And He also said, "'BLESSED [JOYFUL] ARE THOSE WHO ARE PERSECUTED FOR RIGHTEOUSNESS' SAKE, FOR THEIRS IS THE KINGDOM OF HEAVEN. BLESSED ARE YOU WHEN THEY REVILE AND PERSECUTE YOU AND SAY ALL KINDS OF EVIL AGAINST YOU FALSELY FOR MY SAKE. REJOICE AND BE EXCEEDINGLY GLAD, FOR GREAT IS YOUR REWARD IN HEAVEN...'" (Mat. 5:10-12a).

Well, now that Paul has reminded them of God's past faithfulness to them under difficult circumstances (hardships that they had even come through without bloodshed), he continued to encourage them "to keep on keeping on" based on God's future faithfulness! Connected to Matthew 5:12...

VERSE 35: THEREFORE DO NOT CAST AWAY YOUR CONFIDENCE, WHICH HAS A GREAT REWARD.

Paul was urging these brethren to not discard that wondrous **CONFIDENCE** they possessed back in the beginning of their Christian walk; this is reminiscent of 3:6 where he told them to hold fast their confidence to the end ... when the reward of reconciliation and righteousness would be attained.

Per 11:1, "CONFIDENCE" is faith-induced; and in Ephesians 6:16 Paul referred to faith as the shield in a soldier's armor. What's interesting about this is that he may have been alluding to the conduct of weak and cowardly soldiers who, in the day of battle would throw aside their shields and retreat, something considered especially dishonorable.

The phrase **GREAT REWARD** brings to mind First Corinthians 15:58 where Paul wrote, "BE STEADFAST, IMMOVABLE, ALWAYS ABOUNDING IN THE WORK OF THE LORD, KNOWING THAT YOUR LABOR IS NOT IN VAIN IN THE LORD."

> **VERSE 36:** FOR YOU HAVE NEED OF ENDURANCE, SO THAT AFTER YOU HAVE DONE THE WILL OF GOD YOU MAY RECEIVE THE PROMISE.

Just as the faith of chapter 11 was brought to mind in verse 35, now the fortitude of chapter 12 is brought to mind: in 12:5-8 Paul wrote, "'MY SON, DO NOT DESPISE THE CHASTENING OF THE LORD, NOR BE DISCOURAGED WHEN YOU ARE REBUKED BY HIM; FOR WHOM THE LORD LOVES HE CHASTENS AND SCOURGES EVERY SON WHOM HE RECEIVES.' IF YOU ENDURE CHASTENING, GOD DEALS WITH YOU AS WITH SONS. FOR WHAT SON IS THERE WHOM A FATHER DOES NOT CHASTEN? BUT IF YOU ARE WITHOUT CHASTENING, OF WHICH ALL HAVE BECOME PARTAKERS, THEN YOU ARE ILLEGITIMATE AND NOT SONS."

THE WILL OF GOD speaks to their continued faithfulness to the Christ, by persevering under all their trials for His sake.

This blending of confidence (v. 35) and endurance (v. 36) in connection with the attainment of the pledged prize was found earlier in 6:12: "DO NOT BECOME SLUGGISH, BUT IMITATE THOSE WHO THROUGH FAITH AND PATIENCE INHERIT THE PROMISES." So if they wanted to be good little children and not be cut out of their Father's will with the promise of a great reward (cf. Rom. 11), then these Jews simply needed to persevere a little while longer. In fact, quoting Habakkuk 2:3-4...

> **VERSES 37-38:** "FOR YET A LITTLE WHILE, AND HE WHO IS COMING WILL COME AND WILL NOT TARRY. NOW THE JUST SHALL LIVE BY FAITH; BUT IF ANYONE DRAWS BACK, MY SOUL HAS NO PLEASURE IN HIM."

After Habakkuk asked God a question and said something about His judgment against His people Israel (1:12), God replied: "'THE VISION IS YET FOR AN APPOINTED TIME; BUT AT THE END IT WILL SPEAK, AND IT WILL NOT LIE. THOUGH IT TARRIES, WAIT FOR IT; BECAUSE IT WILL SURELY COME. IT WILL NOT TARRY'" (2:3).

Paul began his application of this prophecy here, saying, "YET A LITTLE WHILE," a very strong phrase in the Greek meaning, "yet a little—ever so little—while" (cf. other versions: NIV, NASB, Young's, etc.); in fact, the Greek term μικρον (where we get "micro") is used here.

Consider this: In John 16:16-22, when Jesus talked to His disciples about their future suffering for "A LITTLE WHILE," He used the same term as Paul when He told them that in a "LITTLE WHILE" (μικρον) they wouldn't be able to see Him (i.e. He'd leave them at His ascension), then after another "LITTLE WHILE" (μικρον) they would see Him again (i.e. He'd return for them [cf. John 14:2-3, 16:22, etc.]). The second "LITTLE WHILE" period is what Paul was writing about here in Hebrews: that period, that "LITTLE WHILE" of suffering, was so far gone that, at this time, he could add the phrase οσον οσον ("very very"), meaning that it literally reads, "A VERY VERY LITTLE WHILE." A little while before this Paul told the Christians in Rome that "THE NIGHT IS FAR SPENT; THE DAY IS AT HAND" (Rom. 13:12).

This phraseology clearly indicates that Paul wasn't writing about something 2,000+ years away, but something more like 5 to 7 years away. And what would that be? Christ's AD 70 coming against apostate Israel of course (cf. context, vv. 25ff). After all, this is the coming that would bring major relief to these brethren (cf. Rev. 6:11-12 & even 2 The. 1:6-8). Not only would it bring relief from Jewish persecution, but (since the old physical city of God [Jerusalem] would be razed) it'd also alleviate the temptation to return to Judaism.

The phrase **THE JUST** literally means "the just one," and **ANYONE** should be translated as "he"; in other words, God said, "IF HE [the just one] DRAWS BACK, MY SOUL HAS NO PLEASURE IN HIM," implying, as the entire book does, that a saved person can become lost again. Furthermore, **THE JUST SHALL LIVE BY FAITH** is in contrast to **IF HE DRAWS BACK**, signifying that the phrase **LIVE BY FAITH** here means that he who would escape that judgment would do so because of his faith—and of course the grace of God.

(Side-note: It's interesting that Paul quoted Habakkuk 2:4 various times. In Romans 1:17 he used it to emphasize "THE JUST" part of it; in Galatians 3:11 he used it to emphasize the "SHALL LIVE" part of it; then here in Hebrews 10:38 he used it to emphasize the "BY FAITH" part of it; in fact, chapters 11–13 could be considered a discussion on living "BY FAITH.")

The term **PLEASURE** comes from the word "please," thus God through Habakkuk was saying that the one who chose to become His child then deserted His Christ would very much displease Him; in other words, God wouldn't be able to find anything in His entire being (i.e. His soul) that would keep Him from judging this man along with all the other Jews who rejected His Son. In fact, as Peter wrote, "IT WOULD BE BETTER FOR HIM NOT TO HAVE KNOWN THE WAY OF RIGHTEOUSNESS, THAN HAVING KNOWN IT TO TURN FROM" it (2 Pet. 2:21).

> **VERSE 39:** BUT WE ARE NOT OF THOSE WHO DRAW BACK TO PERDITION, BUT OF THOSE WHO BELIEVE TO THE SAVING OF THE SOUL.

The phrase **DRAW BACK** refers to the desertion of Christianity.

The word **PERDITION** refers to utter/permanent destruction, the very thing promised/prophesied of Jerusalem, indicating that those who drew back would do so to their own destruction.

The term **SOUL** here is the same as above, referring to life as opposed to death (which, in this case, would include both physical and eternal death).

More literally this verse reads, "We are not for shrinking back to destruction, but for faith to the saving of life."

Thus, as though Paul had worked himself up at this point, he concluded this paragraph with what appears to be a pep rally statement of inspiration; picture Paul on the floor of a basketball court, speaking to a discouraged team:

    Paul: **"What are we gonna do?!?!"**

    Paul/Team: **"We're gonna win!!!!"**

    Paul: **"What are we gonna do?!?!"**

    Paul/Team: **"We're gonna win!!!!"**

Don't Depart!
Don't fall away!
Don't neglect your salvation!
Don't cast away your confidence!
Don't drift away!
Don't harden your heart!
How can we neglect so great a salvation? Hebrews 2:3

Hebrews 11:1-7

Beginning at 10:19 and going through the end of Hebrews, Paul wrote of *The Superiority of Christ's Principle (Faith) to Moses' Principle (Law)*. The prior section (10:19-39) teaches that *Faith Is the Proper Response to All the Superior Things* of the previous chapters, perfectly setting the stage for the subject of chapter 11 known as FAITH'S HALL OF FAME.

> **VERSE 1: NOW FAITH IS THE SUBSTANCE OF THINGS HOPED FOR, THE EVIDENCE OF THINGS NOT SEEN.**

Paul concluded chapter 10 with two thoughts in his mind. Firstly he referred to the idea of God's promise that required faith (10:36). He had already written a great deal about the promise of an eternal inheritance (9:15) which was to include a time of reconciliation (6:17-20) and a time of respite (4:1). Beginning in chapter 11 we find him describing faith's relationship to God's promise; in other words, the fact that God had fulfilled every earlier promise should produce the faith that He would fulfill this one (cf. 10:23). Using Abraham as an example in Romans 4:20-21, Paul wrote there that "HE DID NOT WAVER AT THE PROMISE OF GOD THROUGH UNBELIEF, BUT WAS STRENGTHENED IN FAITH ..., BEING FULLY CONVINCED THAT WHAT HE HAD PROMISED HE WAS ALSO ABLE TO PERFORM." Remember, Paul had discussed at length that that which was real was that which was spiritual, not that which was physical; and he had discussed at length that that which was real was that which was being presently fulfilled, not that which was still being practiced in Jerusalem.

Secondly, Paul referred to the idea of living "BY FAITH" (10:38); and he went on in chapter 11 to establish this concept by means of many of their own renowned ancestors (vv. 4-40). The last verse of chapter 10 was a strong encouragement to not draw back, but to press forward in order to save their souls. Now in chapter 11 he abundantly demonstrated the faith of their predecessors who—for the fulfillment of a promise they never experienced—remained faithful for their successors in spite of all sorts of severe difficulties. On the other hand, these brethren were "on the verge" (10:1, etc.) of receiving the fulfillment of God's promise, so—in light of their forefathers—they shouldn't even remotely consider forsaking Christ, for what a slap in their faces that would be!

Regarding the term **SUBSTANCE**, the prefix "sub" means "under," and the base word "stance" refers to a "stand"; so "SUBSTANCE" means "that which stands under, hence a foundation"; thus their faith was the ground upon which hope was built. (The original word for "SUBSTANCE" here is translated "CONFIDENCE" in 3:14.)

The word **EVIDENCE** means "proof"; so (especially in this context) what they knew of the past concerning their God provided faith for any promise yet unfulfilled.

The word **SEEN** means "perceived or experienced" (translated "PERCEIVE" in 2 Cor. 7:8 & "EXPERIENCE" in v. 5 below). So, unlike the "THINGS HOPED FOR" which exclude things of the past and present (cf. Rom. 8:24), the "THINGS NOT SEEN" include "things" of the past, present, and future. This brings two points to mind: {1} even if they ignored it, their confessed faith in Jesus as the Christ (10:23) was evidence concerning whatever they didn't understand about the past (types, shadows, etc.) as well as evidence concerning whatever they couldn't understand about their present (persecution, etc.); and {2} their faith was evidence concerning what they would experience in the future, if they'd just hold on a "VERY, VERY LITTLE WHILE" (10:37).

VERSE 2: FOR BY IT THE ELDERS OBTAINED A GOOD TESTIMONY.

The word **ELDERS** is an antecedent of the ancestors of the Jews to whom Paul was writing (as is evidenced from the lengthy list of them in verses 4-40). There's something important that must be remembered here: Paul was writing to Christians who lived during the time prior to AD 70 when God worked supernaturally to bring about what we now possess, namely the promise just discussed. (Interestingly, miracles are thought of by

God as something for spiritual babies, while that which resulted from them is considered mature/complete, 1 Cor. 13:8ff.) This is broached because verse 2 sets the stage for the rest of the chapter which deals with several supernatural events that would therefore consistently apply to these brethren who had experienced and were still experiencing such events in their lives (cf. 2:1-4 & 6:4-6). In other words, they had no excuse but to be like their forefathers in their faith.

The phrase **A GOOD TESTIMONY** is also translated as "WELL SPOKEN OF" in Acts 16:2 and as "A GOOD REPUTATION" in Acts 10:22. And who spoke well of them and gave them this good reputation? God did: He placed His stamp of approval on their lives lived by faith by blessing them and by testifying of them in His Word; in fact, every individual to whom Paul alluded in this chapter is found in the Old Testament.

It also seems that while verse 3 illustrates the second part of verse 1 about "UNSEEN THINGS," verse 2 illustrates the first part of verse 1 about "THINGS HOPED FOR"; in other words, as is confirmed throughout this chapter, God blessed those who acted on faith for what they hoped for.

> **VERSE 3: BY FAITH WE UNDERSTAND THAT THE WORLDS WERE FRAMED BY THE WORD OF GOD, SO THAT THE THINGS WHICH ARE SEEN WERE NOT MADE OF THINGS WHICH ARE VISIBLE.**

As discussed in 1:2, the word "WORLD" in 10:5 is the Greek term for "planet" (κοσμος); the word for "WORLD" in 1:6 is the Greek term for "inhabitants" (οικουμενε); and the word for **WORLDS** here (as in 1:2) is the Greek term for "ages" (αιον); so, depending on its context, it goes from planet, to an age or the ages of the planet, to the inhabitants of an age or the ages of the planet.

Besides the reality that "ages" is—undeniably—the correct translation here, there are other reasons why it should be rendered "ages." The word is plural: not only does **WORLDS** make this an unnatural statement, but—unless Hebrews is the only place—the Bible never speaks of God creating "the worlds" plural; but, as already seen, this book does concern two covenant ages or two covenant worlds, if one prefers to say it that way. Also, since Paul used the Greek term kosmos (κοσμος) for the physical creation in 10:5 when he wrote of Jesus coming into the world, then he obviously knew the difference.

In fact, there's a clear distinction between these terms in one verse—9:26: Jesus "WOULD HAVE HAD TO SUFFER OFTEN SINCE THE FOUNDATION OF THE WORLD [κοσμος]; BUT NOW, ONCE AT THE END OF THE AGES [αιον], HE HAS APPEARED TO PUT AWAY SIN." Even here (9:26) when Paul wished to express physical creation, he used the word κοσμος not αιον. So a synonym for "AGES" in 11:3 would be the word "TIMES" as in Ephesians 1:10 where the same apostle wrote of God gathering all together in Christ at the fullness of the "TIMES" plural. Besides, the word for **FRAMED** here isn't from the usual word for "created," but from a word which refers to something "arranged in a precise manner," which is likely why it's often translated "perfected."

So all this would mean that Paul was referring to how God arranged the ages or the history of human affairs in such a way as to achieve His spiritual purposes for us.

In fact, if a person thinks about it logically enough, he can actually see that God and His Word aren't concerned with the natural history of mankind in general or even with the history of the Hebrews, but with the redemptive history of man, always pointing toward and focusing on the spiritual, as opposed to the physical! Interestingly, the Jews (those who believed in two primary ages—the Mosaical era and the Messianic era) equated the coming of the Christ (to which Paul had just referred, 10:37) with the changing of ages—ages that were ordered/arranged by God Himself (cf. notes at 1:2).

The phrase **THE WORD OF GOD** literally reads "a" Word of/from God; and the Greek term for **WORD** here is not the usual λογος, but ρημα, referring to "a command," thus meaning that everything in redemptive history occurred by/at God's command and according to His plan or arrangement, no man being able to thwart it.

The word **MADE** is from the term translated "COME TO PASS" or "CAME TO PASS" (KJV) at least 80 times. And everyone knows what this language indicates: the passing of time! By the way, not only did God arrange these things (these ages) by His ρημα, but also Jesus maintains them by His ρημα. So if this is the meaning here, then what does the last part of this verse mean? In other words, how do **THE THINGS WHICH ARE SEEN** and the **THINGS WHICH ARE VISIBLE** fit in? Well, trying to keep it in context, the word "SEEN" is the same term as found in verse 1 where Paul was speaking not about that which may be physically seen with the eye like the cosmos, but about that which can be perceived or understood with the mind. Furthermore, the phrase **ARE SEEN** literally reads "being seen," referring to that which was—in their time—coming into focus ... mentally; before this time, things were types and shadows—out of focus or not clear or **VISIBLE**. (Cf. Eph. 3:3-5, 1 Pet. 1:12, etc.)

* *By faith (and only by faith) they could understand that all of history was orchestrated by God's authority and power to come to pass the way it did in order to effect man's redemption, meaning that (since things were a mystery to them—not clear or visible) they could only sense what was being fulfilled in their time by faith.*

Now that this big picture was before their minds, Paul began his list of ancestor-examples (vv. 4-7) with three men who lived between Eden and the flood: Abel, Enoch, and Noah.

> **VERSE 4:** **BY FAITH ABEL OFFERED TO GOD A MORE EXCELLENT SACRIFICE THAN CAIN, THROUGH WHICH HE OBTAINED A WITNESS THAT HE WAS RIGHTEOUS, GOD TESTIFYING OF HIS GIFTS; AND THROUGH IT HE, BEING DEAD, STILL SPEAKS.**

Again, concentrate on Paul's primary focus—encouraging these brethren to trust in God and His Word which included His promises; after all, trust is what faith is.

With the sufferings of these Hebrews at the hands of their national brethren in mind, consider the similarities of their situation with that of Cain and Abel, recalling first of all that both sets were brothers.

Abel & Christian Jews	Cain & Non-Christian Jews
Just as "BY FAITH ABEL OFFERED A MORE EXCELLENT SACRIFICE THAN CAIN," so "BY FAITH" Jewish Christians "OFFERED A MORE EXCELLENT SACRIFICE THAN" their non-Christian brethren.	Just as Cain killed Abel out of jealousy (cf. 1 John 3:12), so I think we can be assured that many non-Christian Jews were killing their Christian brethren out of jealousy.
Just as Abel's righteousness was God-attested, so the righteousness of these Jewish Christians was God-attested (cf. 2:1-4).	Just as Abel continued to speak though dead, so the dead of these brethren were still speaking: "'BLESSED ARE THE DEAD WHO DIE IN THE LORD.'" ... [For] 'THEY ... REST FROM THEIR LABORS, AND THEIR WORKS FOLLOW THEM'" (Rev. 14:13).

(Side-note: At another time and to another group of people, this same apostle employed the example of Ishmael and Isaac to picture this identical scenario, Gal. 4:21-31.)

Although what these brethren had endured hadn't yet reached bloodshed (12:4), Paul's exhortation to them was that, even if it did, they could be assured that it wouldn't be for nothing; but they (like Abel) would be approved by God as righteous, for "THE RIGHTEOUS SHALL LIVE BY FAITH" (10:38).

VERSE 5: BY FAITH ENOCH WAS TRANSLATED SO THAT HE DID NOT SEE DEATH, "AND WAS NOT FOUND BECAUSE GOD HAD TRANSLATED HIM"; FOR BEFORE HIS TRANSLATION HE HAD THIS TESTIMONY, THAT HE PLEASED GOD.

When it says **ENOCH WAS TRANSLATED**, it means that he was taken from one place (Earth) to another place (cf. 2 Kgs. 2:1 & 11, John 3:13, etc.); Genesis 5:24 simply says, "GOD TOOK HIM" so that he (like Elijah thereafter, 2 Kgs. 2:15-18) couldn't/wouldn't be found. And he was taken because **HE PLEASED GOD**"; Genesis 5:22 says that "ENOCH WALKED WITH GOD," a clause that's described in 6:9 as meaning that he (like Abel) was righteous (cf. similar notation on Noah at v. 7.)

Now consider some similarities here between...

Enoch and First Generation Jewish Christians

Both lived in very sinful times (Gen. 6:1 & Acts 2:40).
Both were the ones who pleased God.
Both were God-approved.
Both escaped God's wrath: Enoch was taken before the flood, while these Christians were taken before Jerusalem's demise (in the sense that they heeded Jesus' warnings and "left town" [cf. Mat. 24:37-41]). (Disclaimer: in Mat. 24:40-41 the term "TAKEN" refers to the condemned [cf. "TOOK" in v. 39]; in verses 40-41 *The Living Oracles* version correctly reads, "ONE SHALL BE TAKEN, AND THE OTHER SHALL ESCAPE." [Cf. 2 Kgs. 24:13ff & Luke 21:36].)

Interestingly, Jude (in vv. 14-15) wrote about Enoch prophesying doom against ungodly people. (The word "MEN" is not in the original of verse 14, indicating the possibility that Enoch was prophesying about the doom of his time that foreshadowed the doom of Jude's time. And surely it isn't just coincidence that Paul went on here in verse 7 to talk about the flood of Noah, Enoch's great-grandson!)

Back to Hebrews 11:5: Before Paul's additional statement about faith in the next verse, it appears that he was telling his audience that whether they suffered death by their Jewish brethren (like Abel) or were allowed to live through the events of AD 70 (like Enoch [cf. 10:37]), God would still bless them *if* they (like Abel and Enoch) remained diligent.

> **VERSE 6: BUT WITHOUT FAITH IT IS IMPOSSIBLE TO PLEASE HIM, FOR HE WHO COMES TO GOD MUST BELIEVE THAT HE IS AND THAT HE IS A REWARDER OF THOSE WHO DILIGENTLY SEEK HIM.**

Perhaps just in case these brethren didn't catch the point that Enoch's pleasing walk with God was (and only could've been) "BY FAITH," he guaranteed them that it's impossible to please God without it.

The phrase **TO PLEASE** is in the aorist tense, emphasizing the word **IMPOSSIBLE** to mean that "WITHOUT FAITH IT IS IMPOSSIBLE TO PLEASE GOD AT ALL OR IN ANY WAY!" Paul put it more succinctly to the Romans when he said that "WHATEVER IS NOT FROM [OR OF] FAITH IS SIN" (Rom. 14:23).

Anyone who desires a relationship with God must believe two things: {1} that God exists and {2} that He's trustworthy; in other words, just as He rewarded Enoch, He'll reward those who are faithful to Him, in spite of how things seem to be going for them (cf. 2 Pet. 3:4 & 9)!

> **VERSE 7: BY FAITH NOAH, BEING DIVINELY WARNED OF THINGS NOT YET SEEN, MOVED WITH GODLY FEAR, PREPARED AN ARK FOR THE SAVING OF HIS HOUSEHOLD, BY WHICH HE CONDEMNED THE WORLD AND BECAME HEIR OF THE RIGHTEOUSNESS WHICH IS ACCORDING TO FAITH.**

The **THINGS NOT YET SEEN** refer to "things that had never been experienced before his time"; in other words, although this warning from God to Noah may have been 120 years in advance (Gen. 6:3), his faith in God motivated him to obey those instructions. Due to this, of these first three men, Noah is perhaps the greatest example of persevering faith.

According to Peter, Noah **CONDEMNED THE WORLD** merely by being "A PREACHER OF RIGHTEOUSNESS" (2 Pet. 2:5), who, according to Paul, thus became an **HEIR OF RIGHTEOUSNESS.**

Lastly, consider some similarities here between...

Noah and First Generation (Jewish) Christians

Both lived in very sinful times (Gen. 6:1 & Acts 2:40).
Both were **DIVINELY WARNED OF THINGS NOT YET SEEN** (cf. Mat. 24).
Both were prepared for imminent destruction (per Eusebius, no Christians were killed in Jerusalem's obliteration).
Both warned their worlds of imminent destruction.
Both were "heirs" of God's rewards.

Hebrews 11:8-19

In the previous section, Paul began displaying <u>FAITH'S HALL OF FAME</u> wherein (per 12:1-2) he portrayed his Jewish-Christian readers as runners in a race within the confines of a coliseum; and within the stadium seats were all the faithful who had run the race before them, cheering them on to victory. Here's the picture: Each generation of the faithful (at least from Abel [11:4] to the fulfillment of the promise [11:39f]) were in a relay race for the prize of reconciliation to God. In this scenario, the baton was in the hands of this first century and last generation of Jewish brethren, and they were on the verge of reaching the finish line; they were winning for all who had gone before them ... and more—those of us who came after them!

When we view it in this manner, we can see how tremendously important it was that these brethren keep pressing on—it wasn't just for their salvation as individuals that they were running, but it was for every child of God before/after them as a collective body as well!

Having begun this discussion with Abel, Enoch, and Noah (vv. 4-7), the study continues with Abraham.

> **VERSE 8:** BY FAITH ABRAHAM OBEYED WHEN HE WAS CALLED TO GO OUT TO THE PLACE WHICH HE WOULD AFTERWARD RECEIVE AS AN INHERITANCE. AND HE WENT OUT, NOT KNOWING WHERE HE WAS GOING.

In Abraham's case, the language is slightly stronger in that the phrase **OBEYED WHEN HE WAS CALLED** actually means "while he was being called, by faith he obeyed"; in other words, he was pictured here as packing while God was speaking (cf. Gen. 12:1-4)!

The clause **THE PLACE WHICH HE WOULD AFTERWARD RECEIVE AS AN INHERITANCE** is important here because it kept the readers' minds focused on the idea of the promise (brought up in 10:36) and how that God has always kept His promises and blessed (or rewarded) those who persevere (11:1 & 6).

The clause **NOT KNOWING WHERE HE WAS GOING** is the most important part of this verse: Abraham had no idea <u>where</u> he was headed or <u>why</u> God was putting him through this (v. 9), especially at his ripe age of 75; he just had faith in God and His promises and submitted. Similarly, these brethren, who claimed (and greatly honored) Abraham as their father, needed to imitate him: they may not have understood exactly <u>where</u> they were headed at this point or <u>why</u> God was allowing them to be put through the ringer, but they needed to have faith in God and His promises, remaining faithful to the end.

> **VERSES 9-10:** **BY FAITH HE SOJOURNED** (LIVED) **IN THE LAND OF PROMISE AS IN A FOREIGN COUNTRY, DWELLING IN TENTS WITH ISAAC AND JACOB, THE HEIRS WITH HIM OF THE SAME PROMISE; FOR HE WAITED FOR THE CITY WHICH HAS FOUNDATIONS, WHOSE BUILDER AND MAKER IS GOD.**

Although Abraham had arrived and was **IN THE LAND OF PROMISE,** his family lived there simply as **STRANGERS AND PILGRIMS** (v. 13), **DWELLING IN TENTS.** But why? There were two reasons: {1} Physically speaking, the promise wouldn't be completely fulfilled to Abraham, Isaac, and Jacob (Acts 7:5a), but to their descendants (Gen. 22:17b); in other words, they had to wait until the sins of the Amorites had reached their limit (Gen. 15:13-16) before God would take the land from them and give it to Abraham's descendants (cf. Jos. 21:43-45). And {2}, spiritually speaking, it's pretty obvious that one reason God had them enter the land prematurely was to provide another example and to create another "SHADOW" to encourage those of Paul's day; in other words, Abraham exemplified the faith they needed, and his life of inconvenience pictured the inconveniences they were having to endure while they also waited upon God.

The clause **THE CITY ... WHOSE BUILDER** (architect) **AND MAKER** (builder) **IS GOD** (cf. NIV, etc.) is an unmistakable reference to that about which Paul had been writing all along, namely ... the coming of the kingdom with all its attendant blessings:

> In 9:11 and 10:1 Paul spoke of all this as "THE GOOD THINGS (μελλω, about) TO COME."
>
> In 6:5 he wrote of "THE AGE (about) TO COME." Similarly...
>
> In 2:5 he wrote of "THE WORLD (about) TO COME." While...
>
> In 13:14 he wrote of the "CITY ... (about) TO COME." And...
>
> In 12:28 he simply called it "A KINGDOM."
>
> Here are some additional designations for the same:
>
> > In 11:14 he called it "A HOMELAND."
> >
> > In 11:16 he called it "A HEAVENLY COUNTRY."
> >
> > In 12:22 he called it "THE CITY OF THE LIVING GOD."
> >
> > In 12:22 he also called it "THE HEAVENLY JERUSALEM."
> >
> > In 12:23 he called it "THE GENERAL ASSEMBLY." And...
> >
> > In 12:23 he also called it "THE CHURCH OF THE FIRSTBORN."
>
> Here are a couple corresponding more to 11:10:
>
> > In 8:2 he called it "THE TRUE TABERNACLE WHICH THE LORD ERECTED AND NOT MAN." And...
> >
> > In 9:11 he called it "THE ... PERFECT TABERNACLE NOT MADE WITH HANDS."

So though there's no clear record of it, Abraham was obviously made aware of this coming kingdom, a kingdom that was on the verge of being completed at the time Hebrews was written (cf. μελλω in first four references above); and when the fullness of the kingdom arrived, then the spiritual side of the promises to Abraham were finally and totally fulfilled (cf. Gal. 3:7-9 & 13-14).

> **VERSE 11:** B͟ʏ ꜰᴀɪᴛʜ Sᴀʀᴀʜ ʜᴇʀsᴇʟꜰ ᴀʟsᴏ ʀᴇᴄᴇɪᴠᴇᴅ sᴛʀᴇɴɢᴛʜ ᴛᴏ ᴄᴏɴ-
> ᴄᴇɪᴠᴇ sᴇᴇᴅ, ᴀɴᴅ sʜᴇ ʙᴏʀᴇ ᴀ ᴄʜɪʟᴅ ᴡʜᴇɴ sʜᴇ ᴡᴀs ᴘᴀsᴛ ᴀɢᴇ, ʙᴇᴄᴀᴜsᴇ
> sʜᴇ ᴊᴜᴅɢᴇᴅ Hɪᴍ (Gᴏᴅ) ꜰᴀɪᴛʜꜰᴜʟ ᴡʜᴏ ʜᴀᴅ ᴘʀᴏᴍɪsᴇᴅ.

Although it doesn't sound like it at first reading, I believe the faith of this verse still has reference to the faith of Abraham, not Sarah; there are at least six reasons for this: {1} The word **ALSO** isn't found in any other case in this chapter, indicating that Paul was enlarging upon the subject of Abraham's faith; besides, "ALSO" (which may be translated as "even") is actually between **FAITH** and **SARAH** in the original, and the addition of the word **HERSELF** lends toward this conclusion. Emphasized accordingly, "even Sarah herself was affected by Abraham's faith." {2} The phrase **TO CONCEIVE SEED** actually comes from a phrase that applies to what a man does (viz. seeds), not to what a woman does (viz. conceives). {3} The term **SHE** in **SHE JUDGED** isn't in the original; a pronoun had to be supplied in harmony with one's interpretation, meaning that the translators could've just as well employed the pronoun **HE**. {4} The next verse continues to speak about Abraham saying, "THEREFORE FROM ONE MAN," emphasizing Abraham's faith, not Sarah's. Besides, {5} Sarah never actually showed much faith when it came to her having children; perhaps it was because that not only was she past the age of being able to conceive, but she couldn't even bear a child when she was young! Lastly, {6} consider the similarity of verse 23 in which the faith of someone besides Moses was spoken of even though it says, "BY FAITH MOSES."

Nonetheless, however verse 11 is interpreted, the main point is still the same: Paul's readers needed to be like Abraham and/or Sarah by judging **HIM FAITHFUL WHO PROMISED!** In regards to Sarah, they just needed to surrender to God's timing (the same thing that the recipients of 2 Pet. 3:4 & 9 needed to do).

> **VERSE 12:** Tʜᴇʀᴇꜰᴏʀᴇ ꜰʀᴏᴍ ᴏɴᴇ ᴍᴀɴ, ᴀɴᴅ ʜɪᴍ ᴀs ɢᴏᴏᴅ ᴀs ᴅᴇᴀᴅ,
> ᴡᴇʀᴇ ʙᴏʀɴ ᴀs ᴍᴀɴʏ ᴀs ᴛʜᴇ sᴛᴀʀs ᴏꜰ ᴛʜᴇ sᴋʏ ɪɴ ᴍᴜʟᴛɪᴛᴜᴅᴇ—ɪɴɴᴜᴍᴇʀ-
> ᴀʙʟᴇ ᴀs ᴛʜᴇ sᴀɴᴅ ᴡʜɪᴄʜ ɪs ʙʏ ᴛʜᴇ sᴇᴀsʜᴏʀᴇ.

According to the literal language, there's indeed very little uncertainty that the phrase **HIM AS GOOD AS DEAD** refers to Abraham's reproductive abilities as being unresponsive (cf. Rom. 4:19). (For an explanation on Abraham's <u>apparent</u> children later by Keturah, consult notes in commentaries by James Burton Coffman or James MacKnight.) So, by means of an impotent man, God miraculously brought forth an innumerable people —the nation of Israel. (And I do believe in this context that Paul had reference to the literal people of physical Israel, not spiritual Israel.) Thus, since Isaac was supernatural, then the Israelite nation was supernatural and thus, in that sense, a "special" people who also brought forth a supernatural person—Jesus.

Coincidentally, just as miracle-baby-Isaac brought physical Israel into God's favor, so miracle-baby-Jesus distanced them from God's favor, superseding them with the melting-pot nation of spiritual Israel.

So the strength of faith in this case was that there was simple confidence in God's fulfillment of a promise when all human probabilities were against it.

> **VERSE 13: THESE ALL DIED IN FAITH, NOT HAVING RECEIVED THE PROMISES, BUT HAVING SEEN THEM AFAR OFF WERE ASSURED OF THEM, EMBRACED THEM, AND CONFESSED THAT THEY WERE STRANGERS AND PILGRIMS ON THE EARTH.**

The phrase **THESE ALL DIED IN FAITH** means that not only did these men <u>live</u> by/in faith, but they also <u>died</u> in it.

The phrase **THE PROMISES** actually refers to the things promised. And what were those things? {1} There would be numerous descendants for Abraham (Gen. 13:16, 15:3-5, 17:2-4, & 22:16). {2} God would be God to him and his descendants (Gen. 17:1-8). {3} An everlasting inheritance would be theirs (Gen. 12:7, 13:15, 15:18-21, & 17:8). And {4} all nations would be blessed through them (Gen. 12:3 & 22:18).

Furthermore, it must be remembered that there were two sides to these promises: a physical fulfillment and a spiritual fulfillment, a physical family and a spiritual family, a type and an antitype.

The clause **HAVING SEEN** the things promised **AFAR OFF** obviously includes both the physical and the spiritual promises fulfilled, and Jesus referred to one of the spiritual ones that they saw when He said, "'YOUR FATHER ABRAHAM REJOICED TO SEE MY DAY, AND HE SAW IT AND WAS GLAD'" (John 8:56).

The word **EMBRACED** is from a word which can be and has been translated as "saluted" as well as "embraced," thus it must be interpreted according to its context; here the word "saluted" or "greeted" would probably be the best rendering due to the clause "HAVING SEEN THEM AFAR OFF" or at a distance, because the word "EMBRACED" calls for closeness, not distance (cf. Young's, ASV, RSV, etc.).

Like the clause "HAVING SEEN THEM AFAR OFF," the clause **CONFESSED THAT THEY WERE STRANGERS AND PILGRIMS ON THE EARTH** literally reads, "HAVING CONFESSED THAT THEY WERE...." Thus this sentence might be better understood today if the last clause were placed first. And, if so, here's how it would read with some comments included: "Having confessed that they were strangers and pilgrims on the earth, these men, having not received the promises, died in expectation of them; but, having seen them at a distance [by the eye of faith], they saluted them." One might look at this as sailors on a ship searching for an island that they were convinced existed, but, because they were torpedoed, could only salute it as they got within eye-shot.

As with verse 11, this verse teaches that true trust doesn't require God to meet our time tables!

VERSE 14: FOR THOSE WHO SAY SUCH THINGS DECLARE PLAINLY THAT THEY SEEK A HOMELAND.

There's very little difference between "STRANGERS AND PILGRIMS" (v. 13): "STRANGERS" are foreigners, while "PILGRIMS" are those who don't have citizenship where they live; Abraham said to the Hittites, "'I AM A FOREIGNER AND A VISITOR AMONG YOU'" (Gen. 23:4a). Why? Because he was looking for "THE CITY ... WHOSE ARCHITECT AND BUILDER IS GOD" (v. 10). (Abraham, even as the first generation of Christians, realized his citizenship was in Heaven, not on Earth, Php. 3:20.)

The phrase "A HOMELAND" here referred to a (spiritual) place in which they would have citizenship and therefore rights as citizens. (The Greek term for "A HOMELAND" is πατρις and may be rendered as "the fatherland" or perhaps even as "the father's country" [cf. p. 217])

> **VERSE 15:** AND TRULY IF THEY HAD CALLED TO MIND THAT COUNTRY FROM WHICH THEY HAD COME OUT, THEY WOULD HAVE HAD OPPORTUNITY TO RETURN.

Besides the fact that their faith was strong enough so as to give them the determination to live as nomads-in-waiting for a homeland that they'd never see, it also gave them the determination to remain as nomads-for-life in a land not their own when they could've easily returned home. It's as if their faith had them so excited about the promises of God that they didn't even consider turning back and losing favor with Him; Abraham, in fact, charged his steward Eliezer to swear that he'd never allow Isaac to go back to Abraham's native land (Gen. 24:1-9).

Surely we can see how this corresponds to Paul's audience! Although at first glance this verse may seem to be somewhat unimportant in the scheme of this chapter, it's perhaps the most significant verse so far. The point is, they (whether Abraham's clan or these Hebrews) were not being forced to follow God's desires for them; if they desired to turn back and were willing to bear the consequences, they were certainly free to do so. But that's just it: there'd be severe consequences in rejecting God's will and gift!

> **VERSE 16: BUT NOW THEY DESIRE A BETTER, THAT IS, A HEAVENLY COUNTRY. THEREFORE GOD IS NOT ASHAMED TO BE CALLED THEIR GOD, FOR HE HAS PREPARED A CITY FOR THEM.**

It's held by some that the term **NOW** is logical, not temporal, meaning some believe (and I agree) that Paul employed it in the form of argumentation, not to necessarily suggest a point in time.

They were desiring **A BETTER ... COUNTRY**, a place better than Chaldea and even better than Canaan, better because it would be of a heavenly nature or from Heaven (cf. 2 Tim. 4:18, Heb. 12:22, & Rev. 21:2 & 10, and perhaps even 1 Cor. 15:44-49 where the "body" &/or the "man" may be viewed as equivalent to the kingdom).

The clause **GOD IS NOT ASHAMED TO BE CALLED THEIR GOD** refers to the idea that God doesn't object to being called things like "THE GOD OF ABRAHAM," or "THE GOD OF ISAAC," or "THE GOD OF JACOB," or "The God of _____," provided they have the kind of obedient faith that Paul had been discussing. (By the way, the lack of shame in God's eyes for His people is reminiscent of the lack of shame in Jesus' eyes for them in 2:11.)

The clause **HE HAS PREPARED A CITY FOR THEM** is prophetic in tone; prophecy is very often spoken as having been accomplished when, in earthly time, it hasn't been (cf. Rom. 4:17b). For examples, in a prophecy about Jesus God said, "'OUT OF EGYPT I CALL<u>ED</u> MY SON'" (Hos. 11:1), and Jesus, a while before He was even sacrificed, said to His disciples, "'I HAVE OVERCOME THE WORLD'" (John 16:33b). (Authors of hermeneutic works refer to this as "already-but-not-yet" language; i.e., it's so certain to occur, that it's spoken of as having already occurred.)

> **VERSES 17-18: BY FAITH ABRAHAM, WHEN HE WAS TESTED, OFFERED UP ISAAC, AND HE WHO HAD RECEIVED THE PROMISES OFFERED UP HIS ONLY BEGOTTEN SON, OF WHOM IT WAS SAID, "IN ISAAC YOUR SEED SHALL BE CALLED"** (GEN. 22:1FF)...

So far Paul has written about Abraham's faith when he didn't know <u>where</u> he was going (vv. 8-10) or <u>how</u> God's will would be accomplished (vv. 11-12) or <u>when</u> God would fulfill His promises (vv. 13-16); here (in vv. 17-19) Paul wrote about Abraham's faith when he didn't know <u>why</u> God was doing what He was doing.

The phrase **WHEN HE WAS TESTED** actually refers to the idea of "when his faith was put to the test." God had worked on Abraham's faith for many years, putting him through various trials (e.g. calling him to leave his native land and relatives to become a wanderer in a foreign land, making him wait 25 years for the promised son, and having him kick Ishmael out of his home). So this case seems to be what proved, once and for all, that Abraham had finally reached a plateau (an area of stability) in his faith (cf. Rom. 4:19-20: "BEING NOT WEAK IN FAITH ... HE DID NOT WAVER...."). This is in the perfect tense indicating "intention," meaning that, in Abraham's mind, Isaac had been sacrificed. There was simply no doubt in his mind that he would obey God's wishes; along that two- or three-day trek to the mountain, it was to him as if it were "already" (though "not yet") all done and over with. Notice just how strong Abraham's faith had become by this time:

> **VERSE 19** TELLS US ABRAHAM WAS **...ACCOUNTING THAT GOD WAS ABLE TO RAISE HIM UP, EVEN FROM THE DEAD, FROM WHICH HE ALSO RECEIVED HIM IN A FIGURATIVE SENSE.**

Not only did Abraham believe **GOD WAS <u>ABLE</u> TO RAISE** [ISAAC] **UP ... FROM THE DEAD,** but a statement he made to his servants <u>appears</u> to even indicate he <u>expected</u> such: "'STAY HERE...; THE LAD AND I WILL GO YONDER AND WORSHIP, AND WE WILL COME BACK TO YOU'" (Gen. 22:5).

Remember the Shunammite woman's story in Second Kings 4? She couldn't have children, so God (through Elisha) miraculously provided her one; when the child died, she thus believed God could also miraculously raise her son from the dead ... which of course He did.

Likewise, Abraham was given a son miraculously, and (by this time in his life) he had come to believe that not only could God miraculously raise him from the dead in order to fulfill His promises, but even that He would raise him from the dead; and because God recognized this confident kind of faith in Abraham, He just saved Himself the trouble (as well as Abraham and Isaac the pain) by stopping Abraham from killing Isaac in the first place.

The term for **FIGURATIVE** here (as in 9:9) is actually the Greek word normally translated "parable," a story or an event that (like a shadow) mirrors something similar to it. So what was being reflected by this incident with Isaac? His rising from the dead, for nothing normally rose from a sacrificial altar.

(Side-note #1: Although I believe that this incident typifies Jesus' death and resurrection, I don't believe that sentence structure or context demands that such was what Paul had in mind when he used the word "figurative" here. If, however, Paul did have Jesus' death and resurrection in mind, perhaps it was at this point that Abraham "SAW" Jesus' day "AND WAS GLAD" (John 8:36); I can only wish I knew when this occurred.)

(Side-note #2: Perhaps Paul was also indirectly indicating to these Hebrews that, "Yes, God may very well expect you to suffer death for His Cause (cf. Rev. 6:9-11); but, then again, He might save you just when things look the most bleak.")

In conclusion to this section, keep in mind that Paul's obvious and primary point through all of this was that his readers, like their forefathers, needed to keep the faith concerning God's promises, because they would be fulfilled ... in God's time (and, in their case, it was actually going to be in just "A VERY, VERY LITTLE WHILE," 10:37 [cf. 2 Pet. 3:3-4 & 8-9]).

Hebrews 11:20-31

In the previous section, Paul began displaying <u>FAITH'S HALL OF FAME</u> wherein (per 12:1-2) he portrayed his Jewish-Christian readers as runners in a race within the confines of a coliseum; and within the stadium seats were all the faithful who had run the race before them, cheering them on to victory. Here's the picture: Each generation of the faithful (at least from Abel [11:4] to the fulfillment of the promise [11:39f]) were in a relay race for the prize of reconciliation to God. In this scenario, the baton was in the hands of this first century and last generation of Jewish brethren, and they were on the verge of reaching the finish line; they were winning for all who had gone before them ... and more—those of us who came after them!

When we view it in this manner, we can see how tremendously important it was that these brethren keep pressing on—it wasn't just for their salvation as individuals that they were running, but it was for every child of God before/after them as a collective body as well!

Having begun this survey with Abel and making it through to Abraham (vv. 4-19), the study continues from Isaac through Rahab (vv. 20-31).

The faith of the next three men (vv. 20-22)—Isaac, Jacob, and Joseph—wasn't only spoken of when they were facing death, but also while facing death when they hadn't received the things promised, something upon which these Hebrews definitely needed to ponder.

VERSE 20: BY FAITH ISAAC [WHEN HE WAS DYING] **BLESSED JACOB AND ESAU CONCERNING THINGS TO COME.**

In reference to his faith in the promises of God (10:36), and in reference to his faith in things he hadn't seen but only hoped for (11:1), Isaac blessed (consecrated or set apart) his twin sons for service; in other words, Isaac sanctified each one of them for the individual part he'd fulfill within God's promises to Abraham about his posterity.

Although blind Isaac was initially upset that he had blessed Jacob as the leader instead of Esau, he didn't revoke it, but trusted that it happened just as God intended.

So as Isaac blindly trusted that God's will would be achieved (even if he didn't understand how or why it would be executed differently than he expected), these brethren needed to trust that God was in control, even of those things they couldn't see/understand.

> **VERSE 21: BY FAITH JACOB, WHEN HE WAS DYING, BLESSED EACH OF THE SONS OF JOSEPH, AND WORSHIPPED [GOD], LEANING ON THE TOP OF HIS STAFF.**

This time Jacob (renamed Israel by God)—in reference to his faith in the promises of God forwarded to him by his father Isaac and in reference to his faith in things he also didn't get to see but only hoped for—blessed Ephraim and Manasseh.

Jacob (who was going blind like his father and who, no doubt, remembering his father at this point) just trusted that he'd bless these boys as God desired them to be blessed, whether he could see them or not. As in Isaac's case, the younger was again blessed as being greater than the firstborn. God was in control, so all things worked out as planned.

The phrase **WORSHIPPED [GOD]** makes one wonder if Paul was thinking about how Jacob gave God praise, even though he knew he would die before the promises were fulfilled.

The **WORSHIPPED, LEANING ON THE TOP OF HIS STAFF** portion of this statement very likely refers to an earlier event (Gen. 47) which occurred when Jacob had Joseph swear that he would bury him in Canaan (the promised land), not in Egypt where he died, for Canaan was where Jacob's faith told him that God's promises would be fulfilled. Besides, his father and grandfather (Isaac and Abraham) were already buried there. This interpretation leads perfectly into…

VERSE 22: BY FAITH JOSEPH, WHEN HE WAS DYING, MADE MENTION OF THE DEPARTURE [LIT. THE EXODUS] **OF THE CHILDREN OF ISRAEL AND GAVE INSTRUCTIONS CONCERNING HIS BONES.**

The phrase **MADE MENTION** is from a term meaning "to recall or remind"; so as he was dying, Joseph not only remembered God's promises regarding Abraham's posterity and reminded Israel of them (Gen. 50:24), but he also informed them about God's prophecy regarding their deliverance from Egyptian bondage which would soon be fulfilled. And when that occurred, Joseph, like his father, wanted to be buried in Canaan; so he instructed Israel to take him with them when they left Egypt for the promised land (Gen. 50:25), and they of course complied (Jsh. 24:32).

Joseph, a great example of unwavering faith(fulness) in the midst of terrible trials, said at the end of his life that God "MEANT IT ALL FOR GOOD" (Gen. 50:20); thus Joseph, like all those Paul has already mentioned, not only lived in faith, but also "DIED IN FAITH" (v. 13). Would these Hebrews follow in the footsteps of their honorable forefathers?

VERSE 23: BY FAITH MOSES, WHEN HE WAS BORN, WAS HIDDEN THREE MONTHS BY HIS PARENTS, BECAUSE THEY SAW HE WAS A BEAUTIFUL CHILD; AND THEY WERE NOT AFRAID OF THE KING'S COMMAND.

The word **BEAUTIFUL** is from a term which means "comely." To whom was Moses "comely"? To God. Stephen, using the same original term, said of Moses that he "'WAS WELL PLEASING TO GOD'" (Acts 7:20).

God evidently revealed to Amram and Jochebed (Moses' parents) that Moses was important to Him and to Israel; so knowing by faith that God was with them, Moses' parents hid him.

Just as Moses' parents weren't afraid of Pharaoh because God was on their side, so these brethren shouldn't be afraid of politicians like Nero or the great Sanhedrin of Jerusalem.

> **VERSES 24-25:** BY FAITH MOSES, WHEN HE BECAME OF AGE, REFUSED TO BE CALLED THE SON OF PHARAOH'S DAUGHTER, CHOOSING RATHER TO SUFFER AFFLICTION WITH THE PEOPLE OF GOD THAN TO ENJOY THE PASSING PLEASURES OF SIN...

The clause **WHEN HE BECAME OF AGE** meant "'WHEN HE WAS FORTY YEARS OLD'" (Acts 7:23), indicating that, according to custom, when Moses became old enough to fully exert his faith, he —by his own free will—refused royalty/riches, joining himself to his native people, the poor/suffering Israelites.

Plenty of opportunity for the **PLEASURES OF SIN** could be found in Pharaoh's court and in Egypt, especially when power and wealth were possessed. But Moses was wise enough to know that those pleasures were fleeting in nature, while the oaths of His God (about which his mother informed him, no doubt, Exo. 2:1-10) were everlasting in nature.

Similarly, these Hebrew brethren, like Paul, needed the attitude of Moses: Paul's attitude can be found in Romans 8:18 when he wrote, "I CONSIDER THAT THE SUFFERINGS OF THE PRESENT TIME ARE NOT WORTHY TO BE COMPARED WITH THE GLORY THAT IS ABOUT TO BE ($\mu\epsilon\lambda\lambda\omega$) REVEALED IN US."

Probably one reason Paul used Moses as an example was to show that there's no middle ground: just as Moses sided with his people by slaying the Egyptian, so there was no middle ground for these Hebrews, meaning they couldn't return to Judaism and concurrently be neutral about Jesus. They either truly believed in Him and His imminent return to fulfill God's promises, or they didn't. It was that simple in the mind of Paul.

> **VERSE 26:** ...ESTEEMING THE REPROACH OF CHRIST GREATER RICHES THAN THE TREASURES IN EGYPT; FOR HE LOOKED TO THE REWARD.

Many, perhaps even most, of the sufferings that Abraham's posterity (God's people) endured were due to who they were; in other words, they likely experienced more captivities, etc. than any other nation from the time of Abraham to Israel's demise in AD 70 because they were God's people through whom would come the promised Messiah. But was it because the other nations knew they were God's favored people and so were jealous? Probably not. As one reads through the Old Testament, it appears that God Himself was behind most of their negative (as well as their positive) circumstances for the grand purpose of successfully bringing His promises to fruition through Jesus. This means that not only did Yahweh arrange things so that the nations of the world would be in existence in a certain fashion when the Christ arrived (Dan. 2:21), but He also arranged things so that the religious world of the Jews would be in existence in a certain fashion when the Christ arrived (cf. Heb. 11:3); everything had to be poised and timed perfectly.

The phrase **THE REPROACH OF CHRIST** was obviously used here in reference to any persecution that anyone suffered who was connected with the promise of God; in other words, the suffering of God's people (v. 25) was equivalent to the reproach of (or due to the coming) Christ (v. 26).

Unlike many of these Hebrews, Moses considered that his maltreatment for God would only result in greater riches than all the treasures of Egypt. In Second Corinthians 4:17-18 Paul similarly wrote, "OUR LIGHT AFFLICTION, WHICH IS BUT FOR A MOMENT, IS WORKING FOR US A FAR MORE EXCEEDING AND ETERNAL WEIGHT OF GLORY, WHILE WE DO NOT LOOK AT THE THINGS WHICH ARE SEEN, BUT AT THE THINGS WHICH ARE NOT SEEN. FOR THE THINGS WHICH ARE SEEN [SUCH AS OUR AFFLICTIONS] ARE TEMPORARY, BUT THE THINGS WHICH ARE NOT SEEN ARE ETERNAL" (2 Cor. 4:17-18).

Thus later when concluding in Hebrews 13:13, Paul, perhaps with Moses in mind, said, "LET US GO FORTH ... BEARING CHRIST'S REPROACH," implying that, if their forefathers could do it for Christ so long before His arrival, surely they could do it then —so soon after His opening coming and so near His closing coming (cf. 9:28 & 10:37).

Robert Milligan made a very astute point when he wrote, "It may be truly said that all reproach suffered for righteousness' sake since the world began has been suffered for Christ's sake"; the reason I find this intriguing is because it makes me wonder if Jesus thought to Himself, "How can I not do whatever it takes to save those who wish to be saved after all the suffering men have endured through the centuries in order to bring Me here for this very purpose?"

The clause **HE LOOKED TO THE REWARD** literally means that "he looked away from" the **PLEASURES OF SIN** and the **TREASURES OF EGYPT** and "intently toward" the **GREATER RICHES** or **THE REWARD** to be possessed by bearing up under **THE REPROACH OF CHRIST**.

This reward is an obvious reference to the eternal one (not the temporal one in the inheritance of Canaan) that was finally about to be realized (cf. Rev. 22:12); in other words, Moses exchanged an earthly possession for a heavenly one.

Speaking of **THE REWARD**, it's very likely that Paul was thinking about how these Hebrews had suffered and were suffering the loss of material things because of Christianity (cf. 10:34 & Rev. 13-16-17), so they needed just this sort of encouragement from the life of Moses.

> **VERSE 27: BY FAITH HE FORSOOK EGYPT, NOT FEARING THE WRATH OF THE KING** (CF. V. 23B)**; FOR HE ENDURED AS SEEING HIM WHO IS INVISIBLE.**

There's a lot of debate as to which forsaking-of-Egypt this concerns (whether it was when Moses left at the age of 40 after killing the Egyptian taskmaster or when he left at the age of 80 with the Israelites in tow); and I don't have an answer.

The phrase **THE KING** here, as in verse 23, is Pharaoh; as far as which Pharaoh Paul had in mind would depend on which forsaking-of-Egypt by Moses he had in mind.

The phrase **HIM WHO IS INVISIBLE** is clearly an allusion to God (who is invisible) as opposed to any of the idols of Egypt (which would of course be visible).

Thus Paul's point to these brethren was that faith not fear is what needed to prevail among them; whether they were afraid or not was much less important than whether they obeyed or not.

These "believers" needed to learn to see, or to focus on seeing, what unbelievers couldn't see; after all, that was Paul's point all along—faith is seeing what can't be seen.

VERSE 28: BY FAITH HE KEPT THE PASSOVER AND THE SPRINKLING OF BLOOD, LEST HE WHO DESTROYED THE FIRSTBORN SHOULD TOUCH THEM.

The word for **KEPT** actually means "to make," hence meaning that Moses instituted the Passover with its attendant blood-sprinkling on Israel. So—although no one had ever heard of such a thing occurring before, and although none of the previous nine plagues had worked—Moses still had faith in God, a faith that prompted him to establish and observe the Passover with the sprinkling of blood in order to keep the death angel from killing any of the firstborn of Israel.

Since this letter concerns the things these Jerusalem Christians were facing that led up to the destruction of AD 70, and since history (EUSEBIUS) claims that no Christians were killed in Jerusalem's annihilation, it makes one wonder if Paul was again indicating that—if they'd just have faith and obey as their ancestors did—they, like those firstborn ones (cf. 12: 23), would escape the wrath of God (cf. Rev. 3:12, 14:1, & 22:4).

VERSE 29: BY FAITH THEY PASSED THROUGH THE RED SEA AS BY DRY LAND, WHEREAS THE EGYPTIANS, ATTEMPTING TO DO SO, WERE DROWNED.

As with verses 11 & 23, I believe this verse is referring to the unwavering faith of Moses, not any "faith" of the Israelites (cf. Exo. 14:11-14). However, if Paul did mean the faith of those Hebrews as they seemed to face a no-way-out situation, surely these Hebrews—by faith—could do the same while facing what seemed to them to be a no-way-out situation.

So either Paul was referring to Moses' faith, or the Israelites' faith, or the faith of the Israelites led by Moses and his faith; the latter appears to be the idea in the next verse concerning the Israelites and Joshua, Moses' successor.

By faith the Israelites passed through the Red Sea, but surely it was only due to their fear of Pharaoh that the Egyptians tried to make it through as well. (This is where one can see the difference between those who act out of faith and those who act merely out of fear.)

So Paul's readers were to learn from Moses that true faith means obeying God no matter how bad things seem to be and no matter what the perceived consequences might be!

(Side-note: According to Paul in First Corinthians 10:1-2, this Red Sea incident pictures baptism. In other words, just as the enemies of God's people were destroyed in the water, alien sins are destroyed by God's power today in the water of baptism [Acts 2:38]. And as the Israelites were saved from Egyptian bondage after they went through the water [Exo. 14:30], lost people today are saved from sin's bondage after they go through the water of baptism [Mark 16:16 & Rom. 6:1-11].)

VERSE 30: BY FAITH THE WALLS OF JERICHO FELL DOWN AFTER THEY WERE ENCIRCLED FOR SEVEN DAYS.

Jericho was the first city taken by Israel once she finally arrived in the promised land; and, though it was a very well fortified city, by faith Jericho's walls simply fell down (Jsh. 6:20).

This is another case which indicates that God's ways aren't man's ways (cf. Isa. 55:8-9); in other words, apparently as another test for His own people (as well as a statement to all the inhabitants of Canaan) God asked His people to do something that seemed ridiculous: march around the city seven days, then blow horns and shout on the seventh day to bring the walls down. Can you picture a general having his troops do that today?

So to do this—perhaps with the citizens of Jericho rolling on the ground laughing at them—required a lot of faith; and, in this case, there wasn't a recorded word of disbelief uttered by the Israelites; by having faith in and obeying God, they overcame, emerging as victors! Would God have brought those walls down had Israel not had faith and obeyed?

> **VERSE 31: BY FAITH THE HARLOT RAHAB DID NOT PERISH WITH THOSE WHO DID NOT BELIEVE WHEN SHE HAD RECEIVED THE SPIES WITH PEACE.**

Rahab is plainly stated to have been a harlot, not just an innkeeper as some claim; but though a harlot and a Gentile, she (as Tamar, Ruth, and Bathsheba) became an ancestor of the Messiah (Mat. 1:5). Why? Because of her righteous treatment toward two of God's people. And why did she take this risk? Because she believed the reports concerning what God had done for His people Israel.

She knew about their deliverance from Egypt and their crossing of the Red Sea (Jsh. 2:8ff), so she said that Yahweh—not some Jerichoan idol—is "'GOD IN HEAVEN ABOVE AND ON EARTH BENEATH'" (Jsh. 2:11).

Furthermore, she knew that the Lord had purposed to give Israel her people's land, so she (unlike the other citizens except her family) yielded to God's will by welcoming and hiding two of God's people with peace—with wholesome motives. In fact, the phrase **NOT BELIEVE** isn't from the common term for unbelief or lack of faith, but from a phrase referring to disbelief which manifests itself in disobedience. In other words, it speaks of the failure on the part of the citizens of Jericho to accept that God was giving their land to the Israelites, manifesting itself in their refusal to surrender.

By the way, Rahab's name reflects her people, for it means insolence, violence, and pride.

So if the Hebrews Paul addressed couldn't have as much faith as a Gentile harlot, then shame on them! Besides, if God rewarded this Gentile harlot for her faith, surely He'd reward these Hebrews for their faith(fulfness).

Hebrews 11:32-40

In the previous section, Paul began displaying <u>FAITH'S HALL OF FAME</u> wherein (per 12:1-2) he portrayed his Jewish-Christian readers as runners in a race within the confines of a coliseum; and within the stadium seats were all the faithful who had run the race before them, cheering them on to victory. Here's the picture: Each generation of the faithful (at least from Abel [11:4] to the fulfillment of the promise [11:39f]) were in a relay race for the prize of reconciliation to God. In this scenario, the baton was in the hands of this first century and last generation of Jewish brethren, and they were on the verge of reaching the finish line; they were winning for all who had gone before them, and more—those of us who have come after them!

When we view it in this manner, we can see how tremendously important it was that these brethren keep pressing on—it wasn't just for their salvation as individuals that they were running, but it was for each and every child of God before them and after them as a collective body!

Having begun this survey with Abel and making it through to Rahab (vv. 4-31), it concludes in verses 32-40 with Paul's brief remarks about the various types of suffering that numerous other ancestors experienced. And, as he stressed earlier then again as this chapter closed, all these people endured their afflictions with only the <u>hope</u> of receiving promised things, whereas these first century brethren were in the process of finally receiving them after 2,000 years of waiting since the promises were initially provided!

> **VERSE 32: AND WHAT MORE SHALL I SAY? FOR TIME WOULD FAIL ME TO TELL OF GIDEON AND BARAK AND SAMSON AND JEPHTHAH, ALSO OF DAVID AND SAMUEL AND THE PROPHETS...**

By posing the initial question here, Paul seemed to be asking, "Do I need to go on with my list?" If he did need to go on, he indicated that he'd run out of time because there were so many faithful to God in their past, seemingly shaming them all the more for what they were becoming branded as—apostatizers (cf. 10:25 & context).

Paul went on to briefly allude to five judges, one king, and the many prophets of Israel in general. And why did he list these particular six individuals? Apparently because of the overwhelming odds that each of them faced, odds that required and (by faith) received God's assistance.

Barak was the one who, with only 10,000 soldiers, defeated the army of the Canaanite king, delivering Israel from 20 years of tyranny. How? By faith. But, as with Sarah (v. 11), Moses (v. 23), and Israel (v. 29)—all who in these cases depended on the faith of another, it seems that Barak carried out his task by the faith of Deborah, Israel's fourth judge (Jdg. 4–5). (Sort of sounds as if Paul were implying that these brethren needed to help/lean on each other [cf. 10:24-25 & 12:12-13]. Huh?)

Gideon, Israel's fifth judge, is known as the one who by faith defeated tens of thousands of Midianites with a mere 300 soldiers (Jdg. 6–8).

Jephthah, Israel's ninth judge, is known for his victories over the Ammonites (Jdg. 11–12 [and he specifically mentioned God's promises in 11:23-24]).

Samson, Israel's thirteenth judge, is known for his victories over the Philistines (Jdg. 13–16), victories that he believed were possible only because of his strength that came from the Lord.

Samuel, Israel's fifteenth and last judge, is known for being a very courageous and virtually perfectly faithful man, regardless of how immoral and idolatrous his circumstances (1 Sam. 1–28).

David, Israel's second and perhaps greatest king, is known very well for his faith in God (1 Sam. 16—1 Kgs. 1), especially in the case of his victory over Goliath and the Philistines.

And by Paul merely saying "AND THE PROPHETS," he realized that these Hebrews knew of the faith of all these men all too well to even name them!

So although none of these people were sinless, at critical times in their lives they boldly trusted God when the odds were against them; and through their obedience to the Lord, God saved His people, the same thing He would do for <u>these</u> Hebrews—they just needed to trust and obey!

> **VERSES 33-34:** ...WHO THROUGH FAITH SUBDUED KINGDOMS, WORKED RIGHTEOUSNESS, OBTAINED PROMISES, STOPPED THE MOUTHS OF LIONS, QUENCHED THE VIOLENCE OF FIRE, ESCAPED THE EDGE OF THE SWORD, OUT OF WEAKNESS WERE MADE STRONG, BECAME VALIANT IN BATTLE, [AND] TURNED TO FLIGHT THE ARMIES OF THE ALIENS.

Joshua subdued the Canaanites; Gideon subdued the Midianites; Jephthah subdued the Ammonites; and David subdued the Amalekites, Edomites, Jebusites, Moabites, Philistines, Syrians, and others.

The phrase **WORKED RIGHTEOUSNESS** could be translated as "enforced justice" (RSV), meaning that it likely has reference to leaders such as Samuel and David for being righteous in the execution of God's laws (1 Sam. 12:4 & 2 Sam. 8:15) not only in Israel, but also among nations of a corrupt nature.

Joshua and Caleb obtained the land of Canaan; Phineas obtained an everlasting priesthood; and David obtained the promise of the kingdom of Israel. In fact, these all saw the fulfillment of promises concerning conquests, land, and children.

Samson, David, Benaiah, and Daniel all survived encounters with lions, the most dreaded beast of their time/region.

Hananiah, Mishael, and Azariah (aka Shadrach, Meshach, and Abednego) were delivered from a violent or powerful fire (**VIOLENCE** is from δυναμιν in Greek, the word from which we get "dynamite"); the reading of this could mean that the faith of some quenched the <u>power</u> of the fire, even though they weren't saved like the three Hebrew children.

Moses escaped the sword of Pharaoh; Elijah escaped the sword of Ahab; Elisha escaped the sword of Jehoram; David escaped the sword of Saul; and Jeremiah escaped the sword of Jehoiakim.

Abraham defeated 4 kings with only 318 men; Gideon defeated tens of thousands of Midianites with only 300 men; Samson took out a city all by himself; and David defeated the nine-foot Philistine champion with a stone; as Jonathan once said, "'NOTHING RESTRAINS THE LORD FROM SAVING BY MANY OR BY FEW'" (1 Sam. 14:6c).

Courage in battle not only can be clearly seen in all the victories referred to earlier, but one can also find numerous others in the books of Joshua, Judges, Samuel, and Kings.

The clause **TURNED TO FLIGHT THE ARMIES OF THE ALIENS** reads better as "PUT FOREIGN ARMIES TO FLIGHT" (RSV); in other words, when nations such as the Ammonites, Assyrians, Moabites, and Philistines attempted to invade Israel's territory, they were made to retreat. How? By faith in Yahweh.

> **VERSE 35:** WOMEN RECEIVED THEIR DEAD RAISED TO LIFE AGAIN. AND OTHERS WERE TORTURED, NOT ACCEPTING DELIVERANCE THAT THEY MIGHT OBTAIN A BETTER RESURRECTION.

There were at least two women who received their dead to life again: Elijah brought back the child of the widow of Zarephath (1 Kgs. 17:17-24), and Elisha brought back the child of the woman of Shunem (2 Kgs. 4:18-37).

In opposition to verse 34 about many escaping the sword, this verse indicates that God didn't always choose to save the faithful—many died of their torture, but even <u>they</u> died in faith; they thought as Job who said, "'THOUGH HE SLAY ME, YET WILL I TRUST HIM'" (Job 13:15), and the three Hebrew children who said that even if God <u>didn't</u> deliver them, they would still serve Him (Dan. 3:17-18).

The original term for **TORTURED** is from the same root term as the English word "tympani," a kettle-drum; so the particular torture to which this referred involved stretching a victim over a large drum-like apparatus and beating him with clubs until he either denied his God or he was pronounced "dead" or both.

So how could anyone read this verse about Old Testament saints enduring torture for their faith and <u>not</u> see the relevance of it for the Hebrews to whom Paul was writing in their first century time of severe persecution?

When Paul wrote of **A BETTER RESURRECTION**, the question is, "A better resurrection than what resurrection?" The answer of course is "the biological/temporal one that the sons of these women experienced." And what would be better than that? Logically the opposite of physical, namely a <u>spiritual</u> one—one in which the reconciliation of fellowship to their Creator in the "HEAVENLY COUNTRY" is enjoyed (v. 16)!

Incidentally, something interesting about this verse (v. 35) is it confirms that Old Testament saints believed in the promise of a resurrection of some sort; and it appears that it wasn't necessarily one of a physical (thus temporary) nature, but one that is "better" than that. And remember, the key term "better" throughout Hebrews is a contrast word for the blessings of the New Covenant as distinguished from the lack thereof under the Old Covenant.

VERSE 36: STILL OTHERS HAD TRIAL OF MOCKINGS AND SCOURGINGS, YES, AND OF CHAINS AND IMPRISONMENTS.

While some were tortured to death on the tympani, there were others who lived to endure an enormous amount of torture of various other sorts: many suffered the emotional anguish of mockings and the physical anguish of scourgings, incidents which generally led to chains and imprisonments. Thus Paul covered the entire spectrum: those who escaped death (v. 34), those who died during torture (v. 35), and those who suffered at length (v. 36).

Samson was scorned and ridiculed by the Godless Philistines (Jdg. 16:25) who also bored out his eyes (16:21); even worse, God's prophets were scoffed at by their own people (2 Chr. 36:16).

Joseph was falsely accused and imprisoned by Pharaoh (Gen. 39:20); the prophet Micaiah was beaten by Zedekiah and imprisoned with only bread and water by Ahab (1 Kgs. 22:24 & 27); and the prophet Hanani was imprisoned in rage by Asa (2 Chr. 16:10).

There was one man who endured all of these and more: Not only was Jeremiah mocked by everyone (Jer. 20:7), beaten (20:2a & 37: 15a), put in chains (20:2b), and placed in prison (32:2 & 37:15), but he was also put into a dungeon (a waterless well) of sludge, into which he sank (38:6). What was so bad about poor Jeremiah's case (as with many other cases) is that nearly all the tragedies he suffered were at the hands of his own people whom he was merely trying to help.

Likewise, the people to whom Paul was writing at this time (AD 63-65) were experiencing most of their suffering at the hands of their own Jewish brethren. The question was, "Would they respond like Jeremiah and their other numerous ancestral heroes of faith?"

VERSE 37: THEY WERE STONED, THEY WERE SAWN IN TWO, WERE TEMPTED, WERE SLAIN WITH THE SWORD. THEY WANDERED ABOUT IN SHEEPSKINS AND GOATSKINS, BEING DESTITUTE, AFFLICTED, [AND] TORMENTED...

Naboth was falsely accused and **STONED** to death (1 Kgs. 21:13-14); and the prophet Zechariah was "STONED" to death for his warnings from God (2 Chr. 24:20-22).

Clarke wrote that, in a Jewish source called the *Yevamoth*, "it is written that 'Manasseh slew Isaiah, for he commanded that he be slain with a wooden saw. They then brought the saw and cut him in two; and when the saw reached his mouth, his soul fled forth.'"

The oldest manuscript we have of Hebrews doesn't include the phrase "WERE TEMPTED" (cf. Ralph Earle's *Word Meanings in the New Testament*), which is why many versions don't include it. However, if it's accepted as genuine, then it probably has reference to the relentless torture referred to in verse 35 which no doubt included coercion (perhaps even threatening family members in the victim's presence) to deny their faith and turn to idols (cf. Dan. 3 & 6 where men were punished for not worshipping something/someone other than Yahweh). (By the way, there were severe consequences for anyone who tried to compel God's people to worship anything/anyone except Yahweh, Deu. 13:6-11.)

Saul had many of God's people killed by the sword for being on David's side (1 Sam. 22:17-19); the prophet Uriah was "SLAIN WITH THE SWORD" (Jer. 26:20-23); and Elijah spoke about Jezebel killing many of God's prophets with the sword (1 Kgs. 19:10) This coincidentally brings up the next thought: just as the one man Jeremiah so perfectly epitomized verse 36, so the one man Elijah, "BEING DESTITUTE, AFFLICTED, AND TORTURED" by Jezebel, perfectly epitomizes much of verse 37.

Because he was driven from his home by Jezebel (1 Kgs. 19:3-14), Elijah was **DESTITUTE** and so had to wear **SHEEPSKIN** (cf. 2 Kgs. 2:13, etc. where *The Septuagint* has the same Greek term as in Hebrews; this is probably why he was called "A HAIRY MAN" in 1 Kgs. 1:8a, not—as supposed by painters—because he had an enormously long beard.)

Paul used the same term for **AFFLICTED** (2 Cor. 4:8) when he said that the apostles were "HARD-PRESSED" on every side.

One can't read the story of Elijah without at least partially feeling the torment he unjustly endured from Jezebel and Ahab, all because he, like John the Baptist (the NT Elijah who also wore hairy clothing), stood for Yahweh against the rulers of Israel.

> **VERSE 38: ...OF WHOM THE WORLD WAS NOT WORTHY. THEY WANDERED IN DESERTS AND MOUNTAINS, IN DENS AND CAVES OF THE EARTH.**

The idea that **THE WORLD WAS NOT WORTHY** of such people implies that there were those who were not only in the world but also of the world, while there were those who were in the world but were not of the world (cf. John 15:19 & 17:14-16).

After the apostle Paul spoke in his defense before the Jews in Jerusalem, they said, "'AWAY WITH SUCH A FELLOW FROM THE EARTH, FOR HE IS NOT FIT TO LIVE'" (Acts 22:22), meaning that they considered men like him as merely "SHEEP FOR THE SLAUGHTER" (Rom. 8:36). That's man's opinion! But if one were to ask God His thoughts on the matter, He'd say just the opposite: "THE WORLD WAS NOT WORTHY" of such fellows! (Cf. Rom. 8:33ff.)

Probably with Elijah still in mind, Paul reminded his readers where these wanderers wandered/lived: they wandered in deserts/mountains and lived in caverns/holes.

When Jezebel pursued Elijah, he hid in a mountain cavern (1 Kgs. 19:9), and when Jezebel was killing the prophets of God, Obadiah hid one hundred of them in caves, only able to feed them with bread and water (1 Kgs. 18:4); and let's don't forget about poor David hiding in a cave from Saul (1 Sam. 24:3). (Surely all this makes one wonder about the veracity of the health-and-wealth doctrine?)

> **VERSE 39: AND ALL THESE, HAVING OBTAINED A GOOD TESTIMONY THROUGH FAITH, DID NOT RECEIVE THE PROMISE...**

Just as Paul began this chapter by speaking of how God indicated His approval of people who lived and even died in faith (vv. 2, 4, & 5), so here he ended it by speaking of the same. Not only did these saints receive God's approval in their faithfulness by which they gained a good reputation among the saints, but (as Paul also wrote of in verse 13) they did so even without receiving the fulfillment of "THE PROMISE" —the promise of the Messiah, His covenant, and His kingdom. (They did receive _some_ of the things promised to Abraham [v. 33], but not _this_ promise.)

An interesting thought here is that, although the promise of a spiritual land or the eternal kingdom and life through the Messiah is usually associated with Abraham alone, those before him (Abel/Enoch/Noah/et.al.) were included, meaning that Paul could've very well had Genesis 3:15 in mind where God said to the serpent (and probably in earshot of Adam and Eve so they would pass it down to their children), "'I WILL PUT ENMITY BETWEEN YOU AND THE WOMAN, AND BETWEEN YOUR SEED AND HER SEED; HE SHALL WOUND YOUR HEAD, AND YOU SHALL BRUISE HIS HEEL.'"

All these saints pleased God because they not only believed He existed, but that He also would reward those who diligently sought after Him (v. 6); in other words, they were convinced that He would indeed fulfill His promises, promises that involved the reward of deliverance from sin and its consequent death.

VERSE 40: ...GOD HAVING PROVIDED SOMETHING BETTER FOR US, THAT THEY SHOULD NOT BE MADE PERFECT APART FROM US.

The phrase **SOMETHING BETTER** refers to New Covenant _life_ as opposed to Old Covenant death (2:14-15); this is the "BETTER" thing that Paul has been discussing all along (cf. v. 35).

The word **PERFECT** means "complete" here, indicating that the Lord's imminent arrival (10:37) to fulfill the promise (10:36) of "THE TIME OF REFORMATION" (9:10) or the "TIMES OF RESTORATION" (Acts 3:21) would bring to completion the plan of God for reconciliation to all mankind!

Another important "re-" word is right here in this context, something without which <u>re</u>formation, <u>re</u>storation, and <u>re</u>conciliation wouldn't be possible—<u>resurrection</u> (v. 35); it's the better thing because it's what makes perfect! Then Paul said of their ancestors that "THEY SHOULD NOT [OR WOULD NOT, NLT, NIV, NASB, ETC.] BE MADE PERFECT APART FROM US," meaning that the reconciling of the Jews, yea the world, would <u>not</u> be apart from/without the first generation saints/the remnant/the elect—the ones who lived in those days of fulfillment.

See, it was God's plan that all of this be worked out over a long period of earthly time, and now these Hebrew brethren were experiencing the fulfillment of it all; as Paul wrote in Ephesians 1:10, "THAT IN THE DISPENSATION OF THE FULLNESS OF TIMES HE MIGHT GATHER TOGETHER IN ONE ALL THINGS IN CHRIST, BOTH WHICH ARE IN HEAVEN AND WHICH ARE ON EARTH." In Luke 10:23-24 Jesus said to His disciples, "'BLESSED ARE THE EYES THAT SEE WHAT YOU SEE; FOR I TELL YOU THAT MANY PROPHETS AND KINGS HAVE DESIRED TO SEE WHAT YOU SEE AND HAVEN'T SEEN IT, AND TO HEAR WHAT YOU HEAR AND HAVE NOT HEARD IT.'" And in First Peter 1:12 Peter wrote, "TO THEM IT WAS REVEALED THAT, NOT TO THEMSELVES BUT TO US, THEY WERE MINISTERING THE THINGS WHICH HAVE BEEN REPORTED TO YOU ... THINGS ANGELS DESIRE TO LOOK INTO."

Thus these Hebrews should've been <u>excited</u> over what they were experiencing, namely a being raised to fellowship-life which would culminate at Jesus' AD 70 consummation of all things.

Hebrews 12:1-3

Thus far the apostle has discussed *The Superiority of Christ's Person* (1:1-4:13), *The Superiority of Christ's Priesthood* (4:14-7:28), and *The Superiority of Christ's Pact* (8:1-10:18). At 10:19 Paul commenced the last major section of Hebrews—*The Superiority of Christ's Principle*.

Within this section about Christ's Principle, Paul not only discussed how *Christ's Faith-Principle Is the Proper Response to Superior Things*, but also how *It Prompts Superior Actions* (10:19-11:40). Beginning with 12:1 he argued that *Christ's Faith-Principle Establishes a Superior Relationship* to what man possessed prior to Christ.

> **VERSE 1: THEREFORE WE ALSO, SINCE WE ARE SURROUNDED BY SO GREAT A CLOUD OF WITNESSES, LET US LAY ASIDE EVERY WEIGHT AND THE SIN WHICH SO EASILY ENSNARES US, AND LET US RUN WITH PATIENCE THE RACE THAT IS SET BEFORE US...**

The **GREAT CLOUD OF WITNESSES** includes all the heroes recorded in the previous chapter; in fact, this phrase likely embraces every faithful saint from Adam to these Hebrews, especially those who had been martyred in God's service.

The Greek term for **CLOUD** isn't νεφελε (an isolated, definable cloud), but νεφος (an indefinable cloud, covering the entirety of the visible sky). The use of "CLOUD" for a mass of people became an idiom: Homer wrote of "a cloud of footmen, a cloud of Trojans," and Themistocles referred to Xerxes' army as "so great a cloud of men." Why? Probably because of the cloud of dust that armies of men, horses, and chariots created in those days of dusty roads.

Hence we shouldn't deem it strange that Jesus spoke of His coming against Jerusalem on a cloud (Luke 21:27) since He would do so via the Roman army led by Titus (cf. Rev. 1:7). For examples: God spoke of the army of Gog attacking Israel as "'COMING LIKE A STORM, COVERING THE LAND LIKE A CLOUD'" (Eze. 38:9, cf. 38:16). When God prophesied about His coming against Egypt, He said, "'THE LORD RIDES ON A SWIFT CLOUD AND WILL COME INTO EGYPT'" (Isa. 19:1). And how did He do that? Via the Babylonian army under Nebuchadnezzar (Eze. 32:11ff, cf. 30:18). Similarly, when Jeremiah prophesied of God's coming against Jerusalem via the Babylonian army under Nebuchadnezzar, he said, "'HE SHALL COME UP LIKE CLOUDS, AND HIS CHARIOTS LIKE A WHIRLWIND'" (Jer. 4:13). Probably because of such apocalyptic language, Nahum said of God, "THE LORD HAS HIS WAY IN THE WHIRLWIND AND IN THE STORM, AND THE CLOUDS ARE THE DUST OF HIS FEET" (Nahum 1:3).

So why would men have a problem with Christ's idiomatic, Jewish language when He spoke of coming against Jerusalem via the Roman army in/on/with clouds (Mat. 24:30, Mark 13:26, Luke 21:27, etc.)?

The point? Interpreters should permit the Bible to explain or expound upon the Bible in every possible case, keeping in mind that, before he can ever accurately apply what he reads, he first must discover how the initial audience understood it; the rule is that <u>a statement can never mean what it never meant</u>.

The term for **WITNESSES** is the word from which we get "martyr." However, by this time in its etymology, it wasn't always used to refer to those who were slain for a cause; it could've also merely referred to those who were (as translated here) "WITNESSES" to/of something. So, in this case, whether they died as martyrs or not, Paul called the Old Testament faithful "A GREAT CLOUD OF WITNESSES." Witnesses of what? Witnesses of what faith can accomplish! In other words, it's unlikely Paul was saying that the dead could literally see these Hebrews; rather, just as God bore witness to the faithfulness of the saints of chapter 11, they were in turn bearing witness of God's faithfulness to these brethren, thus cheering them on.

Incidentally, since chapter 11 is merely an extended parenthetical statement, meaning that chapter 10 actually flows into chapter 12, then one may see how the comments on 10:39 correspond to the comments here. So when Paul said, "WE AREN'T OF THOSE WHO DRAW BACK TO PERDITION, BUT OF THOSE WHO BELIEVE TO THE SAVING OF THE SOUL," he wasn't speaking as if they had no free-will, but as if he were a cheerleader or an inspiring coach saying:

> Paul: **"What're we gonna do?!?!"**
> Paul/Team: **"We're gonna win!!!!"**
> Paul: **"What're we gonna do?!?!"**
> Paul/Team: **"We're gonna win!!!!"**

So doing what Paul did here in chapter 12 (with the "CLOUD OF WITNESSES" and even "JESUS" in verse 3) was a natural form of motivation: just as all subsequent teams try to do at least as well as their predecessors, so these Christians should try to do at least as well as their ancestors, keeping in mind what those forefathers had endured/accomplished to get them to where they were!

The phrase **LAY ASIDE** is also translated as "CAST OFF" in Romans 13:12 where Paul said to "CAST OFF THE WORKS OF DARKNESS" and as "PUT OFF" in Ephesians 4:22 where he said to "PUT OFF ... THE OLD MAN." Concerning Acts 7:58, which speaks of those who stoned Stephen, *Young's Literal Translation* says that they "PUT DOWN" the clothes they had on which would hinder them in hurling rocks.

In the phrase **THE SIN WHICH SO EASILY ENSNARES**, the term "ENSNARES" is from a word which refers to something totally surrounding someone, meaning that it's certain to cause him to stumble and fall; due to this and the context of the book in general, Paul was likely referring to "THE SIN" of apostasy—turning one's back on God altogether.

The **WEIGHT** that Paul advised them to put off is from a word referring to surplus flesh—fat. There are two acceptable interpretations concerning what Paul had in mind by his use of this term:

It could refer to how going back or continuing to observe various Old Testament ceremonies and such is nothing but a hindrance since they no longer meant anything: of the Galatians Paul asked, "BUT NOW, AFTER YOU HAVE KNOWN GOD, OR RATHER ARE KNOWN BY GOD, HOW IS IT THAT YOU TURN AGAIN TO THE WEAK AND BEGGARLY ELEMENTS TO WHICH YOU DESIRE AGAIN TO BE IN BONDAGE? YOU OBSERVE DAYS AND MONTHS AND SEASONS AND YEARS. I AM AFRAID OF YOU LEST I HAVE LABORED FOR YOU IN VAIN" (4:9-11).

Or it could refer to how that they needed to seriously consider trimming from their lives anything that was hindering their progress (regardless of how "lawful" it may have been). This interpretation is reminiscent of how, in his discussion of marrying versus remaining single, Paul wrote to the Corinthian Christians, saying, "TO THE UNMARRIED...: IT IS GOOD FOR THEM IF THEY REMAIN EVEN AS I AM"—single (1 COR. 7:8). Why? "BECAUSE OF THE PRESENT DISTRESS" (v. 26).

So not only were they to put off or put down their sin of unbelief/doubt, but they were advised to even put off or put down things that weren't necessarily sinful in and of themselves—things that might be lawful, but things that would still hinder them on their course; so, spiritually speaking, they needed to "bulk down and buck up"!

The phrase **LET US RUN** is in the present tense, alluding to a day-by-day/life-long resolve; in other words, they were being told that they couldn't set time limits on their God such as by saying things like, "Well, I'll be faithful until such and such a time, but by then things had better be different."

The term for **PATIENCE** isn't the term for mere patience, but for endurance/perseverance; it's that "keep on keeping on" idea that has been the theme of the book, for no one ever won a race by patience. So Paul was telling them to "press forward, not allowing anything or anyone to keep you from the goal of redemption."

To the Galatian Christians who had/were dealing with similar difficulties, Paul wrote, "YOU WERE RUNNING THE RACE SO WELL. WHO HAS HELD YOU BACK FROM FOLLOWING THE TRUTH" (Gal. 5:7, NLT)?

Lastly in verse 1, the word for **RACE** would likely be better translated as "course"; after all, it was something **SET BEFORE** them, Paul said.

> **VERSE 2:** ...LOOKING TO JESUS, THE AUTHOR AND FINISHER OF OUR FAITH, WHO, FOR THE JOY THAT WAS SET BEFORE HIM, ENDURED THE CROSS, DESPISING THE SHAME, AND HAS SAT DOWN AT THE RIGHT HAND OF THE THRONE OF GOD.

After confronting them at length with their faithful ancestors, Paul then turned to confront them with their Messiah—Jesus (which means Savior, Mat. 1:21).

The word for **LOOKING** means "to turn one's eyes/mind from one thing, and fix them on another thing." And this was appropriate here because if a runner took his eyes off his path, even momentarily, he'd lose speed or stumble and fall; he had to have total concentration on his task at hand. (Cf. Peter when he was walking on water, then took his eyes off Jesus, Mat. 14:22-33.)

Likewise, spiritually speaking, these Hebrews had to keep their minds off any weights or sins which would slow them down or cause them to stumble and fall! And what or who was their goal? Jesus.

And by **JESUS** here, Paul didn't just mean Jesus as a person, but everything that Jesus symbolized; in other words, Paul was referring back to the idea in 10:36-37, namely Christ's imminent arrival to wrap up the promises with the fullness of the eternal kingdom!

The term **AUTHOR** is from a word that refers to the leader—the one who began the race and whose example was to be emulated as in our game "Follow the Leader."

Jesus said, "'IF THE WORLD HATES YOU, YOU KNOW THAT IT HATED ME BEFORE IT HATED YOU. ... REMEMBER ... SINCE THEY PERSECUTED ME, THEY WILL ALSO PERSECUTE YOU'" (John 15:18 & 20). "'BUT,'" He went on to say later, "'BE OF GOOD CHEER, [for] I HAVE OVERCOME THE WORLD'" (John 16:33; cf. note on this verse at 11:16).

The Greek term for **FINISHER** means "to bring to an end" then "to complete or perfect"; so Jesus wasn't only the One who started the race (the captain, as it were; cf. note at 2:10), but He was also the One who finished it by bringing all things to their fulfillment. In Romans 10:4 this same writer said that "CHRIST IS THE END (the Consummator) OF THE LAW," and in Revelation 22:13 Jesus calls Himself "'THE BEGINNING AND THE END.'"

The phrase **OUR FAITH** shouldn't be translated subjectively as <u>our</u> faith, but objectively as <u>the</u> faith, referring to the religion of God, especially that of the new/universal/final testament. So while their ancestors were heroes/models of God's religion, Jesus was the author/finisher of it. (By the way, there is such a thing as acceptable religion in the sight of God, Jas. 1:26-27.)

The clause **THE JOY THAT WAS SET BEFORE** Jesus appears to be the prospect of what it would mean to sit **DOWN AT THE RIGHT HAND OF THE THRONE OF GOD**, namely reversing the tragic defeat of humanity portrayed in the Garden of Eden story in Genesis 2–3; in other words, Christ's joy was/is experienced in/by fulfilling His task of "BRINGING MANY SONS TO GLORY" (2:10).

Since the original term translated as **FOR** here is αντι (meaning "instead of"), not εις (meaning "in order to"), some believe that Paul wasn't saying that Jesus endured the suffering of the cross in order to obtain future joy, but that He suffered instead of retaining past joy—the joy of His preincarnate life (Php. 2:6-8). However, since αντι can also mean "for the sake of" (Heb. 12:16), and since the phrase **SET BEFORE HIM** is the same as found in verse 1 with reference to a <u>future</u> course, and since Paul was clearly correlating the two, then **THE JOY** before Christ here must also be a reference to something that was in His future, <u>not</u> in His past.

Crucifixion was considered a shameful death for at least three reasons: {1} it was reserved for the worst of criminals; {2} the victim was crucified naked; and {3} the victim was considered accursed of God (Deu. 21:23 & Gal. 3:13). All this is why Paul said that Jesus was obedient, not just to death, but "EVEN [TO] THE DEATH OF A CROSS" (Php. 2:8).

Thus if Jesus **ENDURED THE CROSS** of shame for these Hebrews, surely they should've been willing to endure their trivial-in-comparison difficulties for Him.

> **VERSE 3:** **FOR CONSIDER HIM WHO ENDURED SUCH HOSTILITY FROM SINNERS AGAINST HIMSELF, LEST YOU BECOME WEARY AND DISCOURAGED IN YOUR SOULS.**

The word **FOR** introduces the reason why these brethren were exhorted to look to the Author/Finisher of their faith.

The term **CONSIDER** means "to calculate and compare"; in other words, they were told to calculate the cost of their salvation by adding up all the hostility and opposition that their Messiah suffered, then compare that cost to the price of remaining faithful to Him and His cause.

The word for **HOSTILITY** refers to "opposition in both word and deed"; this same word is translated **REBELLION** in Jude 11. So Jesus experienced hostile rebellion, the likes of which these brethren certainly hadn't experienced (v. 4) and probably never did.

When concluding his letter to the Galatian Christians who were dealing with similar difficulties, Paul wrote, "LET US NOT GROW WEARY WHILE DOING GOOD, FOR IN DUE SEASON WE SHALL REAP IF WE DON'T LOSE HEART" (6:9). And Peter, who also wrote to encourage suffering Christians, said, "WHEN YOU DO GOOD AND SUFFER FOR IT, IF YOU TAKE IT PATIENTLY, THIS IS COMMENDABLE BEFORE GOD. FOR TO THIS YOU WERE CALLED, BECAUSE CHRIST ALSO SUFFERED FOR US, LEAVING US AN EXAMPLE, THAT YOU SHOULD FOLLOW HIS STEPS" (1 Pet. 2:21).

The word for **SOULS** is from a term that simply means "lives"; some versions even translate it as "minds."

Being **WEARY** refers to "tiredness," while being **DISCOURAGED** refers to "exhaustion," that which results in giving up or quitting; Adam Clarke in his commentary indicated that the original language here is what was used of a contender in a game who, due to weariness and exhaustion, yielded to the opponent.

Let's conclude with remarks by Albert Barnes in his commentary on this verse: Speaking of what Jesus endured, he wrote, "The reference is to the Jews of the time of the Savior who opposed His plans, perverted His sayings, and ridiculed His claims. Yet, regardless of their opposition, He persevered in the course which He had marked out and went patiently forward in the execution of His plans. The idea is that [they were] to pursue the path of duty..., letting the world say what it will about it. In doing this [they could not] find a better example than the Savior. No opposition of sinners ever turned Him from the way which He regarded as right; no ridicule ever caused Him to abandon any of His plans; no argument or expression of scorn ever caused Him for a moment to deviate from His course."

PARAPHRASE OF 12:1-3: *Since we're surrounded by so many witnesses of God's faithfulness and of what faith can do, let's get strict with ourselves: let's not merely rid ourselves of the sin which causes us to leave our God, but let's even cut out of our lives things which just get in our way of reaching His goal for us; and we can do this by taking our eyes off those things and placing them only on Jesus—the One who not only conceived this journey we're on, but who also travelled it and finished it ahead of us. Besides that, consider the extreme difficulty He suffered as our leader in order to aid us in bolstering our determination.*

Hebrews 12:4-13

Hebrews 12:1-3 summed up Paul's point of how that *Christ's Superior Principle of Faith Prompts Superior Actions*. But then again these verses also ease into Paul's main point of chapter 12, namely that *This Principle of Faith Establishes a Superior Relationship* to what anyone ever possessed prior to Jesus.

Paul followed that truth with a discussion in verses 4-13 concerning one of God's purposes for allowing these Christians to experience persecution, especially as it related to this time of transition/transformation from one covenant to another. He began by reminding them that, although they had suffered, it hadn't really even come close to equaling that of their Messiah (the subject of v. 3).

VERSE 4: YOU HAVEN'T YET RESISTED TO BLOODSHED, STRIVING AGAINST SIN.

To **RESIST** is defensive meaning "to stand against," while to **STRIVE** is offensive meaning "to fight"; though many scholars have written that **BLOODSHED** here refers to blood shed in death, such isn't a necessary conclusion. The point seems to be that, while many of their ancestors (cf. chap. 11) such as Stephen, James, and even Jesus had been slain many years earlier, these complaining/apostatizing brethren had yet to even experience bloodshed, implying that their cowardice was that much more inexcusable!

Since the definite article exists before **SIN** here, it's likely that Paul had the sin of verse 1 in mind—the sin of unbelief/doubt in God that leads to apostasy. But, relative to **THE SINNERS** of verse 3 (against whom Jesus fought spiritually), it's possible that Paul was personifying sin as the opponent in the boxing ring of the Roman games; if so, "SIN" here would be an allusion to the enemy of Christ and His people, namely the rejecting

Jews who were presently persecuting these Christians. (This would correlate with Jesus' reference to dissenting Jews as instruments of the enemy [σατανας] in Revelation 2:9 & 3:9.) Then again these two interpretations mesh together so that, in the end, it doesn't matter. Why? Because these brethren were fighting against the temptation to forsake Christ <u>due to</u> the persecution of the enemy; in other words, sin—finding its strength in the old law and its defenders (1 Cor. 15:56)—was attempting to stamp out Christianity before Christ could finalize redemption (Eph. 1:10-14). The Lord once asked His people through Jeremiah in 12:5, "'IF YOU HAVE RUN WITH THE FOOTMEN AND THEY HAVE WEARIED YOU, THEN HOW CAN YOU CONTEND WITH HORSES? AND IF IN THE LAND OF PEACE … THEY HAVE WEARIED YOU, THEN HOW WILL YOU DO IN THE FLOODPLAINS OF THE JORDAN?'"

By his use of the word **YET**, Paul implied that things were only going to get worse before they got better; and from history one can see that clearly, because once Nero became an ally of the Jews against Christians, things did indeed become worse, and soon after this writing. This is why Paul went on to discuss the purpose of the suffering they were experiencing at the present time.

> **VERSES 5-6: AND YOU HAVE FORGOTTEN THE EXHORTATION WHICH SPEAKS TO YOU AS TO SONS: "MY SON, DO NOT DESPISE THE CHASTENING OF THE LORD, NOR BE DISCOURAGED WHEN YOU ARE REBUKED BY HIM; FOR WHOM THE LORD LOVES HE CHASTENS, AND SCOURGES EVERY SON WHOM HE RECEIVES"** (AN ECHO OF SOLOMON'S WORDS IN PRV. 3:11-12).

(Side-note: Even if Solomon was thinking about his own son when he wrote such proverbs, God—when inspiring him to write them—was obviously thinking about His children in relation to Him; at least that's the point Paul seemed to be making in verse 5a by the phrase **SPEAKS TO YOU**.)

The word for **DESPISE** means "regard lightly," and **CHASTENING** refers to "correction"; so they were being warned not to ignore God's discipline. Job 5:17 says, "'HAPPY IS THE MAN WHOM GOD CORRECTS; THEREFORE, DO NOT DESPISE THE CHASTENING OF THE ALMIGHTY.'"

Through the wise man Solomon, God taught in Proverbs 13:24 that parents who refuse to spank their children actually exhibit hatred for their children. Why? Because...

As He taught in 22:15, "FOOLISHNESS IS BOUND UP IN THE HEART OF A CHILD, BUT THE ROD OF CORRECTION WILL DRIVE IT FAR FROM HIM"; and "DO NOT WITHHOLD CORRECTION FROM A CHILD, FOR IF YOU BEAT HIM WITH A ROD, HE WILL NOT DIE ... [BUT] YOU SHALL ... DELIVER HIS SOUL FROM HELL" (23:13-14). See, God, as the Father of these Hebrew Christians, not only reproved/rebuked them through Paul, but He also chastised them via suffering, sometimes severely, as signified by the word **SCOURGE** which means "to whip."

Paul called the truth of this teaching an **EXHORTATION** or an "encouragement through instruction." In other words, their Father was allowing them to experience all such discipline for their own good; thus they weren't to disregard it or become discouraged by it as if God didn't care, but to view it as one of His gifts (cf. Php. 1:29).

So Paul's teaching here essentially implied that it's rank ignorance for a Christian to ask, "Why, if I'm a child of God, does He allow me to suffer so?" Why? Well, it was precisely because they were His children that they're disciplined.

VERSE 7: IF YOU ENDURE CHASTENING, GOD DEALS WITH YOU AS WITH SONS. FOR WHAT SON IS THERE WHOM A FATHER DOES NOT CHASTEN?

Here the word **IF** obviously means "when," and **ENDURE** means "experience"; in other words, Paul was saying, "When you experience adversities, acknowledge that they're actually blessings, for behind your difficulties stands a loving Father who knows what's best for you." Besides, not only did God create all human fathers, but He's also the very epitome of love (1 John 4:8). So "if an earthly father cares enough to know to discipline his children, surely God—the model Father—should be expected to discipline His children as well." Even Jesus, acting as a Father (cf. Isa. 9:6), once similarly said, "'AS MANY AS I LOVE, I REBUKE AND CHASTEN'" (Rev. 3:19).

> **VERSE 8: BUT IF YOU ARE WITHOUT CHASTENING, OF WHICH ALL HAVE BECOME PARTAKERS, THEN YOU ARE ILLEGITIMATE AND NOT SONS.**

Not only was Paul trying to give them confidence relative to their standing with God, but I believe he was even encouraging them to acknowledge the necessity of God's chastening. In other words, it appears Paul was saying that, if they wanted to be those who were "AT EASE IN ZION" (Amos 6:1)—those who didn't "SUFFER PERSECUTION" for Christ's sake (1 Pet. 4:16 & 2 Tim. 3:12), then that would be no different than a child disowning his father, making himself (figuratively) illegitimate. Or perhaps picture this converse scenario: a child needing discipline won't accept it, so his father says, "If you don't accept my discipline, then you're not my child."

Either way, the point is that if they wanted out of the suffering they were enduring for Jesus' sake, especially to the point of forsaking Christ to go back to Judaism, then they were *as* illegitimate children (cf. 2 Pet. 2:20ff).

> **VERSE 9: FURTHERMORE, WE HAVE HAD HUMAN FATHERS WHO CORRECTED US, AND WE PAID THEM RESPECT. SHALL WE NOT MUCH MORE READILY BE IN SUBJECTION TO THE FATHER OF SPIRITS AND LIVE?**

The phrase **HUMAN FATHERS** has reference to those who are fallible, while **THE FATHER OF SPIRITS** has reference to God who is infallible.

Verse 7 was paraphrased to have Paul say, "If earthly fathers care enough to discipline their children, surely God should be expected to discipline His children as well." Now verse 9 may be paraphrased by saying, "If by their discipline fallible fathers merit respect, certainly by His discipline the infallible Father should be respected!" Besides, Paul went on to tell these Hebrews that, just as submission to earthly parents resulted in life (cf. Eph. 6:2-3), submission to the Heavenly Father would/will/was about to result in life.

Earlier in Hebrews chapter 10 (the chapter which actually, as noted earlier, connects to this chapter), Paul had just told them that "'THE JUST SHALL LIVE BY FAITH'" (v. 38) and then in verse 39 that "WE ARE ... OF THOSE WHO BELIEVE TO THE SAVING OF THE SOUL (life)"—primarily in this case living through the destruction of the Jews. (See notes back at 10:38-39.)

VERSE 10: FOR THEY INDEED FOR A FEW DAYS CHASTENED US AS SEEMED BEST TO THEM, BUT HE FOR OUR PROFIT THAT WE MAY BE PARTAKERS OF HIS HOLINESS.

Unlike the Heavenly Father, earthly fathers only have their children for a short time (**A FEW DAYS**) for disciplinary purposes; and even during that time, being human, their discipline is often improper (**AS SEEMED BEST TO THEM**).

Conversely, the Heavenly Father (who has control throughout the entire lives of His created beings) never disciplines improperly and always with the view toward making His children holy as He is holy, meaning that, while an earthly father may discipline a child for selfish reasons, the Heavenly Father never does such a thing.

VERSE 11: NOW NO CHASTENING SEEMS TO BE JOYFUL FOR THE PRESENT, BUT GRIEVOUS; NEVERTHELESS, AFTERWARD IT YIELDS THE PEACEABLE FRUIT OF RIGHTEOUSNESS TO THOSE WHO HAVE BEEN TRAINED BY IT.

No discipline, whether human or divine or whether verbal or physical, is fun to bear, rather it's very unpleasant when being administered. If discipline were pleasant, it wouldn't have any power to produce its desired result—the improvement of the one disciplined. Just think of American "justice" and its lack of results, primarily, in my estimation at least, because of the lack of physical discipline. By the way, the word for **TRAINED** here is from our word for "gym," a place where one trains or is trained.

RIGHTEOUSNESS is **PEACEABLE** because the more righteous a child of God is, the closer his relationship will be with His Father.

However, instead of looking at this on an individual basis, it's likely that Paul had a more general application in mind in reference to these specific brethren in their particular time; in other words, maybe when he spoke of their reaching the goal of "THE PEACE OF RIGHTEOUSNESS" (v. 11) and being "PARTAKERS OF GOD'S HOLINESS" (v. 10), he had in mind their pressing forward through all of their persecution in order to attain their crown of "LIFE" (v. 9) in fulfillment of the promises. In fact, this is what I believe Paul had in mind when he wrote, "OUR LIGHT AFFLICTION—WHICH IS BUT FOR A MOMENT—IS WORKING FOR US A FAR MORE EXCEEDING AND ETERNAL WEIGHT OF GLORY" (2 Cor. 4:17).

> **VERSES 12-13: THEREFORE** (SINCE DISCIPLINE IS FOR YOUR GOOD, THEN)... **STRENGTHEN THE HANDS WHICH HANG DOWN AND THE FEEBLE KNEES, AND MAKE STRAIGHT PATHS FOR YOUR FEET, SO THAT WHAT IS LAME MAY NOT BE DISLOCATED, BUT RATHER HEALED.**

The word for **STRENGTHEN** literally means "to make vertical," but since it's obvious Paul was using the physical to illustrate the spiritual, this word (being plural) means "to encourage one another."

By the phrases **HANDS WHICH HANG DOWN** and **FEEBLE KNEES**, Paul reminded them of the "WEARY AND DISCOURAGED" in verse 3; they were those who (through lack of understanding the purpose of trials and therefore the lack of having the right attitude toward them) had caused themselves to become exhausted by their hardships to the point of reconsidering their Christianity.

The word **STRAIGHT** refers to that which is straight horizontally; so, by the clause "make level or smooth paths," Paul (probably referring back to "THE SIN" and "EVERY WEIGHT" of verse 1) meant for them to clear their courses of all unnecessary obstacles, not just for their own personal good, but also so that the **LAME** (weak ones) following them wouldn't be **DISLOCATED** (fall totally out of the race).

Paul was urging them all to help one another, especially should the strong strengthen the weak (cf. Rom. 15:1 & Gal. 6:2) in order to **HEAL** or save them. This aid may have needed to involve helping them remove some sin or weight from their lives or helping them to regain their "FIRST LOVE" for Christ (cf. Rev. 2:4 & Mat. 24:12).

Paul summed up all of this when he told the Thessalonians (who had come under the impression that the Lord had already come, 2 The. 2:1-2) to "WARN THOSE WHO ARE UNRULY, COMFORT THE FAINTHEARTED, AND UPHOLD THE WEAK" (1 The. 5:14).

As mentioned in reference to 10:39, this is another place in which Paul appeared to be impersonating a cheerleader or an inspiring coach; in other words, "Lift up those hands! Strengthen those knees! Get those lazy feet on the track!" (But then again perhaps in this instance he sounds more like a platoon sergeant!)

In these verses Paul, being led by the master writer—the Holy Spirit, was alluding to a prophecy in Isaiah 35 which perfectly flows right into the latter part of this chapter concerning the New Jerusalem that was on the verge of coming in its fullness: verse 22 in fact specifically told them that "YOU HAVE COME TO MOUNT ZION ... THE HEAVENLY JERUSALEM"—that which Paul called the kingdom they were in the process of receiving (v. 28).

Thus, using Edom's judgment and destruction to picture the judgment and destruction of physical Zion (old Jerusalem) in Isaiah 34, Isaiah went on to contrast that with a picture of the glory which would follow such ugliness in chapter 35. Here are verses 3-4 and parts of 8-10: **3**"STRENGTHEN THE WEAK HANDS AND MAKE FIRM THE FEEBLE KNEES. **4**SAY TO THOSE WHO ARE FEARFUL-HEARTED, 'BE STRONG, DO NOT FEAR! BEHOLD, YOUR GOD WILL COME WITH VENGEANCE, WITH THE RECOMPENSE OF GOD; HE WILL COME AND SAVE YOU.' ... **8a**A HIGHWAY SHALL BE THERE AND A ROAD, AND IT SHALL BE CALLED THE HIGHWAY OF HOLINESS. THE UNCLEAN SHALL NOT PASS OVER IT, BUT IT SHALL BE FOR OTHERS. ... **9b**BUT THE REDEEMED SHALL WALK THERE, **10a**AND THE RANSOMED OF THE LORD SHALL RETURN AND COME TO ZION WITH SINGING, WITH EVERLASTING JOY ON THEIR HEADS."

It appears that not only was Paul explaining to them the purpose and necessity of their trials in order to help them get through them, but it also appears that he was reminding them that Isaiah had specifically predicted that those who were alive as the New Zion was coming to fruition would suffer—a suffering, however, that would turn into joyous redemption!

By the way, all this corresponds perfectly with Paul's earlier admonition to "ENCOURAGE (as in 'strengthen') ONE ANOTHER, AND SO MUCH THE MORE AS YOU SEE THAT DAY APPROACHING" (10:25b).

Hebrews 12:14-21

Following 12:4-11—in which Paul tried to encourage his Jewish Christian addressees in their suffering by explaining and/or reminding them of God's purpose and plan for hardship—he exhorted them in verses 12-13 to help one another through these difficult times, indicating that they were expected to work together as a family, for "no man is an island."

In the paragraph under consideration now, Paul will be seen as continuing to urge them onward—as he himself wrote in Philippians 3:14—"TOWARD THE GOAL FOR THE PRIZE OF THE UPWARD CALL OF GOD IN CHRIST JESUS," still emphasizing the need to help one another under their strenuous circumstances.

> **VERSE 14: PURSUE PEACE WITH ALL MEN AND HOLINESS WITHOUT WHICH NO ONE WILL SEE THE LORD...**

The word **PURSUE** brings back to mind the runner in the race of verse 1, because it comes from a word which means "to run swiftly, to run after, to press on with intensity"; it's the same word as found in Philippians 3:12 where Paul (just before speak-ing of "THE PRIZE OF THE UPWARD CALL") wrote, "NOT THAT I HAVE ALREADY ATTAINED OR AM ALREADY PERFECTED [as some were claiming, cf. 2 Tim. 2:18 w/ Php. 3:10ff]; BUT I PRESS ON THAT I MAY LAY HOLD OF THAT FOR WHICH CHRIST JESUS HAS ALSO LAID HOLD OF ME." So, according to 12:2, 14, & 24, their ultimate goal in this race was a perfected relationship with Christ. But what were their immediate goals at the time Paul was writing that would lead them to their ultimate goal? "PEACE" and "HOLINESS."

In the phrase **PEACE WITH ALL MEN**, there's no word in the original wording for "MEN"; a word must be supplied, but (due to the context) I believe (along with various scholars) the supplied word should've been "brethren," meaning that they were to do their best to keep peace among themselves during those very difficult times, for the more discord they had among themselves, the less help they'd be to one another. (Incidentally, the word translated WITH is often translated "AMONG," cf. Luke 24:5, etc.) Besides, as Jesus said, "'BLESSED ARE THE PEACEMAKERS, FOR THEY SHALL BE CALLED SONS OF GOD'" (Mat. 5:9); so if they wanted to be among those "SONS" in the fulfilled sense of Hebrews 2:10, then they had better be keeping peace among themselves.

They were also urged to help one another in the pursuit of holiness (cf. vv. 15-16). And, due to the modifying phrase ("WITHOUT WHICH NO ONE WILL SEE THE LORD"), this was a reminder of another beatitude of Jesus: "'BLESSED ARE THE PURE IN HEART, FOR THEY SHALL SEE GOD'" (Mat. 5:8).

Another blessing of pursuing holiness was that they could take comfort in knowing that they were being "'PERSECUTED FOR RIGHTEOUSNESS' SAKE, FOR THEIRS IS THE KINGDOM OF HEAVEN'" (Mat. 5:10, cf. 1 Pet. 3:14), the very kingdom Paul went on to discuss. After all, as John wrote of this kingdom, "THERE SHALL BY NO MEANS ENTER IT ANYTHING THAT DEFILES OR CAUSES AN ABOMINATION OR A LIE, BUT ONLY THOSE WHO ARE WRITTEN IN THE LAMB'S BOOK OF LIFE" (Rev. 21:27, cf. Heb. 12:23).

Interestingly, **PEACE/HOLINESS** here correspond to "THE PEACEABLE FRUIT OF RIGHTEOUSNESS" (v. 11), that which comes from having the correct knowledge/attitude/response toward hardship (v. 10). Furthermore, "PEACE" and "HOLINESS" are reminiscent of Christ's high priestly ministry as "KING OF PEACE" and "KING OF RIGHTEOUSNESS" (7:1-2). So it would seem that one of these attributes cannot be successfully acquired apart from the other, one having to do with our relationship to men and the other having to do with our relationship to God.

VERSE 15: ...LOOKING DILIGENTLY LEST ANYONE FALL SHORT OF THE GRACE OF GOD, LEST ANY ROOT OF BITTERNESS SPRINGING UP CAUSE TROUBLE AND BY THIS [THE] MANY BECOME DEFILED...

The phrase **FALL SHORT** is in the present tense, meaning that they were to be watching out for any of their spiritual family members who were in the process of "falling away from the grace of God" or falling out of the race (v. 13), the finish of which was God's gift of His kingdom (v. 28, cf. notes there).

The word **ROOT** is often used in the Bible as a metaphor for a person (cf. Rom. 15:12). Why? More than likely it's because a root produces fruit, whether it be good or bad. So, if someone were to come or rise up among them spreading falsehoods (cf. Acts 20:29), not only would it generate bitterness among them, but it could also cause untold trouble, possibly even leading to the loss of their eternal rewards! (By the way, Judaizers would sometimes become pseudo-Christians in order to do exactly that, cf. 2 Cor. 11:13, Gal. 2:4, & Jude 4.)

(Side-note: When one reads Deuteronomy 29:16-21, it's almost impossible to deny that Paul had that passage in mind when he penned this paragraph, especially since it's the only other place where the idea of "A ROOT BEARING BITTERNESS" [a poisonous plant] is found and at that in the context of the Israelites entering into a covenant relationship with the God who brought them out of Egyptian bondage and kept them from extinction through forty years of wandering in the wilderness.)

Now, because this verse begins with the participle **LOOKING**, it describes or expounds upon the previous verse, meaning that they needed to pursue peace and holiness (v. 14) to keep out trouble and defilement (v. 15). He was essentially saying the same thing here that he said in 3:12-14: "BEWARE, BRETHREN, LEST THERE BE IN ANY OF YOU AN EVIL HEART OF UNBELIEF IN DEPARTING FROM THE LIVING GOD, BUT EXHORT ONE ANOTHER DAILY WHILE IT IS CALLED 'TODAY,' LEST ANY OF YOU BE HARDENED THROUGH THE DECEITFULNESS OF SIN."

> **VERSE 16:** ...**LEST THERE BE ANY FORNICATOR OR PROFANE PERSON LIKE ESAU WHO, FOR ONE MORSEL OF FOOD, SOLD HIS BIRTHRIGHT.**

Apparently out of pure hatred, Judaizers weren't content with just trying to incite Christians to renounce Jesus as the

Christ and return to Judaism, but (perhaps to ruin any reputation they might have) they also tried to incite them to commit immorality: Jude 4 reads, "CERTAIN MEN HAVE CREPT IN UNNOTICED ... MEN WHO TURN THE GRACE OF GOD INTO LICENTIOUSNESS."

Per this verse, a **PROFANE PERSON** was someone who used what was consecrated to God (sacred in nature) in order to obtain what wasn't consecrated to God (material in nature), and Esau illustrated this character perfectly by using/selling his birthright to satisfy a physical appetite.

His birthright meant that he was in line to be the next family priest once his father died, but he had no appreciation for sacred things; so in parting with this religious honor for mere food, he declared himself a non-religious person. So how did this apply to these Jewish Christians? Well, if one of them was incited to become a fornicator for example, he (as one of the firstborn [cf. notes at v. 23]) would in essence be selling his birthright for a physical appetite; he'd lose his privilege of being one of the first ones to be born again and come into possession of the kingdom of Heaven (cf. John 3:3 & 5). According to verses 18-28, it seems that Paul used Esau (and all he failed to value) as a parallel (or another type) of these brethren (and what they would lose) if they acted as Esau. By the way, **A MORSEL OF FOOD** actually refers to "a single meal."

> **VERSE 17:** FOR YOU KNOW THAT AFTERWARD, WHEN HE WANTED TO INHERIT THE BLESSING, HE WAS REJECTED, FOR HE FOUND NO PLACE FOR REPENTANCE, THOUGH HE SOUGHT IT DILIGENTLY WITH TEARS.

How could one not think of the parable of the ten virgins in Matthew 25:1-13? Try reading that sometime with this passage in mind: Jacob representing the first five virgins and Esau representing the second five virgins. This is also reminiscent of a couple of kids: Joe and Ted each have a toy that the other wants, so an agreed upon trade is made; but later when Joe sees how much fun Ted is having with his old toy, he wants it back, but it's too late!

The clause **HE FOUND NO PLACE FOR REPENTANCE** could mean at least three things: {1} It could mean that Esau couldn't conjure up within himself any true sorrow for what he had done, but since the structural antecedent for **IT** in the last clause is **REPENTANCE**, then to say that **HE SOUGHT IT DILIGENTLY WITH TEARS** seems to rule out this interpretation. {2} As with most sins, it could mean that Esau couldn't find a way to change the consequences of his decision, but I know of no historical evidence that Esau tried to convince Jacob to return his birthright; rather, they simply became enemies for numerous years. And {3} in harmony with the *American Standard Version* and many scholars, it could mean that Esau couldn't bring about a change *in his father's mind*, though he tried to do so with passionate tears. This appears to be the most accurate interpretation, chiefly because it perfectly corresponds to Genesis 27:34ff as well as the parable of Matthew 25:1-13.

Thus, if this (third) explanation is indeed correct, then the parallel is that, if these brethren forsook Christ for Moses, they would discover at the judgment that it was then too late to effect a change in the mind of God, which corresponds perfectly to how that Jesus (after He supplied plenty of signs of their end in His Olivet discourse) warned them not to wait too late to take care of things.

> **VERSES 18-19A:** FOR YOU HAVE NOT COME TO THE MOUNTAIN THAT MAY BE TOUCHED AND THAT BURNED WITH FIRE AND TO BLACKNESS AND DARKNESS AND TEMPEST, AND THE SOUND OF A TRUMPET...

Although Paul never used the phrase "Mount Sinai" in this context, by the description he supplied, he left no doubt that Mt. Sinai was the place he had in mind.

The reasoning for listing these various characteristics here seems to be two-fold: {1} Paul wanted to remind them of the awesomeness of the time when Moses received the wondrous yet inferior covenant; and {2} he wanted them to contrast the fear that God meant to instill in them by the giving of a law that could only condemn.

Although the Israelites were told to not touch Mt. Sinai while Moses was receiving the Law (v. 20 & Exo. 19:12-13), that command, in and of itself, implied that this mountain was tangible; Paul wanted these brethren to be sure that they got that point in order for them to clearly see the contrast between the receiving of the Old Covenant on a physical, earthly mountain and the receiving of the New Covenant on a spiritual, heavenly mountain—the Mt. Zion of verse 22.

Not only were these brethren reminded that their ancestors weren't allowed to touch Mt. Sinai, but they were also reminded that it "BURNED WITH FIRE" because "THE LORD DESCENDED UPON IT IN FIRE" (Exo. 19:18); besides that, it was covered in a "THICK CLOUD" (Exo. 19:16), creating a "THICK DARKNESS" (Exo. 20:21). (Ironically, the original word for "BLACKNESS" here is translated "THICK CLOUD" in *The Emphatic Diaglott*.) Then added to that was a "TEMPEST" (storm) and "THE SOUND OF A TRUMPET"; Exodus 19:16 declares that there were "THUNDERINGS AND LIGHTNINGS," and 19:18 declares that "THE WHOLE MOUNTAIN QUAKED GREATLY," and 19:16 & 19 declare that "THE SOUND OF A TRUMPET WAS VERY LOUD," becoming "LOUDER AND LOUDER" until it ceased.

Let's notice a couple of things: {1} Not only here in this text indirectly, but also in the entire book of Hebrews, Paul was dealing with the passing away of the Old Covenant (e.g. 8:13) and the bringing in of the New Covenant. I doubt very seriously that it's only a coincidence that the Old Covenant went out in AD 70 in a similar fashion as it came in. And {2} concerning this trumpet, trumpet blasts were a common signal announcing God's presence and often associated with the giving of a covenant (e.g. Exo. 19:16, 19, 20:18, Mat. 24:31, 1 The. 4:16, & Rev. 11:15), in this instance putting the finishing touches on the New Covenant in the abolition of the old.

> **VERSE 19B:...AND THE VOICE OF WORDS, SO THAT THOSE WHO HEARD IT BEGGED THAT THE WORD SHOULD NOT BE SPOKEN TO THEM ANYMORE.**

The people evidently heard God call Moses up to the mountain (Exo. 19:19-20), because it frightened them to the point that they asked Moses to do the talking to them in God's place lest they die (Exo. 20:19, cf. Deu. 5:25).

The main point of all of these negative characteristics in reference to the giving of the Law is that it could only judge and condemn; it couldn't forgive and save. Now consider a few things here: {1} While the old law was given by God's voice on the mountain of Sinai, it was in essence replaced by God's voice on the mountain of transfiguration by a new law (Mat. 17:1-8). (By the way, just as Moses encouraged the Israelites to not be afraid of God's voice at Mt. Sinai [Exo. 20:20], Jesus encouraged the disciples to not be afraid of God's voice at this mountain.) {2} While God led Moses into a 40-day fast before he began sharing with Israel what we today call the old law (Exo. 34:28 & 20:1ff), the Spirit led Jesus into a 40-day fast before He began sharing with the people of His day what we today call the new law (Mat. 4:1-2 & 5–7). {3} While the old law in its entirety was being given and instilled over a period of 40 years in a literal wilderness, the new law was given and instilled over a period of 40 years (AD 30—AD 70) in a metaphoric wilderness (Rev. 12). And {4} the giving of the old law began with fear, darkness, earth-quaking, a cloud, and a trumpet, then later ended with the same—things that denoted/pictured judgment (cf. Luke 21:26 & Mat. 24:7 & 29-30 & 34-35).

> **VERSE 20:** (FOR THEY COULD NOT ENDURE WHAT WAS COMMANDED: "AND IF SO MUCH AS A BEAST TOUCHES THE MOUNTAIN, IT SHALL BE STONED OR THRUST THROUGH WITH AN ARROW."

The statement that **THEY COULDN'T ENDURE WHAT WAS COMMANDED** doesn't mean that God asked them to do impossible things; it rather means that the command to not even touch the mountain lest they die (Exo. 19:12-13) made this a very awe-inspiring, yea terrifying, experience. But the question is: Why did God command this? There could be at least two reasons: {1} God may have commanded this just to add to the entirety of the phenomenon, cinching the fact that this would not be an experience easily forgotten. And/or {2} sinful man just wasn't allowed to approach God's presence, and God's presence was then concentrated upon Mount Sinai; even Moses was told to not come too close in Exodus 3:5.

Later on this idea was pictured in the tabernacle when it was created with two compartments, the holiest of all being God's room, accessible only to the high priest one day a year; so just as the entrance of a non-high-priest would desecrate the holiest of all, the allowance of anyone except Moses (a priest, Psa. 99:6) to touch Mt. Sinai would've defiled it. In fact, it seems that the reason they had to kill with stones or arrows whatever/whomever touched the mountain was because they weren't even allowed to touch that which had come into contact with it. (This is reminiscent of how the people remained aloof from Moses when he came down from Sinai with his face shining so brightly, Exo. 34:30. Did you ever wonder what would've happened had someone touched him before the glow disappeared?)

VERSE 21: AND SO TERRIFYING WAS THE SIGHT THAT MOSES SAID, "I AM EXCEEDINGLY AFRAID AND TREMBLING.")

The record of this statement by Moses isn't recorded; Paul (as in Acts 20:35) wrote this by inspiration. But, to guess at what point in the narrative of Exodus 19 Moses made this statement, it could be placed at verse 19 for two reasons: {1} It's in the context of the time when (in verse 16) it says that God (by means of all those frightening events, especially the loud horn-blowing) had caused everyone to tremble (just as Moses had done when he first met God on the mountain in Exodus 3 [cf. Acts 7:32]); besides, seeing that their leader was afraid would've surely made the rest of them afraid. And {2} verse 19 declares that Moses said something at the point when the trumpets had become louder and louder, but it doesn't reveal what he said, just like it declares that God answered him, but likewise doesn't reveal what He said.

In conclusion of this section, the Bible student must be sure to remember that Paul's main point in verses 18-21 was to remind these Jewish brethren of the terrifying yet awe-inspiring circumstances that surrounded the giving of the old law so that he could go on to demonstrate through contrast that what they were experiencing in the giving of the new law in their time was even greater than what their forefathers had experienced.

Hebrews 12:22-29

Following the outline in the introduction, this section heads toward the conclusion of Paul's thoughts concerning *Christ's Superior Principle of Faith* (10:19-13:25); more specifically, 12:22-29 wrap up Paul's thoughts concerning how that this principle establishes a relationship superior to that which was possible under Moses. (This implies of course that since God spent thousands of years orchestrating everything in order to get to this point [cf. 1:2 & 11:3], then it would be foolish of Him to accept any type of previously permitted relationship, that is any relationship which dodges Jesus, e.g. returning to the old law.)

So in this section Paul wrote his seventh and last warning of the book: he warned against rejecting God's Christ and the kingdom He was in the process of bringing to fruition. Why? Because only through Jesus and this kingdom could they (and we, of course) have total forgiveness, redemption, and a once-and-for-all restored fellowship to their (and our) Creator, a relationship in which man can serve Him acceptably.

> **VERSE 22:** BUT YOU HAVE COME TO MOUNT ZION AND TO THE CITY OF THE LIVING GOD, THE HEAVENLY JERUSALEM, TO AN INNUMERABLE COMPANY OF ANGELS...

After writing in the previous verses about the awesomeness exhibited in the giving of the Law of Moses, Paul began to contrast something even greater than that! And that which is greater is that of which they as Christians had become part (1 Pet. 2:5); in other words, in harmony with Ephesians 1:10, they were already part of that which was in the process of being expanded to include the Earth: verse 28 below reads, "WE ARE RECEIVING A KINGDOM WHICH [UNLIKE THAT OF MOSES] CANNOT BE SHAKEN" (cf. "ABOUT TO [μελλω] COME" in 13:14).

What a wondrous thing to be part of that which is even greater than what their ancestors were involved in and experienced! These brethren were experiencing the giving of the Law of Christ from Zion instead of the Law of Moses from Sinai (v. 18, cf. Gal. 4:22-26)!

The term ZION was another designation for earthly Jerusalem, sometimes called "MOUNT ZION" since Jerusalem was situated on a hill (hence why the Bible sometimes speaks of going "DOWN" to a place that was actually north of Jerusalem [cf. Luke 10:30]).

As discussed in chapter 9, God dwelled by the Ark of the Covenant, the only piece of furniture in the tabernacle's holiest of all; thus, in a sense, where the Ark was, God was. So, because King David placed the Ark of the Lord in Jerusalem (2 Sam. 6:12 & 17), it became known as "THE CITY OF GOD" or where God dwelt (Psa. 46:4 & 132:13), which in turn of course implies that when God destroyed it He was finished dwelling there (cf. John 4:21).

Since God would ultimately live in another Zion—the New Testament kingdom, the term "ZION" is used numerous times in prophecies to refer to it (e.g., Isa. 1:27, 28:16, 33:5, & 60:14).

The phrase THE CITY OF GOD here is the very city that their most beloved forefathers were looking forward to (cf. 11:16). It was an eternal/spiritual kingdom, not a temporary/physical one like that of David (2 Sam. 5:7 & 9); in other words, it was "THE HEAVENLY JERUSALEM" (not the earthly one) that Abraham looked forward to (11:10). According to 9:8, the old law didn't make any provisions for men to enter into this wondrous city, the same wondrous city referenced in chapters 3 & 21–22 of Revelation, words penned to more suffering Christians of that generation. (Cf. Rev. 3:12 & 21:1 w/ Mat. 24:34-35, 21:2-3, & 9-10.)

Listing the INNUMERABLE COMPANY OF ANGELS here seems to imply that, by becoming members of this heavenly city, they had become part of the kingdom which includes the angels of God, again reminiscent of Ephesians 1:10 (probably the best summary verse of biblical eschatology): "THAT IN THE DISPENSATION OF

THE FULLNESS OF THE TIMES GOD MIGHT GATHER TOGETHER IN ONE ALL THINGS IN CHRIST, BOTH WHICH ARE IN HEAVEN AND WHICH ARE ON EARTH." (There's that "heavens and earth" business again [cf. notes at Heb. 1:10].) Following this statement, Paul went on to write that God has "RAISED US UP TOGETHER AND MADE US SIT TOGETHER IN THE HEAVENLY PLACES IN CHRIST JESUS" (Eph. 2:6).

> **VERSE 23:** ...**TO THE GENERAL ASSEMBLY AND CHURCH OF THE FIRSTBORN WHO ARE REGISTERED IN HEAVEN, TO GOD THE JUDGE OF ALL** [CF. GEN. 18:25], **TO THE SPIRITS OF JUST MEN MADE PERFECT...**

As indicated in other versions (e.g., NIV), **GENERAL ASSEMBLY** actually refers to an assembly of celebration (cf. the English word "panegyric"), and here it's actually directly connected to the angels of verse 22, meaning that verses 22b & 23a should read something more like this: "YOU HAVE COME TO A FESTIVE ASSEMBLY OF MYRIADS [the Greek term] OF ANGELS." But what does that mean or imply? {1} The angels (as part of God's kingdom to which Christians were being joined) rejoiced over salvation and those being saved (cf. Luke 15:10 & Luke 2:13-15). {2} The angels also rejoiced because they were seeing how all God's labor over the centuries was finally working itself out for this salvation (cf. 1 Pet. 1:12 & Mat. 13:17). And {3} while there was terror exhibited in the giving of the Law by angels via Moses (12:18 & 2:2), these first century brethren should've been sharing in the joy the angels were experiencing in the giving of the Law of Christ by the Spirit via the apostles!

The phrase **THE CHURCH OF THE FIRSTBORN WHO ARE REGISTERED IN HEAVEN** is reminiscent of Philippians 3:20 and 4:3 where Paul spoke of Christians as having their citizenship in Heaven ... and in its Book of Life, even though they lived on Earth. (As a reminder, the church is that part of the kingdom which exists only on Earth.) Who are the "firstborn" here? {1} As the complete clause clearly indicates, "THE FIRSTBORN" here isn't a reference to Christ as in 1:6, but to Christians (the Greek term being plural in number). And {2} it isn't a reference to all Christians of all time, but to the <u>first</u> ones, especially the Jews who submitted to Jesus as the promised Messiah before the holocaust of AD 70. In fact, I believe "the firstborn" here are parallel to the remnant of Revelation 14:1-4. (Note specifically John's terms "Mount Zion" and "firstfruits.") So perhaps we today fit better into the numerous Christians of Romans 8:29 in which Paul spoke of Jesus as being "THE FIRSTBORN AMONG MANY." By the way, I also believe there's a shadow/substance correlation between the firstborn of Hebrews 12 and the firstborn of Exodus 12. (You can consider that for yourself.)

The phrase **GOD THE JUDGE OF ALL** (from Gen. 18:25) was placed here probably because He's the One who decided who was to be registered in Heaven as a citizen and who was not to be so registered.

When he wrote of **THE SPIRITS OF JUST MEN MADE PERFECT**, Paul was probably thinking of all the faithful saints who had gone on before these brethren, perhaps with special reference to those he had just delineated in the previous chapter.

> **VERSE 24: ...TO JESUS THE MEDIATOR OF THE NEW COVENANT, AND TO THE BLOOD OF SPRINKLING THAT SPEAKS BETTER THINGS THAN THAT OF ABEL.**

Whereas the Old Covenant was given through Moses as mediator (Gal. 3:19), the new/better covenant established upon better promises (Heb. 8:6) was given by God through His Son who mediates at His right hand (Heb. 1:3, etc.).

Next Paul contrasted Jesus' blood with that of Abel (cf. 11:4). The query is, "Did Paul have in mind the blood of Abel's animal sacrifice or Abel's personal blood shed by his brother?" If he had Abel's animal sacrifice in mind (Gen. 4:1-4), then perhaps he was contrasting blood that couldn't forgive sins (Heb. 10:4) with blood that could (Heb. 9:14 & 10:22). But if he had Abel's personal blood in mind (Gen. 4:10 & 15), then perhaps he was contrasting the blood of the righteous who cried out for vengeance (Mat. 23:29-39, esp. v. 35) with the blood that was shed for forgiveness (Eph. 1:7). Either way, mercy and forgiveness are emphasized.

Now, based on all of Paul's contrasts between the Old and New Covenants in verses 18-24, he went on in verses 25-29 to warn them against renouncing Christ and His kingdom.

> **VERSE 25: SEE [THEN] THAT YOU DO NOT REFUSE HIM WHO SPEAKS. FOR IF THEY DID NOT ESCAPE WHO REFUSED HIM WHO SPOKE ON EARTH, MUCH MORE SHALL WE NOT ESCAPE IF WE TURN AWAY FROM HIM WHO SPEAKS FROM HEAVEN...**

The term for **REFUSE** means "to disown or renounce," and the present tense term for **SEE** means "to see to it on a continuous basis" (translated "BEWARE" in 3:12); so, putting this together, Paul was essentially saying, "You must see to it that you never even consider renouncing Jesus!"

If one fails to read verse 26 with verse 25, he may struggle figuring out how Abel **SPOKE ON EARTH**, since he seems to be the antecedent for the pronoun "HIM" in the phrase **HIM WHO SPOKE ON EARTH**. Verse 26 makes it clear that Paul had returned to talking about God when He came down upon Mt. Sinai to give the Law (Exo. 19:18–20:19 & Heb. 12:18-21) in contrast to His speaking through Jesus from Mt. Zion (cf. Heb. 1:1 w/ 12:22 & 24).

The warning of this verse is actually just a repeat of at least two others found in Hebrews 2:2-3 and 10:23-30; it was a warning based on a logical conclusion: since God didn't let those who refused His previous/inferior law escape punishment (Heb. 3:7–4:5), certainly He wouldn't let these brethren escape an even worse punishment for refusing His superior law of grace/liberty, one that cost Him His only begotten Son!

> **VERSE 26: ...WHOSE VOICE THEN SHOOK THE EARTH; BUT NOW HE HAS PROMISED SAYING, "YET ONCE MORE I SHAKE NOT ONLY THE EARTH, BUT ALSO [THE] HEAVEN[S]."**

The part about God's voice shaking the earth refers once again of course to the time when God gave the Law at Mt. Sinai: speaking of God descending upon Mt. Sinai, Exodus 19:18 says that "THE WHOLE MOUNTAIN QUAKED GREATLY."

The latter part of this verse is a quote from Haggai 2:6, a prophecy that found its ultimate fulfillment when the old law was replaced by the new; that's the context in which Paul placed it here in Hebrews 12 (yea, the entire book of Hebrews), and it also corresponds to Joel 3:16, the context of which speaks of the coming of the New Covenant administration at the destruction of the Old (cf. Joel chapters 2–3). Joel 3:16 says, "THE LORD ALSO WILL ROAR FROM ZION AND UTTER HIS VOICE FROM JERUSALEM [just as we've been discussing, cf. Luke 24:47]; THE HEAVENS AND EARTH WILL SHAKE; BUT THE LORD WILL BE A SHELTER FOR HIS PEOPLE...." By the way, Isaiah 2–3 are parallel to Joel 2–3. And in Isaiah 2:19 & 21 one can read about how God would "SHAKE THE EARTH MIGHTILY" at the time of the exchange of covenant administrations that was obviously fulfilled in the last generation of the Jews between Pentecost and Holocaust (AD 30–70).

When studying Hebrews chapter one earlier, there was a lengthy discussion concerning the apocalyptic/prophetic usage of the phrase "HEAVENS AND EARTH" and how that it was often employed to refer to the demise of one administration for another (see notes at Heb. 1:10). (Cf. Isa. 51:4-6 & 15-16; 65:7 & 17; 66:22; also cf. Mat. 5:17-18, 24:29, & 34-35, verses which can refer to nothing else but the time of AD 70.) So it isn't difficult for one to see that the literal shaking in Exodus became the basis for the Jews' figurative expression ("THE SHAKING OF HEAVEN AND EARTH") which denotes a change in administration or law, that with which Paul had been dealing throughout the book of Hebrews.

(Side-note: I concur with Adam Clarke who said that the prophetic writings often used this terminology: "earth" to describe the land or city of Jerusalem and "heaven(s)" to describe its political and religious constitution. So in AD 70, when Jerusalem and its temple were annihilated, their heaven and earth—*their world*—was removed so that a new heaven and earth could be estab-lished [cf. Rev. 20:11 & 21:1].)

VERSE 27: NOW THIS, "YET ONCE MORE," INDICATES THE REMOVAL OF THOSE THINGS THAT ARE BEING SHAKEN, AS OF THINGS THAT ARE MADE, THAT THE THINGS WHICH CANNOT BE SHAKEN MAY REMAIN.

Paul drew attention to the phrase **YET ONCE MORE** because it implies something that's final, meaning that the new heavens and earth would be the last administration because it would be so perfect that there would never be a need for another.

This verse provides another indication why Paul wasn't referring to the material heavens and earth: whatever would be shaken and removed was <u>in</u> <u>the</u> <u>process</u> of **BEING SHAKEN** at the time he wrote (2,000 years ago), corresponding to 8:13 where, speaking of the first covenant, he wrote that it was —at that time—"BECOM<u>ING</u> OBSOLETE AND GROW<u>ING</u> OLD ... READY TO VANISH AWAY," or, as he said in Second Corinthians, it was in the process at that time (AD 53) of "PASS<u>ING</u> AWAY" (3:7-13).

The **THINGS THAT ARE MADE** or created is obviously a reference to the physical (that which was temporary) as opposed to the spiritual (that which is eternal); in other words, all those physical things like Jerusalem (the specific city to which Jews had to come) and the temple (the specific part of Jerusalem to which the Jews had to come) would all be replaced with something spiritual/eternal.

The things that were being shaken (the old, temporary Jerusalem, etc.) were <u>on</u> <u>the</u> <u>verge</u> of being supplanted with **THINGS** (the New Covenant and its kingdom [v. 28]) which **CANNOT** and will <u>never</u> **BE SHAKEN**, much less supplanted.

In 13:14 Paul said that, in their present circumstances, they had "NO <u>CONTINUING</u> CITY, BUT ... SEEK THE ONE [ABOUT] TO COME." And what would that be but "THE CITY OF GOD ... THE HEAVENLY JERUSALEM" of 12:22?

In 9:11, using some of the same language found in 12:27 and 13:14, Paul wrote, "CHRIST CAME AS HIGH PRIEST OF THE GOOD THINGS [ABOUT] TO COME, WITH THE GREATER AND MORE PERFECT TABERNACLE NOT MADE WITH HANDS, THAT IS, NOT OF THIS CREATION." Thus...

VERSES 28-29: SINCE WE ARE RECEIVING A KINGDOM WHICH CANNOT BE SHAKEN, LET US HAVE GRACE BY WHICH WE MAY SERVE GOD ACCEPTABLY WITH REVERENCE AND GODLY FEAR; FOR OUR GOD IS A CONSUMING FIRE.

The word **GRACE** could be translated as "thankfulness," implying that only service rendered out of gratitude (as opposed to merit, especially via the old law) is acceptable now (cf. NIV, NASB, & Earle's *Word Meanings in the New Testament*); however (and perhaps better corresponding to this context) it should be translated as "gift" (cf. 2 Cor. 8:4, etc.) with reference to the **KINGDOM** as the gift.

The word **HAVE** in the phrase **LET US HAVE GRACE** means "to hold on to;" it's translated as "RETAIN" (Rom. 1:28) and "I HAVE KEPT" (Luke 19:20). So Paul was admonishing them to hold on to the reception of the gift that they were in the process of **RECEIVING**, for only through it could they truly **SERVE GOD ACCEPTABLY**.

The word **REVERENCE** refers to "respect demonstrated by means of humility," and the phrase "GODLY FEAR" is from a single term, the same term used in relation to Jesus in 5:7 where it says that His prayers were "HEARD BECAUSE OF HIS GODLY FEAR." Since we know Jesus didn't fear His Father in the sense of being scared/terrified of Him, then this helps us to see that here it's simply a synonym for "REVERENCE" or humble respect. The word for **GODLY FEAR** here is from δεος which refers to "moving with caution," whereas φοβος is the word that refers to the "terror which seizes one when danger emerges."

Verse 29 is a quote from Deuteronomy 4:24, a verse found just before Moses repeated the Law given in Exodus 20 and after God set fire to Mt. Sinai by His presence (Exo. 19). According to Deuteronomy 4, Moses warned the Jews against idolatry by reminding them of the fire of Mt. Sinai—**GOD IS A CONSUMING FIRE**. And according to Deuteronomy 9:3, Moses also let them know that God would be "A CONSUMING FIRE" for them against their enemies.

Thus these brethren needed to choose if they wanted God to be for them or against them! They needed to decide if they would side with their rejecting brethren and be consumed in their judgment, or if they would side with believing brethren and be saved from condemnation. God isn't only a God of mercy/grace/love (1 John 4:8), but He's also a God of justice! Conclude this study by reading 10:26-31.

(Note: The fulfillment of Daniel 2, 7, & 9 are alluded to in this context.)

Hebrews 13:1-8

After presenting several examples of faith in chapter 11, and after presenting many encouragements of faith in chapter 12, Paul concluded by presenting some evidences of faith, in chapter 13, evidences that God expected to exist in the lives of Paul's addressees if they were really walking by faith.

Another way to view chapter 13 is that (as mentioned in the general introduction) after Paul demonstrated in chapter 12 that *The Faith-Principle of Christ Establishes a Better Relationship with God* than what was possible through Moses, he concluded in chapter 13 by demonstrating that *The Faith-Principle of Christ Is Also the Basis for a Superior Way of Life* to that possible under Moses.

> **VERSE 1: LET BROTHERLY LOVE CONTINUE** (I.E. ENDURE).

The term for **BROTHERLY LOVE** is φιλαδελφια, from φιλια (philia) meaning fondness and αδελφια (adelphia) meaning siblings, literally translated: "from the same womb" and rendered as "BROTHERLY KINDNESS" in Second Peter 1:7.

By this command Paul was signifying at least two things: {1} They were expected to act like siblings, because {2} they were people with the same parent—God, implying that it was love among Christians, not non-Christians, that Paul had in mind. Although siblings may fight, just let a non-sibling come between them and see what happens—one sibling will protect the other! In fact, this is likely the very reason Paul used φιλια (philia) instead of αγαπε (agape) here; in other words, he wasn't referring to how they treated each other as much as he was to how they protected each other from outsiders (e.g. the Jews [and soon the Romans] who were trying to annihilate Christianity, cf. 12:12-17).

Speaking of love and endurance, since Jesus prophesied of these dark days that "THE LOVE OF MANY WILL GROW COLD, BUT HE WHO ENDURES TO THE END SHALL BE SAVED" (Mat. 24:12b-13), Paul, as he concluded his letter, commanded them to actively work on keeping this fire alive. Later Paul wrote of this to Timothy in the mid AD 60s in (what we believe to be) his last letter penned. Notice that the only love some folks would have would be love for themselves: "IN THE LAST DAYS PERILOUS TIMES WILL COME: FOR MEN WILL BE LOVERS OF THEMSELVES, LOVERS OF MONEY, BOASTERS, PROUD, BLASPHEMERS, DISOBEDIENT TO PARENTS, UNTHANKFUL, UNHOLY, UNLOVING, UNFORGIVING, SLANDERERS, WITHOUT SELF-CONTROL, BRUTAL, DESPISERS OF GOOD, TRAITORS, HEAD-STRONG, HAUGHTY, [AND] LOVERS OF PLEASURE RATHER THAN LOVERS OF GOD" (2 Tim. 3:1-4). So while they would love themselves, they wouldn't love others or even God Himself.

VERSE 2: DON'T FORGET TO ENTERTAIN STRANGERS, FOR BY SO DOING SOME HAVE UNWITTINGLY ENTERTAINED ANGELS.

Now, moving from love for those familiar to them, Paul went on to include an admonition to show concern for the unfamiliar—Christian brethren from other places. (Since verses 1 & 3 are about Christians, it's safe to assume, especially during this time [1 Cor. 7:26], that such is his emphasis here as well.) In Galatians 6:10 Paul wrote, "AS WE HAVE OPPORTUNITY, LET US DO GOOD TO ALL, ESPECIALLY THOSE ... OF THE HOUSEHOLD OF FAITH." In James 2:15-17 James asked, "IF A BROTHER OR SISTER IS ... DESTITUTE ... [AND] YOU DON'T GIVE THEM ... THE THINGS THAT ARE NEEDED FOR THE BODY, WHAT DOES IT PROFIT?" And read also Matthew 25:34-40, noting that Jesus employed the term "brethren."

So it seems very likely that Paul's main point to the Hebrews in this verse concerned outpost brethren. In their time there were itinerant preachers who needed places to stay (cf. 3 John 5-8), not to mention brethren who had been driven from their homes (as discussed at 10:33).

Regarding the last part of this verse, it seems very probable that Paul had in mind the accounts of Abraham and Lot who (at least initially) unwittingly entertained strangers who were actually angels (Genesis 18–19).

During the time these brethren lived—the time when supernatural things were coming to an end (yet still in existence, 1 Cor. 13:8ff & Eph. 4:7ff), there may very well have been a chance for them to encounter angels in this way; after all, as noted at 1:14, angels had a closer relationship to them then than they do with us today.

> **VERSE 3:** REMEMBER THE PRISONERS AS IF CHAINED WITH THEM AND THOSE WHO ARE MISTREATED, SINCE YOU YOURSELVES ARE IN [THE] BODY ALSO.

Common sense alone indicates that the command to **REMEMBER** here includes more than just thinking about poor tormented and imprisoned Christians from time to time, for it obviously includes praying for them, even feeding and clothing them when possible. The idea here is much like it is in James 1:27 where the term for "VISIT" means more than just checking on someone from time to time; besides, as stated at 10:34, those in prison were expected to be fed by family and friends.

By saying **AS IF CHAINED WITH THEM** and **SINCE YOU YOURSELVES ARE IN [THE] BODY ALSO**, Paul was reminding them of their Savior's teaching to treat others the way they'd want to be treated if they were in their shoes (Mat. 7:12) in which, especially at this time, they could very well find themselves!

(Side-note: The definite article "THE" before "BODY" isn't in the original, implying that Paul wasn't referring to the church body, but to the physical body; however, if he were speaking about the church body, then such would still make sense because the members of the church were the ones being persecuted.)

One reason why Paul had only Christians in mind in this verse is that he wrote **THE PRISONERS**, (yes, "THE" is in the original before "PRISONERS") not just "PRISONERS" in general; besides, the immediate context (as well as all of Hebrews) suggests that Paul was writing about the encouragement of Christians during this time of persecution.

> **VERSE 4:** MARRIAGE IS HONORABLE AMONG ALL AND THE BED UNDEFILED; BUT FORNICATORS AND ADULTERERS GOD WILL JUDGE.

Although the first part of this verse sounds as though it's merely a declarative statement, it's actually an imperative statement, meaning that the first part of this verse should read, "Let marriage be honorable among all, and let the bed be undefiled." Here are four reasons why: {1} interlinears and most versions render it as a command; {2} such corresponds to the flow of the entire chapter that's full of exhortations to do this or that; {3} every verse immediately surrounding this one indicates that it was also meant to be in the form of a command: "LET BROTHERLY LOVE CONTINUE" (v. 1), "DON'T FORGET TO ENTERTAIN" (v. 2), "REMEMBER THE PRISONERS" (v. 3), and "LET YOUR CONDUCT BE WITHOUT COVETOUSNESS" (v. 5); and {4} before the word **FORNICATORS** Nestle's text has the Greek word γαρ which means "for" or "because"; in other words, let your bed be undefiled because God will punish fornicators.

It has been suggested that the first clause, **LET MARRIAGE BE HONORABLE AMONG ALL**, may have been penned by Paul to counteract the mistaken belief by some (e.g. the Essenes and Origen) that celibacy was more honorable or holy than marriage; after all, since Paul did tell Timothy that some people would come along and forbid marriage (1 Tim. 4:1-3a), perhaps he was preparing these Hebrews for that if it hadn't already begun (cf. v. 9).

What's the difference between "FORNICATORS" and "ADULTERERS"? "ADULTERERS" are those who commit any sexual act against a biblical marriage, while "FORNICATORS" are those who commit any unlawful sexual act period; thus fornication includes adultery, homosexuality, incest, premarital relations, bestiality, and so on, which is why the NKJV usually translates the original term here as "SEXUALLY IMMORAL" (cf. 1 Cor. 5:10, etc.).

> **VERSE 5A:** LET YOUR CONDUCT BE WITHOUT COVETOUSNESS, AND BE CONTENT WITH SUCH THINGS AS YOU HAVE.

Although the word for **COVETOUSNESS** literally referred to the "LOVE OF MONEY" (as in 1 Tim. 6:10), the word came to refer to "a yearning for better circumstances in general," which is obviously what Paul had in mind in this verse for the following reasons: {1} the word for **HAVE** here refers to "that which presently surrounds" someone—their current circumstances, which is reminiscent of Philippians 4:11 where Paul wrote, "I HAVE LEARNED TO BE CONTENT IN WHATEVER CIRCUMSTANCES I FIND MYSELF"; {2} in the immediate context Paul wrote of God being their helper and never leaving them (vv. 5b & 6), as well as the fact that they could find themselves mistreated and in prison (v. 3); and {3} in the remote context (i.e. this entire letter), Paul had been encouraging them to press onward through whatever negative circumstances in which they found themselves for Christ.

Thus, since the phrase **LET YOUR CONDUCT BE** simply means to "live your lives," Paul was in essence telling them to live without yearning for better physical lives under Moses (evading persecution), because that would result in forfeiting better spiritual/eternal lives under Christ and with God.

Why would Paul feel it necessary to give this exhortation? Because the indication back in 10:33-34 was that some of these brethren had lost much for Christ; so Paul was probably encouraging them here to not use up their time and energies trying to get back what they once had, especially at this point in time when things were coming to an end. "Just be content, placing your lives in God's hands."

> **VERSES 5B-6:** FOR HE HIMSELF HAS SAID, "I WILL NEVER LEAVE YOU NOR FORSAKE YOU (DEU. 31:5-8)." SO WE MAY BOLDLY SAY, "THE LORD IS MY HELPER; I WILL NOT FEAR. WHAT CAN MAN DO TO ME (PSA. 118:6)?"

In English a double negative equals a positive; for example, to say "He hasn't eaten nothing" actually means that he has eaten something. However, in Greek the opposite was the case: the more negatives, the greater the emphasis.

In our English translations of verse 5b, there's only one negative—**NEVER**; but in the original there are <u>two</u> negatives before the word **LEAVE**, and <u>three</u> negatives before the word **FORSAKE**. What does this mean? It means that a literal rendering would have God promising with profound emphasis something more like this: "I will never, never leave you! And I will never, never, never forsake you!" (By the way, the word "FORSAKE" is very strong of itself, referring to leaving someone totally helpless or in dire straits.)

The word **BOLDLY** refers to courage, indicating that Paul was saying, "So we, <u>with</u> <u>courage</u>, may say...."

The whole point here then is that, as long as they trusted in God, they needed no one and nothing else; in other words, covetousness (implying anxiety) for better earthly/physical circumstances would—in their case—be detrimental (implying, by the way, that we should be more careful how we apply New Testament statements as found in verse 5a above to folks today)! Especially "in the present distress" (1 Cor. 7:26), Paul's attitude was, "AS HAVING NOTHING, YET POSSESSING ALL THINGS" (2 Cor. 6:10). And we might add to this the comforting promise Paul gave to another group of suffering Christians at this time in Romans 8:28: "ALL THINGS WORK TOGETHER FOR GOOD TO THOSE WHO LOVE GOD," for "THE GOD OF PEACE WILL CRUSH [THE] SATAN (THE ENEMY) UNDER YOUR FEET SHORTLY" (16:20). After all, Jesus did promise His disciples: "I AM WITH YOU ALWAYS, EVEN TO THE END OF THE AGE" (Mat. 28:20). And I love the exclamation of Isaiah 12:2: "GOD IS MY SALVATION! [SO] I WILL TRUST AND NOT BE AFRAID!"

What a wonderful way for Paul to begin closing out his thoughts to these weary brethren! No matter what would happen to them, the Lord would never, never, never forsake them! They had the free-will right/ability to leave Him, but He would never, never, never forsake them!

VERSE 7: REMEMBER THOSE WHO RULE OVER YOU, WHO HAVE SPOKEN THE WORD OF GOD TO YOU, WHOSE FAITH FOLLOW, CONSIDERING THE OUTCOME OF THEIR CONDUCT.

The original term for **REMEMBER** here is slightly different than the one in verse 3; they're synonyms, but because this word is more closely related to the words for "memorial" and "mention," it's believed that Paul used this term instead of the other one because here he was referring to those who were martyred for the Cause of Christ. And this is probably correct for the following reasons: {1} **THOSE WHO RULE** here may be simply translated as "teachers" or "leaders," eliminating the idea of those presently ruling over them (cf. numerous other versions). Besides, {2} the next phrase **WHO HAVE SPOKEN ... TO YOU** is in the past tense, more literally reading, "who spoke to you." {3} The clause **CONSIDERING THE OUTCOME OF THEIR CONDUCT** indicates that they (e.g. James, Acts 12:1f) were dead. And {4} verse 17, being in the present tense, clearly discusses living/ruling leaders.

So Paul charged them to do three things with regard to these teachers/preachers/leaders: {1} Remember/honor them. No, he wasn't telling them to worship or "saint" them, putting them up as idols, but (as he urged the Thessalonians in 1 The. 5:12-13) "APPRECIATE [respect, NIV] THOSE WHO DILIGENTLY LABOR AMONG YOU AND ... GIVE YOU INSTRUCTION ... ESTEEM THEM VERY HIGHLY IN LOVE BECAUSE OF THEIR WORK" (NASB). {2} Follow or imitate them. (The English word "mimic" from this Greek term.) And {3} consider the outcome of their lives. And what was that? The Lord never, never, never forsook them (cf. 2 Tim. 4:16-17); so, as Revelation 14:13 says, "'BLESSED ARE THE DEAD WHO DIE IN THE LORD ... [FOR] THEY REST FROM THEIR LABORS, AND THEIR WORKS FOLLOW THEM.'"

VERSE 8: JESUS CHRIST IS THE SAME YESTERDAY, TODAY, AND FOREVER.

Paul began this letter by quoting God as saying to His Son, "'YOU ARE THE SAME, AND YOUR YEARS WILL NOT FAIL'" (1:12), then he ended it here with the same sentiment. So what's the point in this verse? Well, keeping both the immediate and remote contexts in mind, it seems pretty plain Paul was telling them that, just as the Lord had always been with the faithful in the past, so He would be with these brethren in their time and all others from that time onward.

In other words, putting ourselves in the shoes of these first century brethren, Paul was saying to them, "As a sacrificial High Priest, Jesus—<u>yesterday</u>—offered Himself for your sin (9:23-28); likewise, as a sympathetic High Priest, Jesus—<u>today</u>—represents you at God's throne (4:14-16); besides that, He'll continue to do this for all His people—<u>forevermore</u> (7:23-28)."

So God and/or Jesus is faithful to the faithful; and, because of that, Paul went on in verses 9-17 to discuss just how they could remain faithful.

Hebrews 13:9-17

As mentioned in the introduction of the study of verses 1-8, Hebrews 13 reveals that *The Faith-Principle of Christ Is the Basis for a Superior Way of Life* to that possible under Moses.

Also, as mentioned in the conclusion of the previous study, since God and Jesus are faithful to the faithful, Paul went on in verses 9-17 to share a little with his readers about how they could remain faithful.

> **VERSE 9: DO NOT BE CARRIED ABOUT WITH VARIOUS AND STRANGE DOCTRINES. FOR IT IS GOOD THAT THE HEART BE ESTABLISHED BY GRACE, NOT WITH FOODS WHICH HAVE NOT PROFITED THOSE WHO HAVE BEEN OCCUPIED WITH THEM.**

The clause **DO NOT BE CARRIED ABOUT** could literally be translated "stop being carried away," indicating that many or all those brethren who had already forsaken Christ did so by falling prey to **VARIOUS** (different) and **STRANGE** (foreign) **DOCTRINES** (teachings). What doctrines? Judaistic doctrines (aka "DOCTRINES OF DEMONS," 1 Tim. 4:1).

These brethren needed to become those who were "NO LONGER CHILDREN, TOSSED TO AND FRO AND CARRIED ABOUT WITH EVERY WIND OF DOCTRINE BY THE TRICKERY OF MEN" (Eph. 4:14, cf. Luke 7:24); remember, according to 5:12—6:2, being children in their comprehension was part of their problem.

The last sentence of this verse implies an obvious contrast: what's **GOOD** is that which purifies the heart and conscience —the New Covenant (9:14 & 10:22), not that which never purified them—the Old Covenant (9:9-10).

Paul oft wrote against eating (and even <u>not</u> eating) for religious reasons: "FOOD DOES NOT COMMEND US TO GOD; FOR NEITHER IF

WE EAT ARE WE THE BETTER, NOR IF WE DO NOT EAT ARE WE THE WORSE" (1 Cor. 8:8). In order to compromise with the Jews who refused to let go of Judaistic teachings, many Christians allowed their beliefs into the church just as Paul predicted (1 Tim. 4:1-5), even to the point of specifically mentioning that some would bind eating and/or not eating. But Colossians 2:16 says, "LET NO ONE JUDGE YOU IN FOOD OR DRINK," for—Romans 14:17 says—God's "KINGDOM IS NOT FOOD OR DRINK" (which would be a "DOCTRINE OF MEN," Col. 2:22), BUT RIGHTEOUSNESS, PEACE, AND JOY."

VERSE 10: WE HAVE AN ALTAR FROM WHICH THEY WHO SERVE THE TABERNACLE HAVE NO RIGHT TO EAT.

The pronoun **WE** refers to New Testament priests (i.e. Christians, 1 Pet. 2:9); the pronoun **THEY** refers to Old Testament priests.

An **ALTAR** was that upon which a sacrifice was made for sin and in worship to God; and, as the student will soon see, the "ALTAR" of this verse (based on typology) is a reference to Christ Himself (cf. E. W. Bullinger's *Figures of Speech in the New Testament*). So the assertion Paul made here (and that he went on to validate) was simply that Christians (like the Old Testament priests) have an exclusive altar. But as has been the case throughout Hebrews, the difference is that, instead of it being a tangible altar, it's an intangible altar.

Furthermore, being exclusive means that Old Testament priests—yea all Jews represented by those priests—have no right to Christ and His blessings (e.g. salvation). Why was/is this true? Well, before going on to the reason Paul submitted in this context, recall John 6:53-56 in which Jesus spoke figuratively of eating/drinking—assimilating—His teachings (v. 68); and to do that they needed to have faith in Him (v. 64). So, since to have faith in Him meant that they believed His claim of Messiahship, then to continue worshipping at the altar of Judaism while claiming to be Christians was totally unacceptable (cf. principle of Mat. 6:24a & 9:16-17).

(Side-note: While the Jews could not eat of sin-offerings because such would signify that they were forgiven when they weren't, Christians can eat of Jesus because they have been forgiven [cf. Adam Clarke's notes on this verse].)

Now on to Paul's reason for why Old Testament priests had no right to Christ and His blessings. Paul applied his reasoning by means of typology.

> **VERSE 11: FOR THE BODIES OF THOSE BEASTS, WHOSE BLOOD IS BROUGHT INTO THE SANCTUARY BY THE HIGH PRIEST FOR SIN, ARE** [NOTE THE PRESENT TENSE AGAIN] **BURNED OUTSIDE THE CAMP.**

In both verses 10 & 11, Paul was alluding to Leviticus 6:30 & 16:27 wherein God said, concerning bloody sin-offerings (e.g. on The Day of Atonement), that {1} the priests were not to eat of them, rather {2} they were to be taken outside of the camp of Israel and burned.

Now with that in mind, certainly what Paul went on to say here (i.e. how he went on to apply this) were fighting words to any Jew who rejected Jesus as the Christ. Listen:

> **VERSES 12-13: THEREFORE JESUS ALSO, THAT HE MIGHT SANCTIFY THE PEOPLE WITH HIS OWN BLOOD, SUFFERED OUTSIDE THE GATE. THEREFORE LET US GO FORTH TO HIM, OUTSIDE THE CAMP, BEARING HIS REPROACH.**

So here was Paul's point as well as the proof for his assertion that insistent temple-servants have no right to Christ and His blessings: When the Old Testament priests were submitting to the regulation of taking the sacrificial sin-offering outside the camp to burn it, they had no idea that they were picturing that one day they would likewise take their own Messiah and kill Him outside of Jerusalem and thus also outside of the temple—the two main symbols of Judaism!

Thus, since the Messiah was killed outside of that which represented Judaism, that in itself was a sign that Judaism would (soon) cease and that God would ultimately accept non-Jews as well as Jews as His people.

Two other points Paul made here: {1} Jesus' blood was shed outside the temple instead of inside of it as with the Old Testament animal sacrifices, indicating that He gave Himself as our sacrifice. This is perfectly consistent with John 2:19-21: 'THE JEWS [ASKED] HIM, 'WHAT SIGN DO YOU SHOW TO US SINCE YOU DO

THESE THINGS?' JESUS ANSWERED ... 'DESTROY THIS TEMPLE, AND IN THREE DAYS I WILL RAISE IT UP.' THEN THE JEWS SAID, 'IT HAS TAKEN FORTY-SIX YEARS TO BUILD THIS TEMPLE. AND WILL YOU RAISE IT UP IN THREE DAYS?' BUT HE WAS SPEAKING OF THE TEMPLE OF HIS BODY"—that which He gave willingly (John 10:15-18). And {2} those who claimed to be Christians, those who desired the benefits of Jesus' death, were to forsake Judaism by meeting Christ where He died —outside the camp (John 19:17 & 20); in other words, to eat and drink Christ, one had to leave the camp of Israel, for to go back into the camp—to go back to Judaism—would be (as Paul said in 10:26) to leave the one and only acceptable sacrifice for salvation.

So what was Jesus' **REPROACH**? It was His exclusion—being cast out, which is why He was crucified **OUTSIDE** the holy city and which also may be connected to why dying on a cross was considered shameful (Gal. 3:13). (Outside the city they'd let the bodies go unburied for more than one day [cf. Deu. 21:23].) As those outside the camp carried a stigma either because of uncleanness (Lev. 13:45-46) or excommunication (Num. 15:30) or guilt demanding death (Lev. 24:14 & Num. 15:35), early Jewish Christians were exhorted to remain faithful to Christ and accept a similar status of disgrace; in other words, they were to identify with Moses who—even 1,600 years before Jesus was born—esteemed "THE REPROACH OF CHRIST GREATER RICHES THAN THE TREASURES OF EGYPT" (Heb. 11:26, cf. 1 Pet. 4:14).

By the way, while Paul was obviously urging his readers to **GO FORTH ... OUTSIDE THE CAMP** of Jerusalem in a figurative sense, it wouldn't be long (around five years) until they'd have to take this advice literally. In fact, Albert Barnes commented on this verse: "The *object* of the writer seems to be to comfort the Hebrew Christians on the supposition that they would be driven by persecution from the city of Jerusalem and doomed to wander as exiles. He tells them that their Lord was led from that city to be put to death, and they should be willing to go forth also; that their permanent home was not Jerusalem, but heaven; and they should be willing, in view of that blessed abode, to be exiled from the city where they dwelt and made wanderers in the earth."

So why did Paul exhort these brethren to "GO FORTH ... OUTSIDE THE CAMP, BEARING CHRIST'S REPROACH"?

> **VERSE 14:** BECAUSE HERE WE HAVE NO CONTINUING CITY, BUT WE SEEK THE ONE TO COME.

The word **HERE** means "in this situation" or "under these circumstances." What situation/circumstances? The state of Jewish rule; i.e., due to God's plan from the very beginning that Judaism be temporary, under the Jewish administration there never would've/could've existed a **CONTINUING** or a spiritual/eternal **CITY** or kingdom of God (cf. 12:26-28).

In this statement Paul employed the Greek term μελλω for the last time in this epistle: McReynold's Interlinear (*The Word Study Greek-English New Testament*) reads, "not for we have here staying city, but the one being about to be we seek after" (i.e. "here we have no enduring city, so we seek the one that's on the verge of arriving"), which plainly indicates that soon the old/earthly/temporary Jerusalem would be supplanted by the new/heavenly/eternal Jerusalem; soon the old/temporary covenant of Moses from Mt. Sinai would be completely supplanted by the new/eternal covenant of Christ from Mt. Zion (cf. 12:18-19 & 22-24). (Cf. notes at 2:5.)

> **VERSE 15:** THEREFORE BY HIM LET US CONTINUALLY OFFER THE SACRIFICE OF PRAISE TO GOD, THAT IS, THE FRUIT OF OUR LIPS, GIVING THANKS TO HIS NAME.

The word **BY** here means "through, by means of," implying that, instead of continually offering unprofitable and unacceptable animal sacrifices to Yahweh as Old Testament priests did and stubbornly continued to do, Christians (as New Testament priests) were/are expected to **CONTINUALLY OFFER ... PRAISE ... TO HIS NAME** through or by means of Christ—the once-for-all-people-and-time accepted and therefore profitable sacrifice. Peter agreed with Paul when he wrote to Christians: "YOU ... ARE ... A HOLY PRIESTHOOD TO OFFER SPIRITUAL SACRIFICES ACCEPTABLE TO GOD THROUGH JESUS CHRIST" (1 Pet. 2:5).

Giving God **PRAISE** is called a **SACRIFICE** here in order to retain the parallelism; in other words, merely audibly extolling God isn't much of a sacrifice, but by calling that action **THE FRUIT OF OUR LIPS**, Paul paralleled it with the fruit of the field—the firstfruits—and/or the fruit of animal-loins—the firstborn.

The phrase **GIVING THANKS** here is from a term found 23 times in the New Testament and is always translated as "CONFESSING" or "PROFESSING" ... except here. So the idea Paul meant to express was "confessing or professing His name," not **GIVING THANKS TO HIS NAME**; if "GIVING THANKS" were the best rendering, then it should read as "giving thanks to Him," not "TO HIS NAME." So it isn't about speaking to God, but about speaking of God ... through Jesus! Yes, of course thanksgiving in prayer is a way to praise God; that just wasn't Paul's point in this statement.

But while thinking about offerings of gratitude, it's interesting to note that, whereas the thank-offerings were only presented on certain stated occasions (according to Leviticus 7:11ff), the praise of Christians may be—and is even expected to be—offered **CONTINUALLY** (cf. Rom. 12:1-2 & 1 The. 5:17).

One other interesting point is this: It's quite evident that Paul was quoting one of the Jews' most respected rabbis (Rabbi Menachem) who wrote, "In the time of the Messiah, all sacrifice shall cease except the sacrifice of praise." By alluding to this, Paul was indicating that this very declaration had been fulfilled, meaning that now (in the mid AD 60s) was the time of the Messiah. And, since that was true, then {1} Jesus was that Messiah, {2} the Jewish sacrificial system was in the process of being abolished, and {3} no other sacrifice would be accepted by God, save the sacrifice of praise for the gift of His Son (cf. additional notes in Adam Clarke's commentary).

> **VERSE 16: BUT DO NOT FORGET TO DO GOOD AND TO SHARE, FOR WITH SUCH SACRIFICES GOD IS WELL PLEASED.**

These Christians were cautioned to not allow their praise of God to cause them to neglect the more physical things; even the New Covenant requires a few things of a physical nature. This is reminiscent of the New Covenant passage of James 2:15-17: "IF A BROTHER OR SISTER IS NAKED AND DESTITUTE OF DAILY FOOD, AND ONE OF YOU SAYS TO THEM, 'DEPART IN PEACE, BE WARMED AND FILLED,' BUT YOU DO NOT GIVE THEM THE THINGS WHICH ARE NEEDED FOR THE BODY, WHAT DOES IT PROFIT? THUS ALSO FAITH BY ITSELF, IF IT DOES NOT HAVE WORKS, IS DEAD." So these Hebrew brethren were to be careful to not delude themselves into thinking that spiritual sacrifices excluded everything of a physical nature (cf. 1 Pet. 2:5 again). Philippians 4:10-20 confirm this because Paul referred to the physical aid that the Philippian brethren sent to him as "AN ACCEPTABLE SACRIFICE, WELL-PLEASING TO GOD" (v. 18).

These brethren (as all brethren, of course) needed to remember that "THE FRUIT OF THE HANDS" (Prv. 31:31) is as important as "THE FRUIT OF THE LIPS"; besides, there's normally more sacrificing (e.g. in time/talent/treasure) involved in "THE FRUIT OF THE HANDS."

Nothing should've been more important to these brethren (especially at this precarious time) than to make their Creator and Judge pleased with them; they needed to imitate Enoch who "PLEASED GOD" (11:5, same Greek word), something this text teaches was to be accomplished by praising Him with their lips and serving Him with their lives.

So combining verses 15-16, Paul was in essence saying that praise of God in word and deed are inseparable, or, as First John 4:20 puts it, "IF SOMEONE SAYS 'I LOVE GOD' YET HE HATES HIS BROTHER, HE IS A LIAR; FOR HE WHO DOES NOT LOVE HIS BROTHER WHOM HE HAS SEEN, HOW CAN HE LOVE GOD WHOM HE HAS NOT SEEN?"

> **VERSE 17:** OBEY THOSE WHO HAVE RULE OVER YOU AND BE SUBMISSIVE, FOR THEY WATCH FOR YOUR SOULS AS THOSE WHO MUST GIVE ACCOUNT. LET THEM DO SO WITH JOY AND NOT WITH GRIEF, FOR THAT WOULD BE UNPROFITABLE FOR YOU.

As discussed at verse 7, the phrase **THOSE WHO HAVE RULE** refers to leaders; since he called Jesus **THE CHIEF SHEPHERD** in verse 20, Paul probably had elders in mind, but that isn't a necessary conclusion, meaning that this injunction likely applies to all leaders. (While verse 7 is about leaders of their past, this verse is about those who were still alive and presently leading them.)

The word **OBEY** means exactly that—"to listen to and comply with"; Paul made this demand because, in our world, rulers possess their authority by their subjects, meaning that if those subjects refuse to obey them, those rulers cannot be effective —they cannot rule/lead. Applying that here, if these members refused to listen to and comply with the teachings and admonitions of their leaders, then the God-ordained government of the first generation church would've been rendered ineffective. Why? Because God just doesn't force His way against man's free-will.

The term for **BE SUBMISSIVE** is different from the one for "OBEY" in the sense that being submissive carries with it an attitude, an attitude of humility, indicating that one can obey without being submissive, but not vice versa.

The word **WATCH** here literally means "to lose sleep over" and refers to the idea of staying awake to nurse a critical case; and this is exactly what leaders were expected to do—to carefully watch over the congregation (Acts 20:28ff).

The word **GRIEF** refers to the miserable feeling of one who's trying to fulfill a duty, all the while reflecting on how unappreciated and perhaps even opposed his work may be. Why would causing "GRIEF" to the leaders prove to be **UNPROFITABLE** (which means "disastrous") for the members? For at least two reasons: {1} it could've caused them to fulfill their duties in a resentful manner (cf. 2 Cor. 9:7), bringing on nothing but hostility among everyone concerned; and {2} it could've caused the loss of reward at the time of accounting. Why? Because just as submitting to parents or civil leaders is submitting to God, so submitting to congregational leaders is submitting to God (cf. John 13:20, etc.). Again, Paul wrote, "APPRECIATE [RESPECT, NIV] THOSE WHO DILIGENTLY LABOR AMONG YOU AND ... GIVE YOU INSTRUCTION ... ESTEEM THEM VERY HIGHLY IN LOVE BECAUSE OF THEIR WORK" (1 The. 5:12-13, NASB; concerning how to respond toward leaders, cf. 1 Tim. 5:19-20.) However, when leaders required approaching, they were to be approached like anyone else (Mat. 18:15-17, cf. 1 Tim. 5:19-22).

Thus Paul's point here was that the members of the church were obligated by God to cheerfully obey their congregational leaders, unless they could clearly/biblically demonstrate that those leaders were in error; by doing this, the leaders would be able to fulfill their duties and give account to God ... with joy.

Hebrews 13:18-25

As mentioned in the introduction of the study of verses 1-8, Hebrews 13 reveals that *The Faith-Principle of Christ Is the Basis for a Superior Way of Life* to that possible under Moses.

Now while considering the last few verses of Hebrews, the student will find that Paul, as he was wont, concluded with various greetings, blessings, and miscellaneous exhortations; so he began to end by asking them to pray for him.

> **VERSE 18:** PRAY FOR US, FOR WE ARE CONFIDENT THAT WE HAVE A GOOD CONSCIENCE IN ALL THINGS DESIRING TO LIVE HONORABLY.

The word **PRAY** here is in a tense that indicates they were already praying for Paul, so he wanted them to continue that noble deed: "keep praying for us" is the idea.

Since Paul couldn't vouch for the conscience of others, and since in the next verse he applied this to himself, the pronouns **US** and **WE** here are likely editorial in their rhetoric (employing "we" instead of "I" is more pleasing when one is asking for something of a selfish nature). Even with that said, however, one shouldn't be so dogmatic as to claim that Paul wasn't also including his colleagues in these plural pronouns.

The **HAVE A GOOD CONSCIENCE** clause is modified by the **TO LIVE HONORABLY** clause, indicating Paul seemed to be saying that he was living his entire life with only honorable motives, and that included the writing of this letter with its many warnings/instructions. So since Paul only had their spiritual/eternal welfare at heart, that should have motivated them to want to continue praying for him.

An interesting thing to note here is that, even after all the chidings/warnings in this letter, Paul demonstrated that they were still at this point in covenant relationship with God; otherwise, it's very doubtful Paul would've asked for their prayers. Isn't it amazing what God puts up with? This should make us feel better about our relationship to Him.

> **VERSE 19: BUT I ESPECIALLY URGE YOU TO DO THIS THAT I MAY BE RESTORED TO YOU THE SOONER** [I.E. AS SOON AS POSSIBLE].

Where was Paul when he wrote these Jewish Christians in Jerusalem? That will be discussed at verses 23 & 24.

This verse indicates that Paul had been with these brethren at some point in the past and that he was planning on returning to visit them soon; so since this was important to him, he asked that they specifically remember to pray for that plan to see fruition. Yes, he wanted their prayers in general, but (probably due to their precarious/spiritual circumstances) he especially wanted them to pray that his return trip might be expeditious. Why might his return to them not be expeditious? Perhaps he was in prison in Rome; or perhaps he was in the middle of something he didn't feel he could leave incomplete; or possibly he just desired to arrive without another ship wreck or similar delaying mishap.

Nonetheless, what is very apparent from these last few verses is that these Hebrew brethren knew exactly who this writer was, and they knew him well, obviously recognizing him to be one with authority.

> **VERSE 20: NOW MAY THE GOD OF PEACE WHO BROUGHT UP OUR LORD JESUS FROM THE DEAD, THAT GREAT SHEPHERD OF THE SHEEP, THROUGH THE BLOOD OF THE EVERLASTING COVENANT...**

This is a prayer; so after Paul asked them to pray for him, he penned his prayer for them.

Since Paul called God **THE GOD OF PEACE** in connection with His raising up of His Son ("THE PRINCE OF PEACE," Isa. 9:6) "FROM THE DEAD" (Acts 2:24 & Rom. 1:4), then he very likely had vertical peace (i.e. man's peace with God), not horizontal peace (man's peace with man), in mind here (cf. Rom. 5:1). As Colossians 1:20 teaches, God made it possible for man to be at peace (i.e. in harmony) with God by virtue of the blood shed by His Son on a cross. In other words, sin—that which separated man from God (Isa. 59:2)—is that which Jesus took upon Himself and with which He died (Rom. 6:6), thereby making it possible for any free-will individual to be reconciled to his Creator (Rom. 6:10-11).

The phrase **FROM THE DEAD**—being plural—literally means "out from among the dead ones"; in fact, this phrase is found 56 times in the NKJV, and it means this every time. (Check it out and study each context from that perspective sometime.) So the precise idea here isn't that Jesus' physical body was raised from the state of death, but that He—Jesus Himself—was raised up out from among the dead ones, namely all those who were yet to be judged. *This point is significant because it demonstrates that Jesus' spiritual, not His physical, resurrection was the chief goal!*

Although in English it looks as if the phrase **GREAT SHEPHERD OF THE SHEEP** is connected to **THE GOD OF PEACE**, in the Greek it's clear that it's a reference to Jesus who called Himself "THE GOOD SHEPHERD" (John 10:11 & 14) and whose coming was prophesied (Ezekiel 34, etc.); furthermore, Peter called Jesus "THE SHEPHERD" (1 Pet. 1:25), as well as "THE CHIEF SHEPHERD" (1 Pet. 5:4) who he said, in language-agreement with Paul (at that time in the mid AD 60s), was "ABOUT TO BE REVEALED" (v. 1).

The phrase "THE BLOOD OF THE EVERLASTING COVENANT" is in the locative case, meaning that Jesus' blood is (figuratively, of course) found in ("OF" = "in") "THE EVERLASTING [NEW] COVENANT" as opposed to the temporary (old) covenant.

According to the original construction (cf. Albert Barnes), the phrase **THROUGH THE BLOOD OF THE EVERLASTING COVENANT** seems to be connected with this verse not the next, meaning that Jesus was made the "GREAT SHEPHERD OF THE SHEEP" by shedding His "BLOOD" for those sheep, corresponding perfectly with Acts 20:28 which, incidentally, is also in the context of shepherding sheep.

> **VERSE 21:** MAY THE GOD OF PEACE... **MAKE YOU COMPLETE IN EVERY GOOD WORK TO DO HIS WILL, WORKING IN YOU WHAT IS WELL PLEASING IN HIS SIGHT, THROUGH JESUS CHRIST, TO WHOM BE GLORY FOREVER AND EVER. AMEN.**

Concerning the first part of this verse, some other versions render it more clearly as "MAY GOD EQUIP YOU WITH EVERYTHING GOOD TO DO HIS WILL" (cf. ESV, NIV, RSV, etc.). Through what means might He accomplish this? Let's remind ourselves of the context: He'd perform this through {1} His Word (2 Tim. 3:16-17, cf. Heb. 13:22), {2} prayer (2 Cor. 13:9, cf. Heb. 13:20-21), {3} suffering (1 Pet. 5:10, cf. Heb. 12:5-11), {4} spiritual members (Gal. 6:1, cf. Heb. 12:12-15), and {5} leaders (Eph. 4:11-12, cf. Heb. 13:17). And, with that in mind, one must not forget that these brethren lived during miraculous times (cf. 1 Cor. 14). So, since these brethren were in need of maturity (5:11ff) which would aid them to be faithful through their difficulties, Paul prayed for that here.

The idea of God **WORKING IN** them **WHAT IS WELL PLEASING IN HIS SIGHT THROUGH JESUS** indicates that, apart from God and His Son, man cannot please His Creator; in other words, after exhorting them concerning what they needed to do, he then asked for God to help them wherein they lacked. (By the way, the word "WORKING" may be translated as "producing.") As Paul wrote in Philippians, "IT IS GOD WHO WORKS IN YOU BOTH TO WILL AND TO DO FOR HIS GOOD PLEASURE" (2:13); but, on the other hand, as the verse just prior indicates, God won't do this apart from man's free-will: "WORK OUT YOUR OWN SALVATION WITH FEAR AND TREMBLING" (Php. 2:12), meaning that God helps those who help themselves, doing for them what they cannot do alone.

Besides, not only can man not please His Creator apart from God and Christ, but Hebrews 13:21 also indicates that God does not and cannot work on/in/by/with/through/for man apart from Jesus (cf. John 14:6)—the very One many of those brethren had forsaken.

The last clause about **GLORY** grammatically applies to God the Father, but it may also describe the Son (cf. 2 Pet. 3:18).

> **VERSE 22: AND I APPEAL TO YOU, BRETHREN, BEAR WITH THE WORD OF EXHORTATION, FOR I HAVE WRITTEN TO YOU IN A FEW WORDS.**

W. E. Vine wrote in his dictionary that the verb form of the original term for **EXHORTATION** here means "to urge one to pursue some course of conduct"; so it's a strong word related, in fact, to the term translated as "APPEAL" here in the clause **I APPEAL TO YOU…**! Our English word "EXHORTATION" is from the Latin word "hortatorius" which refers to that which incites or provokes someone to behave in a particular manner. So, interestingly, while we today (due to our ignorance of Jewish thinking/understanding/custom, etc.) may primarily think of this letter in nature as <u>didactic</u> (informative/instructive), Paul, by calling this letter his **WORD OF EXHORTATION** to them in their time, indicated that he regarded it in nature as <u>hortative</u>—that which was meant to provoke them to remain faithful to their confession of Jesus as the Christ (cf. 4:14 & 10:23).

Another one of the numerous reasons I believe Paul was the author of Hebrews is because he used this exact same phrase in the only other place it's found: in Acts 13:15 he used it to speak of a hortatory speech. Much like that kind of speech, Hebrews is a letter which could've been a mere hour-long hortatory sermon. Actually, if Paul meant for this letter to be didactic in nature, it probably would've been much longer when one takes into account the weightiness of the subject-matter: concerning just one topic, in 9:5 Paul made the statement that "OF THESE THINGS WE CANNOT NOW SPEAK IN DETAIL."

This is probably why Paul thought of Hebrews (which is longer than most of his others) as one of **FEW WORDS**; in other words, it was considered short because it only <u>touched</u> on very deep Old Testament topics (about which they already knew something) merely in order to exhort them to persevere.

The phrase **BEAR WITH** is a kind way of charging them to simply do what he asked of them; in fact, the exact opposite phrase is found in Second Timothy 4:3 where Paul wrote about those who would "NOT ENDURE (or bear with) SOUND DOCTRINE."

The clause **I HAVE WRITTEN** is from the Greek term επιστελλω, the verb form of the noun επιστολε—the origin of the English word "epistle." It has been said that there are folks who think that epistles were wives of apostles. Although we know that epistles aren't people and therefore cannot be related to human beings in such a fashion, yet the words "epistle" and "apostle" are related in the sense that they both carry with them the idea of something/someone being "sent." In other words, an epistle was a <u>letter</u> that has been sent from one party to another, while an apostle was a <u>person</u> who was sent from one party to another.

> **VERSE 23:** KNOW THAT OUR BROTHER TIMOTHY HAS BEEN SET FREE, WITH WHOM I SHALL SEE YOU IF HE COMES SHORTLY.

Since the phrase **HAS BEEN SET FREE** comes from a term that can refer to a release from prison or to being sent away on a mission, one shouldn't be dogmatic as to its meaning here. Since Timothy was probably Paul's closest companion, it certainly isn't a stretch to believe that Timothy, just as Paul, spent some time in prison. However, it's also believed that it was at this time when Paul sent Timothy on a mission to Macedonia to ascertain how the brethren there were faring (Php. 2:19-24). For the reasons presented by Albert Barnes (which won't be repeated here), it's very likely that Paul had reference to this (or some other) journey from which Timothy would soon return.

Either way, Paul's main point is clear: his plans were to visit these Hebrew brethren as soon as he and Timothy met up once again.

> **VERSE 24:** GREET ALL THOSE WHO RULE OVER YOU AND ALL THE SAINTS. THOSE FROM ITALY GREET YOU.

The term for **GREET** (like the Hawaiian word "aloha") could be used to say (in the American vernacular) "hello" when meeting, or "good-bye" when parting; it meant, "I hope you're doing well," or "I hope you do or <u>fare</u> well."

Unless someone has set out to prove that Paul wasn't in Italy (Rome) when he wrote this letter, this sentence would be taken in its <u>natural</u> manner: he was writing from Italy, and those from Italy wished their Hebrew brethren well. See, a few hold that Paul merely had some Italian brethren with him when he wrote this letter. So, perhaps in order to alleviate a problem that they have with the word "FROM," some versions read, "THOSE <u>OF</u> ITALY GREET YOU." In addition, the same Greek wording exists in Acts 17:13: in that case Paul referred to "THOSE <u>FROM</u> THESSALONICA" while they were still <u>in</u> Thessalonica. This means that, just as in our language today, the word "FROM" in such a case may refer to people who are <u>in</u> the place where they are <u>from</u>.

Besides, usually when Paul meant to refer to those who were with him in his travels (as opposed to those with whom he was working in a given location), he would say something like, "ALL WHO ARE WITH ME GREET YOU" (Titus 3:15, Php. 4:21, & Gal. 1:2).

> **VERSE 25:** GRACE BE WITH YOU ALL. AMEN.

The term for **GRACE** here is the Greek term from which is derived the English word "charity," having reference to favor which one party would bestow on another. In the original it actually reads, "the grace," indicating grace from someone in particular, that someone of course being God. Paul was therefore sharing another prayer of sorts: his prayer to God that He'd show favor on Paul's Hebrew Christian brethren who were under so much pressure.

The word **AMEN** is a transliteration meaning "certain" or "true" (cf. every time Jesus said "truly" in the NKJV); it confirms something stated. So, by using this word here, Paul (and anyone who used it and knew what it meant) was signifying his sincerity in what he desired of God. Incidentally, this was Paul's way of signing off—his signature, if you will (Rom. 16:20; 1 Cor. 16:23; 2 Cor. 13:14; Gal. 6:18; Eph. 6:24; Php. 4:23; Col. 4:18; 1 The. 4:28; 2 The. 3:18; 1 Tim. 6:20; 2 Tim. 4:22; Phi. 25; & esp. Titus 3:15). With so many evidences of Paul's authorship throughout this letter, it's astonishing that anyone could doubt it!

EPISTLE SUMMARY:

Hebrews was written by the apostle Paul to Jews who had become Christians. Because they had accepted Jesus as the Christ (the One most Jews rejected as the prophesied Messiah), they were being fiercely persecuted in order to cause them to renounce Jesus and Christianity, then return to Moses and Judaism. So in order to motivate them to remain steadfast in their profession of Jesus as the Christ, Paul demonstrated that Jesus was indeed the prophesied Messiah and that He and His path were therefore much superior to Moses! (Cf. outline in the introduction for an effective abridgment.)

While Paul's motivations included six warnings (against neglect [2:1-4], unbelief [3:7-9], carelessness [4:1-13], immaturity [5:11–6:20], willful sin [10:26-31], and desertion [12:14-29]), they also included seven blessings in connection with the very-soon-to-come promised kingdom age (salvation [1:14], reigning [2:5], good things [9:11 & 10:1], less persecution [10:27], fulfilled promises [10:36-37], a spiritual/eternal city [13:14], all summed up in the phrase "THE POWERS [BLESSINGS] OF THE AGE ABOUT TO COME" [6:5])!

So of all the first century Christians who needed to pray the prayer of Matthew 6:9-13, these brethren needed to pray it: FATHER ... YOUR KINGDOM COME. YOUR WILL BE DONE ON EARTH AS IT IS IN HEAVEN ... FOR YOURS IS THE KINGDOM AND THE POWER AND THE GLORY FOREVER. AMEN.

Made in the USA
Charleston, SC
16 May 2012